XV - 223

The Papacy in the 19th Century

A Part of " The History of Catholicism
since the Restoration of the Papacy"

By

Friedrich Nippold

Translated by

Laurence Henry Schwab

Rector of the Church of the Intercession
New York

———

G. P. Putnam's Sons
New York and London
The Knickerbocker Press

1900

The Knickerbocker Press, New York

CONTENTS

iii

PART II

CATHOLICISM AND PAPALISM IN ENGLAND AND AMERICA

PART I

THE PAPACY AFTER THE RESTORATION IN 1814

INTRODUCTION BY THE TRANSLATOR

"THE Roman Church is only Roman and everywhere anti-national; she endeavours to force everything into her own forms and formulas and does not rest until she has obliterated the national character of the Church and stifled all national life in the Church. . . . The Roman Church is everywhere a foreigner, even in Italy; for she everywhere pursues tendencies which are opposed to the tendencies of the country." The truth of these words, spoken by Bishop Herzog, is confirmed by the history of the Papacy in this century as Professor Nippold has set it forth.

The average Protestant, when he thinks of the dangers of Romanism, is apt to bring before his mind pictures of Smithfield fires, the horrors of the Inquisition, or the cruelties of Alva. Even so great an historian as Ranke seems to have had something like this in mind when, in the Introduction to his *History of the Popes*, he wrote that the Papacy " no longer exercises any essential influence — the times are past in which we had anything to fear." True: we need no longer fear bodily harm, and those who are anxious only to save their skin may set their minds at rest. But are there not other considerations that may appeal with equal force to our anxious solicitude? Is not the possibility of national decay something to care about? The danger from the Church of Rome to-day is not the stake or torture; but it is the danger from insidious moral and spiritual forces threat-

3

ening to stop a nation's progress, to corrupt a nation's ethical standard, to darken a nation's intellect. The greatest task which God has appointed to the religious forces of this country to-day is to build up a government in city, state, and nation, which shall be pure and just; and the papal system is the most determined enemy to the accomplishment of that task.

Nippold has sketched the history of the Papacy in this century as it is; he has dealt with the facts according to the common rules of evidence followed in secular history. This method is to be clearly distinguished from the method so frequently adopted by writers of ecclesiastical history, who handle facts according to *à priori* preconceptions, who look at Church history through the medium of a theological, æsthetic, or sentimental haze, who depict events and men as they ought to be or as they would like them to be, not as they are. From such this volume will receive no welcome.

The essential purpose of this history is to rescue Catholicism from its papal caricature and to maintain its importance as a corrective to Protestant individualism.

In order to explain and emphasise this distinction between Catholicism and papalism, it will be well to place before the reader certain portions of the three additions to the faith which the modern Papacy has imposed upon the Church of Rome and which differentiate by a clear line of demarcation the "papalism" of our time from the Roman Catholicism of former generations: the Decree of the Immaculate Conception, promulgated by the sole authority of Pius IX. in 1854, the "Papal Syllabus of Errors," likewise resting upon the sole authority of the pope and issued by Pius IX. in 1864, and the Decree of Papal Infallibility, nominally pronounced by the Vatican Council in 1870, but in reality, like the other two documents, imposed upon the Church by the pope and the Jesuits. These three formularies are to-day just as binding upon the Roman Catholic as the decrees of the Council of Trent or any other creed or dogma, and will furnish the official answer to the question, What is modern Romanism ?

I quote from the English version of Schaff's *Creeds of Christendom.*

According to the Decree of the Immaculate Conception the Blessed Virgin Mary has been " from the first instant of her conception, by a singular grace and privilege of Almighty God, in view of the merits of Christ Jesus the Saviour of mankind, preserved free from all stain of original sin." Those who think otherwise " have made shipwreck concerning the faith " and they " subject themselves to the penalties ordained by law, if, by word or writing, or any other external means, they dare to signify what they think in their hearts."

The " Syllabus " of Pius IX. is a collection of eighty errors which the pope condemns. Schaff says concerning it in a prefatory note: " This document, though issued by the sole authority of pope Pius IX., Dec. 8, 1864, must be regarded now as infallible and irreformable, even without the formal sanction of the Vatican Council. It is purely negative, but indirectly it teaches and enjoins the very opposite of what it condemns as error." Nippold states that the " Syllabus " has been expressly declared infallible by Leo XIII. The following are among the errors condemned :

(11) The Church not only ought never to animadvert upon philosophy, but ought to tolerate the errors of philosophy, leaving to philosophy the care of their correction.

(13) The method and principles by which the old scholastic doctors cultivated theology are no longer suitable to the demands of the age and the progress of science.

(14) Philosophy must be treated of without any account being taken of supernatural revelation.

(15) Every man is free to embrace and profess the religion he shall believe true, guided by the light of reason.

(17) We may entertain at least a well-founded hope for the eternal salvation of all those who are in no manner in the true Church of Christ.

(18) Protestantism is nothing more than another form of the same true Christian religion, in which it is possible to be equally pleasing to God as in the Catholic Church.

(24) The Church has not the power of availing herself of force, or any direct or indirect temporal power.

(27) The ministers of the Church, and the Roman Pontiff, ought to be absolutely excluded from all charge and dominion over temporal affairs.

(39) The commonwealth is the origin and source of all rights, and possesses rights which are not circumscribed by any limits.

(42) In the case of conflicting laws between the two powers, the civil law ought to prevail.

(45) The entire direction of public schools, in which the youth of Christian states are educated, except (to a certain extent) in the case of episcopal seminaries, may and must appertain to the civil power, and belong to it so far that no other authority whatsoever shall be recognised as having any right to interfere in the discipline of the schools, the arrangements of the studies, the taking of degrees, or the choice and approval of the teachers.

(47) The best theory of civil society requires that popular schools open to children of all classes, and, generally, all public institutes intended for instruction in letters and philosophy, and for conducting the education of the young, should be freed from all ecclesiastical authority, government, and interference, and should be fully subject to the civil and political power, in conformity with the will of rulers and the prevalent opinions of the age.

(48) This system of instructing youth, which consists in separating it from the Catholic faith and the power of the

Church, and in teaching exclusively, or at least primarily, the knowledge of natural things and the earthly ends of social life alone, may be approved by Catholics.

(55) The Church ought to be separated from the State, and the State from the Church.

(74) Matrimonial causes and espousals belong by their very nature to civil jurisdiction.

(77) In the present day, it is no longer expedient that the Catholic religion shall be held as the only religion of the State, to the exclusion of all other modes of worship.

(78) Whence it has been wisely provided by law, in some countries called Catholic, that persons coming to reside therein shall enjoy the public exercise of their own worship.

(80) The Roman Pontiff can and ought to reconcile himself to, and agree with, progress, liberalism, and civilisation as lately introduced.

The decrees of the Vatican Council are recorded in a document of considerable length. The last two chapters are entitled, " On the Power and Nature of the Primacy of the Roman Pontiff " and " Concerning the Infallible Teaching of the Roman Pontiff "; the latter ending abruptly in the pronouncement of papal infallibility. The very make-up of the document witnesses to the purpose for which the council was called and to whose accomplishment it was ruthlessly directed. Exclusive emphasis has been laid upon the last chapter declaring the infallibility; but Mr. Gladstone — one of the few weighty public men who have recognised the importance of the ecclesiastical factor in the national life — has pointed out the far-reaching and practically important nature of the claims made for the pope in the chapter next to the last, " On the Power and Nature of the Primacy of the Roman Pontiff." Here we read that

full power was given to him in blessed Peter to rule, feed, and govern the universal Church by Jesus Christ our Lord. . . .

Hence we teach and declare that by the appointment of our Lord the Roman Church possesses a superiority of ordinary power over all other churches, and that this power of jurisdiction of the Roman Pontiff, which is truly episcopal, is immediate; to which all, of whatever rite and dignity, both pastors and faithful, both individually and collectively, are bound, by their duty of hierarchical subordination and true obedience, to submit not only in matters which belong to faith and morals, but also in those that appertain to the discipline and government of the Church throughout the world, so that the Church of Christ may be one flock under one supreme pastor through the preservation of unity both of communion and of profession of the same faith with the Roman Pontiff. This is the teaching of Catholic truth, from which no one can deviate without loss of faith and of salvation.

Equally emphatic statements follow, and no claim to unconditioned and unquestioning obedience could go further than that which is made in this chapter in behalf of the pope.

The statement of papal infallibility follows in the next chapter. After an introduction of some length, the dogma is affirmed, the closing sentences reading as follows:

Therefore — we teach and define that it is a dogma divinely revealed: that the Roman Pontiff, when he speaks *ex cathedra*, that is, when, in discharge of the office of pastor and doctor of all Christians, by virtue of his supreme apostolic authority, he defines a doctrine regarding faith or morals to be held by the universal Church, by the divine assistance promised to him in blessed Peter, is possessed of that infallibility with which the divine Redeemer willed that his Church should be endowed for defining doctrine regarding faith or morals; and that therefore such definitions of the Roman Pontiff are irreformable of themselves, and not from the consent of the Church.

But if anyone — which may God avert — presume to contradict this our definition: let him be anathema.

Extraordinary short-sightedness is manifested in the estimation of these papal documents. Whether the pope has ever issued an *ex cathedra* infallible pronouncement is a matter of absolute indifference. The significance of these three documents lies in the fact that they represent both the evidence and the means of an unheard-of centralisation of power in the hands of one man backed by a powerful society, and that this power enables him and the society to shape the development and give direction to the energies of a vast system — the Roman Catholic Church; and that furthermore the first two documents, the Decree of the Immaculate Conception and the Syllabus, indicate the spirit in which and the ends towards which this power is being used. The consequences are the same in America as in Europe: the introduction of a subtle, dangerous poison into the national life. Nippold has described the corrupting action of this poison.

It is the distinction between the Roman Catholic Church as such and the Roman Catholic Church as she has become a helpless tool in the hands of the Papacy that invests Nippold's book with its peculiar interest. And as one realises what injuries this subjection to an alien power has done to the nations of Europe, one is moved to ask whether these injuries — of which we have had a foretaste — may not be averted from us by the one act which alone can bring about this desirable object. There is hardly any single event which could confer such a boon upon this country as the return of the Church of Rome in America to a true Catholicity, by sundering the chain that is dragging her at the heels of a foreign despot and by declaring herself independent. The Church of Rome in America has in prominent and influential positions men who unite high gifts with ardent patriotism and pure devotion. But their labour is largely a labour of Sisyphus while the yoke of Rome is upon them.

King of Corinth — see Longfellow's *Masque of Pandora*

Will there be enough virility in the Roman Church in America to throw off this yoke ? Perhaps it was a happy augury for the future that at the Council of the Vatican, of the only two votes which at the final decision were cast against the infallibility, one was that of an American, Bishop Fitzgerald of Little Rock, Arkansas.

NOTE: The original of this translation, forming the second volume of Nippold's *Manual of the Latest Church-history*, is entitled *The History of Catholicism since the Restoration of the Papacy*. It consists of three parts: The Papacy, the History of Catholicism outside of Germany, and the History of Catholicism in Germany. The first of these parts and six chapters of the second are presented in this translation. The last chapter in the translation has been transposed from its position in the original and rewritten.

The translator has found it necessary to condense in some places and to leave out parts that would be intelligible and interesting to German readers only. The footnotes have been added by the translator where explanation seemed called for. Seignobos' *Political History of Europe since 1814*, translated by Macvane, is an admirable volume to refer to for the general history of the period covered by Nippold.

The translation has been made with the sanction of the author ; he is not responsible, however, for the selection of those parts which are here presented.

CHAPTER I

THE RESTORATION OF PIUS VII., ITS SIGNIFICANCE AND CONSEQUENCES [1]

THE restoration of the Papacy stands at the threshold of a new epoch, and marks a new departure in the history of that ancient institution. The after-development of Catholicism, and hardly less of Protestantism, even that of the state and of civilisation, was led into new channels by this departure. The pope had returned after but a few years' absence. What makes the difference between this return and the many similar occurrences of the Middle Ages, so that the after-effects of this return surpass even those of the return from the exile at Avignon? This question forces itself upon us, and is easily answered. For the cause which gave so widespread a significance to this single fact was the well-known reactionary tendency which sprang from the Revolution and dominated the entire following period.

A direct result of the counter-revolution, the restora-

---

[1] Pius VII., elected pope in 1800, formed the concordat with Napoleon and crowned him emperor ; then quarrelled with Napoleon, was arrested in 1809, kept a prisoner at Savona and Fontainebleau ; was restored and returned to Rome after the peace of Paris in 1814.

The year 1814 marks the most important turning-point in the history of the nineteenth century. It saw Napoleon conquered and banished, the Bourbons returned in the person of Louis XVIII., and the Congress of Vienna, consisting of the plenipotentiaries of the various states, convened in order to rectify the much-disturbed map of Europe. The era of revolution is over and the era of legitimacy and reaction begins.

tion of the Papacy appears not as an isolated fact,
affecting only the city of Rome or the states of the
Church, but as one natural result of certain universal
tendencies.   The conception of sovereignty as such
seemed to find its firmest support against the ideas of
the Revolution in the primacy of the Roman bishop, independent as it was of any democratic influence.   The
emancipation of this primacy from Napoleonic oppression
was therefore looked upon as the climax of all the victories
won over the Revolution.   The decrees issued from the
threshold of the apostle's grave bore the seal of " divine
right " more directly than the mandate of any other
monarch, and it was owing to the support which the
principle of absolutism found in the Papacy that the
spirit which now took possession of Rome spread its influence over one land after another.   Therefore let us
consider the restoration of the Papacy first in its own
character and meaning, and then trace its consequences.

The allied armies had not yet entered Paris when Pius
VII., released from his prison at Fontainebleau, arrived
in Italy.   At precisely the same time that Napoleon,
after his abdication on the 11th of April, 1814, began his
melancholy retreat to the island of Elba, the pope entered
his ancient capital and attracted multitudes of devoted
souls from far and near.   Former political enemies also
paid him their homage: Murat, with Charles IV. of
Spain, the queen of Etruria and the king of Sardinia.
But the people of Italy received him with no less joy,
and his entry into Rome on the 24th of May, 1814, was
like the return home of a victorious emperor.   Even the
Protestants living in Rome wanted to raise a monument
to perpetuate the memory of a renewed Papacy.   These
may have been enthusiasts—artists, half proselytes, or
perhaps secret converts; yet their action was but the
expression of the prevalent temper.

The fact that this feeling of admiration for the Papacy was especially strong in the artistic world proves how great an attraction the residence of the pope, in the new peace-era, exerted upon the art of all cultured nations. The dearly bought peace had at last made it possible for men to indulge the longing for Italy which Winkelmann and Goethe had awakened, and very few gave heed to the system of papal cæsarism which, with its plans of a world-empire only temporarily in abeyance, had once more set up its throne in the ancient capital of the world. Men saw only the return of the days of the Renaissance, the days of Leo X., the days of Raphael and Michael Angelo. One nation after another sent its greatest masters to school in Rome, and the many biographies of artists which treat of this period appear to witness to a second Renaissance.

Rome became at the same time the home or the object of pilgrimage for many noble persons. The old kings of Spain and of Sardinia and the family of Napoleon came to live there. The former found in the restored Papacy a guarantee of legitimacy, the latter trusted to the gratitude of the pope. The relatives of the fallen emperor, especially his mother, Lætitia, and his brother, King Louis of Holland, had in the time of their splendour allied themselves with the papal interests, and now found in Rome not only an asylum for themselves, but also the hope of a happier future for their families. Even the reigning house of Prussia had a representative in Rome in the person of Prince Henry, who, in spite of his delicate health, was a man of some influence.

At no previous time had the salons of the Roman *nobili* seen more numerous and more influential guests. The first princes of Europe, one after another, went on pilgrimage to Rome: the emperor of Austria, the king of Prussia, the Prussian, Bavarian, Danish crown princes. Each of these visits was celebrated with festivities, in which the artistic interests played a prominent part, but which at the same time served the papal policy well. In fact, all those personal connections which were then begun were used to serve the purposes of the Curia. The youthful diplomats who won their spurs in Rome soon learned to know the advantage which a word of re-commendation from the Roman secretary of state to their ministry at home gave them.

As the paradise of artists, the Mecca of princes, the favourite stepping-stone of future statesmen, Rome seemed once more the capital of the world; and it was inevitable that the veneration paid to the holy city should be attributed to the influence of the Roman bishop. For the master of Rome, master in the temporal as well as the spiritual sphere, was no other than the pope-king. Since the time when Constantine yielded the seat of empire in the old Rome and the Roman bishop took the emperor's place as his legitimate successor, the condition of things had perhaps never been more promising.

" It was the deep humiliation, the long misery, of the Church herself, that had changed public feeling in her favour; she who had once been feared had become an object of pity and sympathy." So says Gervinus.[1] And this sympathy, as he points out, was given to Pius VII. personally. His long imprisonment had made him appear as a martyr, and the patience and mildness which he had shown had everywhere won men's hearts. Everybody was ready for concessions, and few remembered that these concessions were made, not to the good-natured person of the pope, but to the callously selfish hierarchy. Indeed, the sacrifices made to the Papacy were not felt as such. The revolutionary chaos which had lasted a full quarter of a century had awakened such a longing for peace and at the same time for authority, that the pre-tended rock of St. Peter appeared in a manner as the

[1] *History of the Nineteenth Century*, 1858.

altar upon which thank-offerings were paid to God for the return of peace. Pius was celebrated not only as one who had suffered most from the demon of the Revolution, but also as the representative of counter-revolutionary and conservative interests.

The Papacy derived its greatest advantages, however, from the victories of non-Roman Catholic nations. For the arms of England, Russia, and Prussia had made its restoration possible. And after the pope had been restored their princes did all they could to strengthen his throne. Alexander I. of Russia, much given to emotional politics, saw in the pope only the princely martyr. Prussia insisted upon the restitution of the states of the Church more strenuously than did Austria; the latter with all its legitimacy would gladly have kept a piece for itself. Even the regent of England entered into correspondence with Pius, and in spite of existing laws received his ambassador with particular favour.

In the introduction to the memoirs of this ambassador (Consalvi) there is a collection of characteristic letters from other illustrious Protestants, who far surpassed born Catholics in the glorification of the papal idea. The latter had known enough to discriminate to a certain degree between Catholicism and Papalism. The ignorance of born Protestants in Catholic matters had made no such distinction. It is no mere chance that the biographies of such papal autocrats as Leo I., Nicholas I., Gregory VII., Innocent III. were written by converts; and it shows to what extent principles formerly held dear were forgotten, that not a few Protestant historians—both secular and ecclesiastical—became instrumental in preparing the way for the restoration of the papal power.

In the Catholic world De Maistre and his associates had cultivated the soil by preaching papal infallibility as the only sure support for the power of princes. The German

Romanticists, too, who out of the clear atmosphere of the
present dreamed themselves back into the incense clouds
of the Middle Ages, proclaimed the pope as the ultimate
arbiter of national differences.

The ruling statesman of the following era himself stood
under the influence of a tendency which was just as much
opposed to the Reformation and all that the Reformation
stood for as it was favourable to the Papacy.   A master
of social form, adroit and facile, with an excellent knowledge of human nature, understanding how to judge and
treat each man aright, Prince Metternich was not a man
of creative ideas.   His policy, which was bent upon the
outward preservation of the existing status, was blind to
the existence of ideal motive powers.   His opposition to
the modern world of ideas made him an enemy to the
foundation of that modern world in the Reformation.
Metternich's frivolous private journalist, Gentz, the
representative of world-worn voluptuousness without
moral principle, was a useful instrument in carrying out
this policy.   By name a Protestant, he outdid the anti-
Reformation attitude of the chancellor.

Under such auspices Austrian statesmanship, which
since Austria's accession to the alliance against Napoleon
had reached the acme of influence, showed itself, where
political interests did not run counter, sympathetic
and helpful to the pretensions of the Papacy.   As the
only Catholic state of the first order in the alliance
against Napoleon, Austria at once sent its own ambassador to Rome, who became the first adviser of the
pope.

The restored dynasties met the renewed Papacy with
even greater sympathy.   The principle of the solidarity
of throne and altar had become the accepted doctrine,
and the Bourbons of France, Spain, and Naples and the
king of Sardinia outdid one another in devotion to the

Holy See. On the other hands, the ancient tradition of the national churches fell into disrepute as the products of unbelief and revolution.

It need hardly be said that this universal love of the Papacy had not the remotest connection with religious motives. At the founding of the Holy Alliance [1] such ideal motives had played a part; but the pope himself, in company with the sultan of Turkey, had refused to join the alliance because it was based upon the equal rights of the several Churches. And the diplomats of the Congress of Vienna were quite as much above transcendental weaknesses as the fallen emperor whose spoils they parted among themselves. In all the bargaining which took place, in which the German and Italian peoples were treated as mere geographical ideas, and where hardly any but such political creations as contradicted the nature of things could count upon general consent, ecclesiastical levers served merely as means to an end; and religious aspirations received even less consideration than did the interests of national life.

But the attempted subjugation and gagging of the independent national spirit needed for its effectiveness the

---

[1] 1815, between the emperors of Austria and Russia and the king of Prussia.

By this act the three sovereigns, "having reached the profound conviction that the policy of the powers, in their mutual relations, ought to be guided by the sublime truths taught by the eternal religion of God our Saviour, solemnly declare that the present act has no other aim than to manifest to the world their unchangeable determination to adopt no other rule of conduct . . . than the precepts of that holy religion, the precepts of justice, charity, and peace." This high ideal was completely belied by subsequent events, which, in view of these lofty pretensions, show the extent to which Christianity may be abused to serve base purposes. Religion, as interpreted by the sovereigns, became a means towards reaction and absolutism.

This very interesting document may be read in full in the *Translations and Reprints from the Original Sources of European History*, published by the University of Pennsylvania (series of 1894).

2

spiritual police not less than the political, and the only point of view under which religion was of any value consisted in the inculcation of blind obedience to the divine rights of the privileged orders. For this purpose the *modus operandi* of the Jesuit order proved far more useful than the faith of the Reformation,— the latter resting upon personal conviction,— and the Danish historian Nielson [1] aptly characterises the kind of religion which the Congress of Vienna recognised when he distinguishes " between the perfumed court and congress-Christianity and that of the apostles and the early Church."

So far as the result was concerned, however, it mattered far less what were the motives by which the ecclesiastical policy of the Congress was guided than what was the disposition of the political rulers. And there is no doubt that this was the most favourable possible to the pretensions of the Papacy.

We have also to consider, as a matter of extreme importance, the attitude of the restored Papacy towards the conditions and problems of the time. The pope might have taken the same stand as his predecessors in the Middle Ages, who knew how to assume the leadership and give direction to the leading ideas of the time. Could not, therefore, the pope even now place himself at the head of the great national movements and thereby once more gain a controlling influence ? With the widespread demand for a reconciliation of the old and the new, for constitutions and popular representations, was not the opportunity given into his hand of making himself master of this tendency, and as supreme shepherd calling upon the princes for the fulfilment of this demand ? Could he not in this way have won the lasting sympathy of the nations, following the example of the

---

[1] *History of the Papacy in the Nineteenth Century*, translated into German—a very excellent work.

powerful popes of the Middle Ages, in the struggle of princes and peoples ? This is the question which Gervinus puts.

Let us add to the question put by this illustrious historian his own answer. In the Middle Ages it was possible for the pope to stand at the head of the spiritual movement, because the whole civilisation of the Middle Ages was nourished and supported by the Church. At that time it was perfectly natural that the pope should make himself the herald of the ruling sympathies and antipathies, and that by calling men to war for the glory of God and of the Church he should render himself terrible to all temporal princes, and that he should reap popularity by his efforts.

But now, such identity of interests between people and pope was simply impossible. The Papacy was by its whole tendency since the Reformation too closely identified with opinions opposed to the popular wishes, and the dominant liberalism was intimately associated with a freer way of thinking in religion; for the enjoyment of political liberty led to the desire for ecclesiastical liberty, and among a free people no limits could be set to enlightenment. Thus the restored Papacy must consistently with its own character assume a reactionary attitude towards all the popular aspirations of the time.

But the opposition of the Papacy to political liberalism, to the demand for popular representation and similar measures was, after all, a mere incident in the general stand which it took and by which it expressed its unwavering enmity to the modern world of ideas. Indeed, the Papacy was never consistent in its opposition to any one set of ideas or any one institution. We shall find hardly any political or social movement with which the Papacy has not entered into some sort of alliance in order to make it useful to its own purposes. We find even an approach to the political-liberal tendencies of the times, as the reigns of Clement XIV. and Pius VI. (the latter at least in its first half) prove. Even Pius VII. personally, as bishop of Imola, had made considerable concessions to the Revolution; Napoleon characterised the sermon which he preached touching the invasion of the French in 1797, as a Jacobite sermon.

It is evident, therefore, that in order to discover what is essential and fundamental in the character of the restored Papacy, we must go deeper; and we shall not understand the Papacy, with all its religious and ecclesiastical pretensions, until we have learned to recognise in it the revival of the old Roman cæsarism under the name of St. Peter, claiming sovereign rights over land and people, so that all concessions and gifts made to the Papacy were in reality only a restitution of what was rightly its own, and had been only for a time alienated. And under the ecclesiastical mask of this new cæsarism there was included that absolutism in the religious sphere which denied the right of every adverse opinion.

Since the era of " Illumination "[1] there had been less antagonism than ever between the original Catholic ideal of Christian universalism and the Protestant principle of Christian individualism. But so soon as the restoration had given it a free hand, papal absolutism was forced in consistency with its own character to wage a war of extermination against so-called heresy. Its opposition to constitutionalism and liberalism was only the result of this ecclesiastical absolutism. And in obedience to the same impulse the Church placed itself in antagonism to the principles of free scientific research; for the latter would appear just as dangerous as the spirit of a pure and

---

[1] " Illumination," or " illuminism " (*Aufklärung*), denotes the general intellectual movement in Germany towards the end of the last century, which was characterised by great activity of thought and a breaking away from ancient traditions.

free religion to a power whose entire growth rested upon a chain of the most outrageous deceptions.

The endeavour to destroy nonconformists by force had become so entirely second nature to the Papacy that even amid the storms of the Revolution every moment favourable to this purpose was used. Gallicans and Theophilanthropists[1] were the first victims. Immediately after Consalvi's departure with the new French concordat (1801), the national synod of the French Church was dissolved, and the first announcement with which Talleyrand greeted the new nuncio, Caprara, was that the public worship of the Theophilanthropists had been closed. Among the papal conditions of the emperor's coronation one of the first had been the demand that Catholicism should be declared once more the ruling religion of the state. This rude insult to the ideas of 1789 failed of being put into effect. But the clergy of the Revolution were obliged to render a humiliating recantation, and the right to preach was taken from married priests, who thus were as far as possible deprived of their means of existence. Similar measures were attempted outside of France. When, with the accession of King Louis Napoleon, Roman influences had gained the upper hand in the Netherlands, an attempt was made to deprive the old Catholic Episcopal Church of its bishops. The difference between the epoch of restoration and the years of revolution consists therefore only in this, that oppression and persecution, which had been sporadic and temporary, after the Restoration became the ruling principle which determined the development of the whole following period.

For a short time it seemed as if at least the most general reforms which followed the French domination — in spite of its revolutionary and anti-national character — would meet with toleration in Rome. At first there was some talk of the necessity of administrative improvement

---

[1] A sect formed in France in 1796.

and the reform of abuses in ecclesiastical orders, but only too soon were such efforts branded as revolutionary tendencies. And more and more the restored papal rule inclined to recognise as valid only the old condition of things before the Revolution and before the era of Illumination.

Nevertheless, in comparison with the reign of his successors, that of Pius VII. enjoys, with those who allow themselves to be deluded by the sound of words, the name of a liberal government. The cardinals were divided into two parties, the Zelanti and the Liberali. It was the latter party which, through Consalvi, who was again made secretary of state, gave its name to the papal policy under Pius VII. It is extremely important, however, not to be misled in our judgment by a foreign use of language. For both parties were equally representative of the specifically papal idea; both stood with equal emphasis for the immutability of the papal Church system; both were equally unwilling to give up any former claims. The Liberali were only inclined to momentary concessions in consideration of the conditions and needs of the present, although they were careful to make their concessions so prudently that the appearance of papal infallibility did not suffer. The Zelanti, on the other hand, clung to the most antiquated pretensions and would give their consent to no kind of sacrifice; they knew but one object — unconditioned restoration of the old.

The latter outnumbered their opponents in the restored Curia from the beginning, and their chief, Cardinal Pacca, enjoyed to a high degree the confidence of the pope. But no less did Consalvi stand well in the latter's favour; his wise statesmanship had made him indispensable. And so the play of intrigue, which was never absent in the Curia, revolved about the greater or less influence of these two factions, although they were in perfect agreement as to the ultimate end. During Consalvi's absence, as ambassador of the pope in England and at the Congress of Vienna, the Zelanti had a freer hand. But even after his return, when he again took the control of affairs, the spirit of the government remained the same, and the liberal phraseology of which Consalvi was master, while all illiberal measures were put upon others, served only to deceive good-natured and ignorant people as to the real ends sought.

Among the diplomats of the nineteenth century Consalvi may claim, with Talleyrand and Metternich, a place in the first rank. His early education — as the special *protégé* of Cardinal York, the last legitimate successor of James II.—had initiated him in political secrets. Not long afterwards, in the social circle of the exiled aunts of Louis XVI., he had entered into close relations with the most influential representatives of the opposition to the Revolution. As the secretary of the conclave at Venice (which elected Pius VII.), he had his first opportunity of showing his diplomatic skill. He appealed simultaneously to the protection of Austria and Russia, wrote to the nominal king, Louis XVIII., and understood how to neutralise the suspicion of the republican leaders.

When he returned to Rome, Pius VII. made him his secretary of state. Immediately afterwards, when the French concordat was drawn, he showed his strategical dexterity. The celebrated contradictions between the despatches which he wrote then and the memoirs drawn up during the later conflict with Napoleon have given much occupation to the learned world. The attempts to solve these contradictions start from the naïve presumption that for Consalvi language served another purpose than for Talleyrand.

Yet a peculiar value attaches to these memoirs for the expressions they contain of the author's bitter animosity against Napoleon.   It was owing to this very feeling that soon after the fall of Napoleon Consalvi became most influential among the allies.   He was assiduous in cultivating the relations with England which he had entered into in his younger years (through the mediation of Cardinal York), so that English statesmen took him into their confidence, and that even in the divorce trial of Queen Caroline he officiated as the confidant of the court.

But his greatest services, next to the French concordat, belonged to the Congress of Vienna; here he not only took formal precedence of all other ministers, but his intimate relations with the leaders of Austrian and French politics, his amiable flatteries for the representatives of Russia and England, the prudent use he made of the ladies' salons, gave him a decisive influence in the most important questions.   His celebrated note of the 23d of October, 1814, in which he demanded the re-establishment of the Papacy in its full possessions, including Avignon, made impossible demands; but it certainly effected a richer harvest at the final settlement.   And the non-fulfilment of the other claims gave occasion to a protest similar to that once made against the peace of Westphalia,—protests which not only belong to the nature of the so-called Curial language, but which, as soon as the favourable moment has come, are made the basis of new claims on the part of the Papacy, which never desists from its divine rights, and is therefore infallible.

Upon his return from the congress Consalvi once more took the headship of the Roman government.   The protest which he had made in Vienna was still more impressively repeated in a papal allocution.   In the restored states of the Church the same administration continued as during his absence.   After the restoration of the temporal power of the pope, Italy was looked upon and treated as a conquered land, of which the powers at Vienna disposed with sovereign authority.

The dexterous hand of Consalvi is traceable in the rejection of the endeavours which the noblest and the most devoted German Catholics made for a more closely united German national church, in the restrictions placed upon the liberty of the press, and in the interference in the affairs of the German Confederation. The fine, smooth handwriting of his letters is, indeed, characteristic of this smooth diplomat, to whom the Romans themselves gave the name of Siren, and who understood admirably how to make the most of the fable of a liberal Papacy. And the master's dexterity was shown by his pupils: above all, Bernetti and Capaccini, whose heartiness and *bon_hommie* delighted the diplomats, while they made every effort to nullify the inner-Catholic reform aspirations, quite after the manner of Loyola.

As to the reform notions of Consalvi, so highly praised by Niebuhr and Ranke, there remains no more doubt about their true value since Curci's [1] remarkable revelation concerning the suppressed plan of reform made by Cardinal Sala. During Consalvi's absence in the year 1815, Sala had rewritten and begun to publish his fundamental propositions (*Piano di riforma umiliato a Pio VII.*). Consalvi had all the copies destroyed. The greater part of the work is completely lost; only an extract from a small part has become known, through the memoirs of Sala, published in 1880, by Professor Cugnoni. [2] The only reason for this action on the part of Consalvi appears to have been his fear that the author might become dangerous to himself. Sala's propositions give evidence of superior ability. Curci adds to his account of this chapter of history the significant sentence: " To such miserable jealousies does God sometimes grant the decision

---

[1] A Jesuit, expelled from the order ; wrote on the relations of Church and State, upholding Italian nationality ; suspended ; submitted, and was reconciled in 1884.

[2] *Memorie della vita e degli scritti dei card.* G. A. Sala, 1880.

concerning the highest interests of the Church and of Rome.''

In contrast to Consalvi and his party, Cardinal Pacca, the head of the opposite party, has the reputation of an eager zealot. The real difference lies perhaps in his greater honesty and frankness. At least the hatred which he cherished to the Revolution and to all that he confounded with it did not make him blind to the imperfections of the Church. On the other hand, his own experiences would naturally lead him to view in the same light Revolution and Illuminism or the tendency towards national churches.

As nuncio in Cologne, hardly twenty-five years old, he had been able to counteract the Punctations of Ems [1] by awakening the jealousy of the bishops against the archbishops. The university of Bonn, founded by the archbishop of Cologne, as well as the diocesan synod called by his colleague of Mainz, [2] with the enlightened teachers of the one and radical reform tendencies of the other, found in him an energetic opponent. He foresaw the fate of the pre-revolutionary Church more clearly than others, and for that very reason demanded all the more thoroughgoing energy, and would know nothing of half-measures or of forbearance towards other forms of belief. The arguments by which the restoration of the order of Jesuits was pushed are traced to his inspiration. And

---

[1] A conflict between the pope and the archbishops of Germany was occasioned by the assumptions of the nuncios. At the Congress of Ems in 1786 the archbishops of Mayence, Treves, Cologne, and Salzburg demanded the old episcopal rights; conceded to the pope only the primacy of honour; denied appeals to him; and demanded the abolition of the nuncios. This act was called the " Punctation of Ems."

[2] This synod discussed a partial abolition of clerical celibacy; only those that had the cure of souls were to be bound to celibacy; the use of the vernacular in the Church service, restriction of the adoration of saints, the reading of the Bible and the repeal of the existing law against it were also treated.

with all this, we find nowhere such a lack of higher considerations, especially of religious ideas,—such as characterises the curialistic diplomacy in general,— as in the memoirs of Pacca.

Standing in the middle between the two diplomats, of whom one represented a watchful prudence, the other an energetic aggressiveness, Pius VII. comes personally to the front only when it was intended to make an impression through his mild, amiable personality. In early life he had suffered severe trials; as bishop of Tivoli he had devoted himself to an ascetic piety. The sermon which he preached at the entrance of the French into Imola,[1] and the concessions which he had made during his imprisonment, had drawn bitter words from De Maistre. But when he returned to Rome, he was looked upon as an unflinching martyr.

It is not on record that his piety ever took offence at the means which his political advisers considered necessary. On the other hand, every single country was soon made to feel that the old curialistic spirit again ruled in the Vatican. In Rome all sails were set to make the best of the favourable wind. Rarely (so says Gervinus) has the Vatican proved its old accustomed all-seeing activity and its dexterity in seizing the right moment better than at this time.

As the first result of the restoration of the Papacy there meets us the re-establishment, though now only for the states of the Church, of the old congregations of cardinals. First of all, that of the Index and of the Inquisition. The congregation of the Index in 1815 forbade all political books. The same fate befell even Alfieri's patriotic poems. In the congregation of the Inquisition there were in a short time 724 charges of heresy pending. After these congregations had been again set up came

[1] See page 20.

the turn of the dissolved monasteries. By a single edict there were restored 1824 monasteries and 622 nunneries. The founding of new institutions soon assumed almost greater dimensions than in those epochs of flourishing monasticism which are illustrated by the names of the Benedictines, the Cluniacs, the begging friars, and the legion of orders which arose in the struggle with the Reformation.

Of a similar character were the prohibitions and condemnations which accompanied these measures. The larger part was directed against the freemasons. And in a class with the secret associations were placed the Bible societies that had arisen during the last ten or twenty years. The first official condemnation of the latter, which was subsequently followed by a series of others, finally put together in the Syllabus of 1864, is pronounced in the briefs of July 29 and September 3, 1814, sent to the archbishops of Gnesen and of Mohilew. In these dioceses a new translation of the Bible had been spread, one of the translations into all the Russian dialects made by the aid of Alexander I. There is hardly a sharper contrast conceivable than that between this Russian emperor, seeking to make the word of salvation accessible to his subjects, and the so-called vicar of Christ in Rome, who forbade it to laymen. The Bible societies are characterised by Pius as

a pest, godless machinations of innovators, a crafty invention to shake the foundations of religion, a new kind of tares which the enemy has sown. . . . The people are to be warned, that they may not fall into the traps which are prepared for them to their eternal perdition. It is for the common welfare that such attempts, which are made by its enemies for the destruction of holy religion, be frustrated. The translations of Holy Scripture in general do more harm than good, and none is to be tolerated which is not sanctioned by the Holy See and furnished with explanations by the Church-fathers.

The restored Papacy could not define its "religious" tendency more distinctly than by this anathema upon the reading of the Bible. The examples which Pius herein followed are unmistakable. Innocent III. (1198–1216), the greatest world-ruler among the popes, had given the first prohibition of Bibles, and a few years later the synod of Toulouse (1229)—and this was the most significant of all its proceedings against the Albigenses and Waldenses—had anathematised the reading of the Bible by the laity. After this, it was not until the era of the counter-Reformation that similar measures were again taken. The anti-Protestant decrees of the Council of Trent concerning the Bible, its reading and interpretation, were soon followed by the first edition of the Index under the authority of Pius IV. (1564), in which the reading of the new translations of the Bible in the vernacular was threatened with eternal damnation. After this, it is not until the time of the Jansenist disputes that we meet with equally decided expressions of enmity to the Bible, in the most notable of the bulls directed against the inner-Catholic reformation — the Unigenitus bull (1715).

On the other hand, in the period of the Illumination at the end of the last century, even among Catholic populations, the Bible had been spread abroad through the influence of the bishops, who at that time were more Christian Catholic than Roman Catholic; and the religious revival which in England and America represented the counterpart of Continental revolutionary tendencies, had, by means of various religious associations, produced a marked effect among foreign Catholics. Against this danger Pius, after his return, thought it necessary to make his first stand, and he took up again the policy of Innocent III. Following it, he thought himself able to cope with Revolution and Reformation.

But even the condemnation of Bible societies might

appear as an isolated event, of more theoretical than
practical significance.   That which gave to the restoration of Pius VII. for all time its ominous significance
was the first act of world-wide importance which he
undertook after his return—the restoration of the Society
of Jesus.   For not only was this, far more than the prohibition of the Bible, an unmistakable sign of the spirit
in which the renewed Papacy undertook its task; we see
in the influence which the Society at once began to exert
upon all conditions the source of that great stream which
drew the entire further development of Catholicism into
its current.   It will therefore be our next task to trace
this stream in its many windings.

From the same source we shall observe a second stream
to flow, which drew European and non-European countries alike within the sphere of the Curia's power.   The
concordats which followed under the same pope have
exerted a hardly less intense influence upon the relations
of Church and State than the restoration of the Jesuits
exerted upon the development of the Church.

And besides these two tendencies we should not forget
a third, which, beginning at the same time, powerfully
affected the development of the religious life of the
people under the dominion of the Jesuits and of the concordats: the alienation of the life of the people from the
Church which outwardly ruled it.   And here, too, we can
trace in one single sphere the type of what happened
in all countries influenced by the Vatican; for there is
no place where the moral nature of the restored Papacy
appears so distinctly as in the states of the Church.

CHAPTER II

THE RESTORATION AND RENEWED EXPANSION OF THE ORDER OF JESUITS

O N the 24th of May, 1814, Pius VII. arrived in Rome. On the 7th of August of the same year he went in solemn procession and — as Pacca tells us — amid the acclamations of the multitude to the Church of the Jesuits, and there read mass at the altar of St. Ignatius. Immediately afterwards, in the neighbouring oratory, in the presence of numerous cardinals and bishops and of the Sicilian Jesuits and their provincial, the pope caused the master of ceremonies to read the bull, *Solicitudo omnium ecclesiarum.*

The care of the churches confided to him lays upon him the duty of using all the means in his power to meet the spiritual needs of Christendom. Since for this reason, by the briefs of May 7, 1801, and July 13, 1804, the Society of Jesus had again been sanctioned in Russia and in the kingdom of both Sicilies, the unanimous wish of almost all Christendom has caused active and energetic demands to be made for the general restoration of the order; especially since there have been diffused on all hands the very abundant fruits which the Society has produced in those regions where it existed. The scattered stones of the temple and the destruction of discipline, caused by the late calamities and misfortunes, demanded his consent to such unanimous and right wishes. He would become partaker in grievous sin towards God, if in

the midst of the heavy storms which were raging round the
vessel of Peter he turned away the strong and experienced
rowers who offered themselves to break through the raging
billows which every moment threatened inevitable ruin.
Therefore he had resolved to carry out what had been his
dearest wish since his elevation to the apostolic throne and by
his present irrevocable decree commands that the orders before given touching Russia and both Sicilies should from this
moment be extended to all parts of the states of the Church as
well as to all other states and dominions. This decree shall
remain for all time unchangeable and inviolable; any action
contrary thereto, proceeding from any person whatsoever, is
declared to be null and void, and especially is the decree of
Clement XIV. pronounced invalid and of no application.

We should not omit to note the remarkable contrast
between the *ex cathedra* decree of Pius VII. and the *ex
cathedra* decree of Clement XIV. of July 21, 1771. For
after Clement XIV. had expressly ordered that no restoration of the order should ever be valid, Pius nevertheless undertook this restoration. But aside from this,
it would be difficult to conceive of a more decided contrast than that presented by the reference of the one
pope to the petitions addressed to him from all sides for
dissolution and the appeal of the other to petitions likewise directed to him from all sides for restoration, than
between the picture which one draws of the good fruits
of the order and that which the other presents of its evil
deeds and its abominable sentiments.

These violent contrasts, however, in the verdicts of two
equally infallible popes admit of a simple explanation, if
we bear in mind the great change in the spirit of the
times brought about by the intervening Revolution. It
was simply the fruit of the Revolution which fell into the
lap of the order as well as of the Papacy.

In our time it may seem peculiar to the candid student
of history that men suddenly seemed to recognise the

deliverer from the Revolution in the same order which by its war of extermination against Huguenots and Jansenists had been chiefly instrumental in preparing the way for the Revolution. But amid the terrors of the Revolution its underlying causes had been forgotten. Men were influenced by what was nearest, and the reasoning of the papal brief was widely echoed. With an increasing sense of triumph it was everywhere published abroad that the only reason why the insolent philosophy of the century had risen against its rulers was that the Society of Jesus, the ancient bulwark of throne and altar, had been destroyed, and these had thus been deprived of their surest support. Only by making haste to raise from its grave the order which understood, as no other body did, how to keep the people in obedience to their divinely appointed spiritual and temporal shepherds, was there any ground to hope that the straying might be brought back and the faithful preserved from infection by the revolutionary poison.

This reasoning, however, was not allowed to pass wholly without contradiction. In a manner truly prophetic, to which after-experiences have given a most telling force, Wessenberg [1] foretold the consequences of the restoration of the Society:

The causes why the order of the Jesuits in its modern development is wholly irreconcilable with the welfare of the Christian Church as well as that of nations and of the agreement between the two, are so numerous and of such force that

[1] "One of the noblest representatives of liberal Catholicism in the beginning of the present century" (Schaff-Herzog). Appointed vicar-general of the diocese of Constance. Elected bishop of Constance in 1817, the pope refused to confirm him, and he retired to private life. "The reasons of the Curia's aversion to him were, that he advocated the establishment of a national church of Germany, and the revival of general councils, and that as vicar-general he had introduced the German language into the liturgy and choir-singing of the churches of his dioceses, and sent his seminarists to Pestalozzi to learn the new method of instruction."

3

it must appear in the highest degree astonishing, that the heads of states should now again see in the order a powerful support of their authority.   Its principles are of such nature that they must inevitably corrupt Christian faith and morals and unsettle the relation of Church and State.   All kinds of unbelief, heathen and Pharisaic opinions, are cherished by them.   The doctrine of probabilities, of the *reservatio mentalis*, and the sanctification of the means by the end, of the invalidity even of oaths, when a supposedly higher end makes this probable, and others, which the order has invented and which it every-where maintains, destroy the foundations of all Christian morals.   The Jesuit-ultramontane doctrine of Church-law is inconsistent with the maintenance of any real secular authority and with the independence of national government.   For this order, true to its character and the spirit of its teaching, as the experience of centuries proves, aspires to an universal despot-ism over all minds, over all organs of State and Church life, so that none but a stone-blind man can fail to see that this order is the most mighty and the most dangerous secret society for grasping the actual power of Church and State.   Should the order succeed in again winning a position for itself in Germany, we may look forward to a bitter and long struggle of light with darkness, a struggle which will become dangerous to the peace of the Church as well as to the quiet of nations.

Even statesmen, especially Catholic statesmen, were at this time not so friendly to the Jesuits as they after-wards became.   It is asserted upon good authority that in the beginning Prince Metternich and the Emperor Francis were little inclined to the restoration of the order.   In Bavaria we find the same temper prevailing, shared even by the romantic crown prince.   In Italy and in Spain the order met with serious suspicion from all independent men.   Portugal and Brazil made decided resistance to the reception of the followers of Loyola. And even Consalvi thought it prudent to give evidence of his liberality by a criticism of the measures adopted during his absence.

But the world stood before an accomplished fact. The Vatican had executed the secretly prepared stroke, and opposition was disarmed. The settlements of the order, which had been allowed to remain, in Russia and Sicily, had already served as stations for new recruits. The former Russian provincial, Brzozowski, had only to assume the name of general in order to connect the new with the old organisation. In the city of Rome itself a considerable number of Jesuits soon came together. On the very day that the Society was restored it received back the three palaces which it had formerly possessed in Rome. The following year saw the foundation of new colleges in Viterbo, Urbino, Orvieto, Ferrara, Terni, Tivoli, Fano, Feventino, and Benevento.

At the same time affiliated orders began to group themselves around the Society. The orders of the Fathers of the Faith and the Redemptorists and the congregations of the Sacred Heart of Jesus formed auxiliaries. Out of the many associations with masonic, liberal, and revolutionary labels, into which the ex-Jesuits had retired, there issued new congregations for all classes and strata of the people, but all placed under the supreme direction of the Company. Even the older monastic orders, which until then had formed a counter-influence to the Jesuits, one after another succumbed to its authority, and were obliged to modify their former independent constitutions according to the Jesuit model.

It is a problem of considerable historical importance to trace the secret activity of the Company in the interval between its dissolution and its restoration; but we are still without the requisite data for even an approximate solution of this problem. The most important plans of the leaders have very rarely been intrusted to paper. Only meagre fragments exist of contemporary literature during the wars of the Revolution, in which there is any mention

of the attempts repeatedly made under Pius VI. for
the restoration of the Jesuits.   We should not even know
that these attempts were considerably increased immediately after the enthronement of Pius VII., if he had not
himself testified that even at that time he had been
favourable to the idea.   And all that is known to us of
any further steps taken to carry out the plans for the
restoration of the order is the promise given by Pius
upon Pacca's request at Fontainebleau, August 7, 1812,
to restore the order after his own liberation.   But although we may not be able to trace the devious ways in
which the abettors of the Jesuits sought to accomplish
their ends, it is now our task, as with the old order so
with the new, to learn to know the tree by its fruits.
These very soon become plain enough.

Since the restoration of the order the Papacy itself has
become its auxiliary in a sense different from before.   In
the history of Catholicism from 1540 to our own day
popes friendly to the Jesuits have alternated with those
who were opponents of their tendencies.   The act of
Pius VII., however, precluded the possibility that
another Clement XIV. should ever lay violent hands
upon the order; and under the reign of his successors
the order has carried out one by one the plans which before it had attempted in vain.   Any possible fluctuation
of the papal policy in the future has now been provided
against.   For the " pious opinions," of which none had
any more authority than any other, have been replaced
by formulated " dogmas "; the condemnations, hitherto
isolated and without system, have been put together in
the system of the Syllabus of Pius IX.; the ecumenical
council, which to the Catholic Church of old stood as the
highest court of appeal, has been obliged to pronounce
its own abdication.   And thus the Papacy, made infallible and declared incapable of improvement, has been degraded to the level of the Company of Jesus, just as the

autocratic cæsarism of Rome at the summit of its absolutism became the prey of the Prætorians.

Along with the Papacy, the bishops also succumbed
to the rule of the Jesuits, although not till after long
struggles. The opposition, apparently suppressed, again
and again gave astonishing signs of life. But all these
inner-Catholic attempts at reform have always been defeated by Jesuit strategy, which knew how to find abettors everywhere. The political leaders of the so-called
Catholic parties could soon without fear of contradiction
identify Catholicism and Jesuitism. Bishops, who found
their support not in their dioceses but in Rome, maintained that a good Catholic must be a friend of the
Jesuits, and characterised every act of self-defence on
the part of Protestantism against the eternal war which
the Jesuits had sworn as an attack upon the Catholic
Church.

The new order, even more than the old, threw its
energies into a war to the death against evangelical
liberty of conscience. The battle against the Revolution
and revolutionary ideas was held to be a continuation of
the old battle against the Reformation. In order to suppress the former, the results of the latter were marked for
destruction, and the character of the new crusade which
the order at once inaugurated against the Evangelical
churches is in nowise distinguished from the intrigues
which brought about the Thirty Years' War and the
revocation of the Edict of Nantes.

It has been elsewhere asserted,[1] with entire justice,
that all abetment and recognition of the principles and
the activity of the order on the part of a Protestant
Christian is not an act of justice, but a betrayal of his
own past and future and an act of ethical laxity. And
yet there are among the rulers of the Protestant churches
many who accept the designation of Protestant Jesuits

[1] In an article by Steitz in Herzog's *Real-Enzyklopaedie*, vi., p. 56.

as an honourable one; and in the war of extermination
against the ancient Catholic traditions the order is now,
as formerly, supported by the ignorance of Protestant
statesmen.

The evidence of the order's activity in modern society
forces upon the candid observer this conclusion, that
there is no more significant and no clearer turning-point
in contemporary history than the restoration of the
Society of Jesus. And we find evidence, astonishingly
soon, not only of the spread of the order's influence, but
also of the character of that influence upon science and
religion.

In opposition to independent research, such as had
begun to flourish, especially among German Catholics, a
new scholasticism was taught as the only correct theology.
In place of independent and impartial historical study,
history became again the handmaid of polemics. Awkward historical documents were systematically destroyed,
and a very extensive literature proceeding from the Jesuit
school sought to preclude the reading of independent
works.

Antiquated fanciful cults were brought forward again.
The worship of the Sacred Heart was spread through all
civilised languages by means of " living rosaries " and
" monthly roses "; the Madonna cult, worship of relics,
and exorcisms, first performed in private, then more and
more publicly, were accredited by miracles. And such
systematic externalisation of dogma and cult was soon
followed by the proper ethical fruits.

The parish clergy were either won over to their interest
by the emissaries of the order, or, where they would not
yield, they became a prey to the worst persecutions. In
Catholic congregations, the civil existence of all who did
not show themselves ready to identify Jesuitism and
Catholicism was zealously undermined, and a disposition
was developed towards those of another faith which made

their injury and defamation appear the first duty of Christian charity.

The new order followed the old in devoting its greatest activity to the education of the young, to the training up of a generation devoted to its own interests. To this end served, as before, the colleges and seminaries for clerics, who upon the completion of the course, and especially at the taking of the doctor's oath, vowed fidelity to the order, and in return, if they appeared at all useful, received the reversion of bishoprics, canonries, and professorships. To these schools for the clergy were soon added all kinds of institutions for the training of youth, especially for the children of the higher orders.

It was particularly for the latter that the Jesuit system of study was calculated. The strict coherence of the system, its logic which shrank from no consequences, the ready judgment concerning everything that plays any part in human development, and in general the standpoint of infallibility: all this was calculated to impose upon the youthful mind. If to this were added family traditions, by which a youth saw himself called to a position of authority over the servile, unthinking masses, we need not be surprised to find the modern pupils of the Jesuits spellbound within a magic circle, just as was the case in the days of Ferdinand II. and III. and the Thirty Years' War. Among the first of these institutions, that of Klinkowstroem in Vienna deserves mention, which, however, is antedated by the English college at Stonyhurst.

The new order as well as the old produced a considerable number of able specialists. In the domain of the exact sciences, especially, the modern Society of Jesuits counted many real celebrities. And no more than the learning, is the ascetic piety of many individual Jesuits to be undervalued among the forces over which the leaders of the order disposed. In the precepts of Loyola himself, together with a fantastic romanticism and a certain worldly wisdom, there is noticeable the manner in which his thoughts attach themselves to the words of Jesus. The success of the new order is quite unintelligible if one does not appreciate the whole power of this enthusiastic devotion.

All this learning and piety, however, are in the service of a system which not only presents the sharpest contrast to the gospel of Jesus, but which undermines the foundations of all morality. It is no mere chance that the manual of Gury, which teaches how to evade the moral law and how to defy the civil laws, has become the favourite schoolbook of the Jesuits and their associates. And Jesuit morality will remain proverbial until the order succeeds in suppressing the sources of real morality in the public conscience.

It may succeed in doing this if the independent responsibility of conscience is sacrificed to an infallible authority. But wherever the national conscience gains utterance, it will always express itself in the same way as it did in the laws of the Swiss confederation, of the new German empire, and of the French republic. We must consider the decrees of these national representative bodies as a moral verdict upon the order, and this moral verdict was not the outcome of sectarian polemics, but is based upon numerous original works of the first Catholic scholars, which set before us the real fruits of the renewed as well as of the dissolved order. Protestant representations might be charged with sectarian bias. But such a picture as — to choose one out of many— Father Curci draws of the Jesuit " fruits " is even less liable to a reproach of this kind than are the researches of Döllinger.

It would be difficult to find a more competent judge of the order than Curci,[1] — for forty years a member, the

[1] See Chapter I., page 25, note 1.

founder of the principal Jesuit organ, the *Civiltà Catholica*, and the writer of the most eloquent defence of the order against the attacks of Gioberti. Even after his celebrated proposals for reform (rejected by Pius IX., adopted in all essential points by Leo XIII.), Curci declares expressly that he does not give up his former devotion and admiration for the Society, even though with bleeding heart he must make public the causes by which the order, " at least apparently, has become the unhappy cause of the dire evils which to-day are visited upon the Church in Italy." But this historic fact forces him (in his *The New Italy and the Old Zealots*) to " disclose the network of deceptions, which owes its power to the fact that it is hidden and little known." An arrogant and superstitious faith in its power and perfection has made the order depraved beyond redemption.

It has covered with its authority and name all the base plans that have been formed and executed by the group of agitators and ambitious characters to the injury of the Church and the desecration of the Holy See, and so has stained itself with one of the worst blots of infamy which darken history.

A large share of the blame, Curci thinks, he must ascribe to his former organ, the *Civiltà Catholica*. On the methods of Roman journalism generally (including those of the Jesuit press-bureau) he makes this remark:

Its character is such that in time it destroys in the soul of the reader all respect for truth, one might almost say, for justice, and drags him down to the level of all kinds of falsifications and juggleries and sophistries and calumnies and invectives, and especially to the level of its own low ruffian-manners, in which unworthy means it is not far behind the worst of its opponents.

Curci adds in the same connection an account of how he himself before the year 1870 sought to effect a reorganisation of the order, with the aid of the order's superiors outside of Italy. But he was met with the same *Sint ut sunt aut non sint* which the last general of the order had opposed to the alternative of dissolution or reform. A provincial, to whose influence over the general Curci appealed in behalf of his proposed reform, gave the answer: " There is only one remedy, but the general cannot apply it."—" Why not ? "—" Because the only effective remedy would be to dissolve the order."

It is no exaggeration to say that modern national development hinges upon the national attitude towards the Jesuits; for the order or against the order, is the shibboleth of contemporary history. Moreover, in future the history of the Jesuits and that of the Papacy may be treated as one and the same, and we shall now endeavour to bring into view the threads of the network which the order spread during the reign of its restorer, Pius VII., starting from Rome and extending over all countries.

Next to the states of the Church the other restored Italian states, where it had been hated more than anywhere else, were soon blessed with the renewed order. In Sicily it had been restored since 1804. From there it was brought to Naples by Ferdinand I. after his victory over Murat (1814); and here, under him and his successors, it steadily gained in influence. In Piedmont, under Victor Emmanuel I., and in Sardinia, under Charles Felix, it acquired great influence. Yet among the most energetic and the best educated Italians opposition to the order grew in proportion to the spread of its power. In the Austrian dependencies its progress was somewhat slower. But here, too, Jesuit influences were at work in the suppression of dissent. In Modena, where the censorship was put into their hands, they took all obnoxious books even from private libraries. In Tuscany, the reforms of Bishop Ricci [1] stood in the way of

---

[1] The reforming bishop of Pistoya (1780). In 1791 Ricci was compelled to abdicate, and retired to private life.

the order's progress; but here, too, they were in the end successful.

As the Italian, so the Spanish restoration. Ferdinand VII. reversed the act of expulsion passed by Charles III. (1767), and declared all charges against the Jesuits to be fabrications by the " enemies of the religion of Christ." Excess of reaction led in Spain sooner than elsewhere to a revolution, and the revolution was directed principally against the Jesuits. After the French invasion and the second restoration of Ferdinand (1823) their power increased. The seed which they had sown soon bore fruit in the wars of the Carlists.

In Portugal affairs took at first the opposite course. King John VI. ($+$ 1826) declared his resolution never to suffer the Jesuits in his dominions. His son Don Pedro followed in his footsteps, and, like his father, leaned upon the liberal anti-Jesuit party. But during the usurpation of Pedro's brother, Don Miguel, the Jesuits were able to steal into the country.

In order, however, to approve itself as the counter-agent of the Revolution, which, according to the papal brief, was the principal object of its restoration, it was a matter of especial importance to the order to gain a firm foothold in France, the land of the Revolution. The restored Jesuits became hardly less fatal to France than the old society. All subsequent political disturbances in this country are intimately connected with the victories and the defeats of the order. Let us trace its first appearance in France after the Restoration.

Before this time, even under the reign of Napoleon, Jesuits were not wanting in France, though they were concealed under other names. As the conflict between emperor and pope grew more pronounced, especially during the imprisonment of the latter in France (1809–1814), the ex-Jesuits gained increasing influence over

Pius, and his scruples about the open restoration of the
order were quieted.   Even in the family of the Bonapartes, the Jesuits found favour with Cardinal Fesch,
Napoleon's uncle.   Yet not until after the legitimate
monarchy had been set up again in France, under the
protection of foreign troops, could the restoration of the
Company of Jesus be carried out.   Then there immediately began a rapid invasion of the conquered country by
the Jesuits.

The order was still nominally prohibited by the law of
the land; nevertheless the government took measures to
help its return.   In October, 1814, Louis XVIII. issued
an ordinance concerning the small seminaries, which
withdrew the superintendence over them from the universities and gave to the bishops full liberty in the choice
of teachers.   The result was to render ineffective the old
decrees against the Jesuits.   A second ordinance, of September, 1816, by which, to remedy the lack of preaching,
missions were organised, gave them a still greater advantage.

They understood well how to use these missions for
their own advantage, especially to arouse the fanaticism
of the lower classes.   The last act of the solemn services
was generally the setting up of a huge cross, to which the
converted attached hearts of lead graven with their
initials.   At the same time the people were excited
against the Protestants, and the hatred thus inflamed led
to horrible massacres, especially in the south of France.
Every effort was made to render the revolutionary and
Napoleonic epoch hateful to the lower classes, and this
effort was eminently successful.

But still more successful was another effort—the institution of Congregations of the Affiliated, of Jesuits *à
robe courte*, or in dress-suits, which served the purposes
of the order without taking the vows.   These congregations were masterfully calculated to influence the minds

of those whom it was desirable to win. There were various such congregations for the various classes. Count Artois and his daughter-in-law, the duchess of Angoulême, stood at the head of the congregation composed of the highest nobility. The higher and middle classes, artisans, domestics, soldiers, even children, had their special sodalities. And how varied was the list of names, how innocent the objects: " for the propagation of the faith," " for the defence of religion," " for the defence of the holy mysteries and the holy sacraments." Besides these there were the societies " of the sacred heart of Jesus or Mary," " of the holy rosary," " of the holy sepulchre," also the " society of regenerated France."

The centre of these congregations was the Pavillon Marsan (the seat of Count Artois), and there, even under Louis XVIII., they formed a secret government alongside of the constitutional authorities. Under Charles X. their tendencies became dominant. Their full influence, however, upon political as well as ecclesiastical conditions must be studied in connection with the history of the French Church.

With the history of the Jesuits in France their progress in the smaller neighbouring countries is intimately associated. Among the mixed peoples of the Southern Netherlands their successes were almost greater than in France itself. Of all the countries in which the Reformation had been suppressed through Jesuit influence, the provinces of the Netherlands which Spain had reconquered had been most deeply impregnated with the poison of the order. By means of the Inquisition and the Index, with the help of learning and art, a bulwark had been thrown up against the dangerous desire for liberty which prevailed in the Northern Netherlands. And the inner-Catholic movements towards reform, in the land which long cherished the traditions of Erasmus, had been subdued in the persons of Jansen and his friends.

The Company of Jesus was lord over all conditions of life, as in a second Paraguay. Even after the dissolution of the order, its spirit remained supreme, as is plainly shown by the revolution against the Emperor Joseph II. (1790). Soon after this the French arms carried Jacobite rule into this land, the first which yielded to the arms of the Revolution. But as in France, so here, too, the excesses of the Revolution prepared the way for a counter-revolution. After the Restoration Belgium immediately becomes one of the most important centres of the order.

For the interests of the Jesuits nothing could have been more opportune than the suicidal decree of the Congress of Vienna, which riveted together the Northern and the Southern Netherlands [1]—in every way the antipodes the one of the other. The Jesuits were in the forefront of the agitation immediately set on foot against the Protestant dynasty of William I. At the same time the old States-General were opened to their settlement. Two of the first four generals of the new order, Roothan and Beckx, were born Belgians. The Dutch Jesuit institute in Katwyk, with its numerous dependencies, is a model of modern Jesuit strongholds. In the revolution of 1830, in the constant increase of Jesuit intrigue in Holland, in the repeated attempts to subject the neighbouring Prussian provinces to the same tendencies, we shall again and again have to follow up the footprints of the Jesuits.

At the same time the Jesuits pushed westward, into the Catholic cantons of French Switzerland. Fribourg had opened its gates to them in the year 1818, and they

---

[1] The Congress of Vienna in 1815 formed the kingdom of the Netherlands, comprising the former republic of Holland and Austrian Belgium, under King William I., the former stadtholder.

at once undertook to demolish all that the last generation had with much labour achieved. The Franciscan father, Girard, working in the spirit of Pestalozzi, but upon a positive and churchly basis, had so greatly promoted the interests of education in Fribourg, that his work was generally accepted as a model. But Girard's work found no favour in the eyes of the Jesuits. In its place a great Jesuit school (aided by a bequest of a million and a half) was founded. Fifty-seven priests and fifteen professors, almost all foreigners, have here laid their magic spell upon thousands of boys, chiefly of noble parentage. In Fribourg the most influential Jesuit pupils of Austria and Germany were trained; and from Fribourg proceeded the efforts to bring the other Swiss cantons under subjection to the Jesuits.

In Northern Switzerland the order was not officially introduced until later. But Vulliemin, in his *History of the Swiss Confederation*, gives the following instructive picture of the condition of affairs immediately after the Restoration in those places which had been given over to the Jesuits:

A new spirit came over the Catholic cantons. The same spirit began to prevail simultaneously in the German and the French parts of Switzerland. In villages where the children of both confessions had lived together in daily intercourse, parents and children were commanded in future to avoid mixing with Protestants; in places where the same building had served as a place of worship for members of both faiths there arose rich churches solely for the Roman worship. The nuncio came out of the obscurity in which he had long remained. His manner was the same as that which Rome had cultivated in the last century. The bishops prohibited the reading of the Bible and withdrew their sanction of mixed marriages. Associations spread tales of miracles and appeals for pilgrimages over the land. Religious zeal everywhere found ready means to accomplish its purpose. The severe discipline of the army, the general at the head, was to lead to victory. The plan, according to the watchword given, was to destroy Carthage and to build Rome.

In the following generation the fruits of this sowing had ripened. The war of the Sonderbund,[1] similar in its beginning to the revolution in Belgium, resulted in the defeat of the Jesuits. But the work begun under Pius VII. in Fribourg was not without lasting results.

It took longest for the order to gain a foothold in Germany. The repeated attempts at reform which German Catholicism made bear witness to the failure of Jesuit influences at the time. Even in Austria their progress was slow, and they had to hide themselves for a time under other names—Liguorians, or Fathers of the Faith. In Bavaria, King Maximilian and King Louis were long suspicious of the Jesuits. In Prussia the order received no official sanction during the reign of Pius VII., although the Rhine province felt the influence of the neighbouring Belgium. Dresden was one of the first centres of operation of the order in Northern Germany, and from here proceeded a strong missionary influence. The conversions of the dukes of Köthen and of Gotha were followed by numerous others among the nobility.

Whichever way we turn, everywhere we see the order immediately after its restoration devoting its accustomed energy to the founding of new strongholds, and in all countries we trace the operations of the pious fathers, especially in the greatest crises and the bloodiest wars. And yet it is a remarkable fact that the pontificate of Pius VII., which had restored the Company, saw its downfall in the country where it had remained in existence after the

---

[1] The seven Catholic cantons, under the leadership of the Jesuits, wished to establish a separate confederacy ; this led to the war of the Sonderbund, 1847.

dissolution under Clement XIV. In Russia, Catherine, and her successors, Paul I. and Alexander I., had all been favourably disposed to the order, and it had flourished. So great was the confidence of the order in its own future throughout Russia, that a comprehensive plan had been formed to bring the whole educational establishment of the empire under its power. But their first successes made them forget their prudence, and they called down upon themselves the vengeance of the orthodox Church.

In the year 1820 they were expelled for ever from the empire. The following causes are named in the decree of banishment: "Their political wrangling, their pro-selytising, their peace-destroying intrusion into the family life of noble houses, the gross use they made of the weaknesses of the female sex." This banishment made an end of their open, but not of their secret, activity. Poland became, as formerly, their headquarters, from where with untiring zeal they stirred up new revolutions. But the motives which prompted Alexander I., so long their friend, to expel them are thoroughly typical of what happened in all those countries which sooner or later were obliged to adopt the same course.

Thus the restoration of the order opened an era of counter-reformation, as in the year 1540. In the choice of means the new Jesuits were no more scrupulous than the old. The latter had formulated the murder of tyrants into a doctrine, and had found willing hands for their theories, as in the murders, quickly following one upon the other, of William of Orange (1584), Henry III. of France (1589), and Henry IV. (1610), and in the repeated attempts upon the life of Elizabeth of England. The new Jesuits found zealous instruments in many Poles and Irishmen. There is hardly a revolution in which they did not have a hand. When the revolution was succeeded by the inevitable reaction, they knew how to

4

make themselves conspicuous as the deliverers from the revolution. The military and irresponsible management of the order made it the special favourite of the military sovereigns, who were for controlling spiritual movements by means of the drill-sergeant's discipline. And there was nowhere a parallel to the compact organisation of the order.

The history of the restored Company of Jesus teaches us to realise the significance of the fact that several thousands of educated, in part learned, men, associated for a common purpose as instruments without a will of their own, seconded by hundreds of thousands of affiliated members, with great financial means, with favour from above, guided by prudent calculation, with unparalleled dexterity in the use of all circumstances, wage daily and hourly war against modern culture.[1]

[1] " To the general characterisation given in Chapter II. should be added a copious collection of quotations, for which, however, it is to be regretted, space is wanting. But we must here insist most emphatically upon the necessity of a systematic study, by Protestant scholars, of the writings of the Jesuits themselves, very much more thorough than has hitherto been made. Besides the Catholic historians, there are few who have even a superficial knowledge of the Jesuit literature " (Extract from the author's note in the literary-critical supplement). In this note the author gives a brief review of the comprehensive literature dealing with the topic of this chapter.

CHAPTER III

THE ERA OF THE CONCORDATS UNDER PIUS VII.[1]

THE restoration of the order of Jesuits was, according to the bull of Pius VII., prompted by the havoc of the Revolution and the need of some weapon against it. The same cause lies behind the second great phenomenon of the time, whose connection with the first now demands our attention. The period which saw the Jesuits resume their open activity was also the period of the new concordats between the Vatican and the several states, which brought to the Curia unexpected triumphs over the secular powers as well as over the ancient national churches. These great triumphs, like the restoration of the Jesuits, are chiefly due to the counter-revolutionary spirit of absolutism which was prevalent, whose influence was everywhere felt. In the concordats ecclesiastical and political absolutism entered into alliance, against independent religious and national development, against the principles of the Reformation as well as those of the Revolution.

As we study the history of each separate country, we are led again and again to this absolutism as the final cause of the political and ecclesiastical disorders which followed. The spirit of the Restoration, prevalent among the ruling classes, placed itself in direct opposition to the

---

[1] The era following the restoration of Pius VII. in 1814, during which he made "concordats" with all those governments in Europe and America where the Church was allied with the State.

ideals of national progress. But we must not neglect to notice other secondary causes which contributed to produce the disorders. They are to be found in the ignorance of ecclesiastical affairs among statesmen; in the continued influence of the Napoleonic concordat of 1801, and in the prudent use by the Curia of present conditions.

The ignorance among the negotiators (mostly Protestant) as to the true conditions of Catholicism, is almost incredible. The consequence of this ignorance was an utter incapacity to follow the tortuous path of curialistic reservations. German ministers proceeded upon the assumption that the Febronian [1] liberal views, to which they were accustomed in Germany, were everywhere in vogue. Most statesmen remained in absolute ignorance of Roman principles, and they never realised that these principles were the very same as those that had prevailed in what was to the statesman a forgotten past. "When they began negotiations with the Curia,"—says Otto Mejer in his *History of the Roman-German Question,—* "they left entirely out of view the character and relations of the opinions accepted at Rome and the range of thought which directed the negotiations on the part of the Curia."

Still more fatal was the ignorance and consequent neglect which especially the Protestant negotiators manifested in regard to the national aspirations of Catholicism. The confusion, customary in Protestant theology, of the infallibility of the Church and the infallibility of the pope,

[1] Bishop Hontheim, of Treves, in the year 1763, published a work *On the State of the Church and the Legitimate Power of the Roman Pontiff*, under the pseudonym "Justinus Febronius." Hontheim stood in connection with the Jansenists and his work was an effort to transplant the Gallican system into Germany. He upheld the episcopal against the papal system; the pope does not represent the Church, the ecumenical council is the true representative. The bishops are the successors of the apostles. Catholic princes are called upon to combine for the restriction of the papal power.— These opinions were long held and taught by Hontheim · but in the end, at eighty years of age, he was obliged to recant.

gave no little impulse towards the final adoption of the latter dogma. In the same manner it was considered an axiom by Protestant diplomats that the office of bishop had its source in the higher office, in the divine right of the Papacy. The pope created bishoprics and sanctioned bishops. Most of these gentlemen had probably never heard of the constitution of the ancient Church, the very reverse of this (as it is found especially in Cyprian, the real originator of Catholic Church principles), and were ignorant of the independence of the original Germanic churches (according to the energetic testimony of Columban and Willibrord, the true apostles of the Germans).

Just as little did they seem to know of those indispensable foundations of an independent state, about which the disputes in the Middle Ages concerning investiture centred, or of the endeavours for reform within the Church made by the great councils of the fifteenth century. The thorough investigations of Protestant historians of the eighteenth century concerning State and Church (Plank, Moser, Walch, Le Bret) were as good as non-existent for the politicians of the Restoration. Did they not date from the period of unbelieving, revolution-breeding rationalism, whose products were to be so soon as possible forgotten?

The principles in vogue within the Catholic Church itself in the era before the Revolution were looked upon as especially heretical. Rome did not wish to be reminded of these principles; and to bring to remembrance awkward historical data, which did not agree with Roman dogmas, was at Rome considered in itself heretical. The diplomats, to whom heresy and the spirit of revolution were synonymous, thought this quite in order. It was therefore an easy matter by the use of heretical epithets, such as Jansenism, Febronianism, Josephinism, to impress the revolutionary stamp upon all efforts to maintain a certain independence of national churches.

One must go far back in history to find parallels to
these methods.   We discover their prototype in the second third of the fifteenth century, when the acquisitions
of the great reform councils of Constance and Basle were
bargained away; and in the time of the counter-reformation, when, at the Council of Trent, opposition to the
Reformation was bought at the price of the triumph of
papal principles.   The same concentration of Catholicism
in the Papacy, which had brought to a standstill the independent expansion of national life, which had smothered
the aspirations of councils and of the Reformation, was
now counted upon to act as a dam against the Revolution.

There was only this difference between the present and
the former periods: in those times it was Catholic and
mostly spiritual statesmen who, with an eye to their own
end, lost sight of the impairment of ancient Church
liberties; while now Protestant statesmen in the ignorance
of a childlike faith placed themselves at the service of the
Curia.   When the agents of the states proceeded upon
the assumption that the pope nominated bishops and
created sees, they conceded claims which the older
Catholicism had always disputed.

We must not leave out of sight the special pattern
which was, consciously or unconsciously, followed by the
diplomats of the Restoration.   All the concordats were
but imitations of that which Napoleon Bonaparte as first
consul had concluded in the beginning of the century.
By this concordat the ancient French pre-revolutionary
Church had been suppressed, its legal bishops deposed,
the new bishops made the subject creatures of the pope,
the great mass of the clergy degraded into curates *ad
nutum episcopi*, and the congregations turned over to the
mercy of the clerics who were drilled in the new seminaries.   And this entire new Church system was simply
a copy of the political absolutism under which the son of

the Revolution had humbled a people that dreamed of liberty and equality. The restored powers had but to walk in his footsteps, both in regard to the end sought and to the means by which that end was to be accomplished.

We are not in ignorance of the motives which prompted Napoleon in this matter. He was guided by the same principles as in the negotiations just previous to this with the Mohammedan Muftis, to whom he spoke of himself as a good Mohammedan. This is what he said to the philosopher Cabanis: " The concordat is a religious vaccination ; in fifty years there will be no more religion in France." Nevertheless, it was of the highest importance to his policy that he should appear before the people as the saviour of an endangered religion; and to the pope, when he invited him to the coronation, he spoke of the concordat as "the regeneration of Christianity in France." The necessity of this regeneration of Christianity is explained in a speech of Portalis delivered in the legislative body (after the expulsion of the members from whom opposition was expected):

Because the morality of citizens is necessary for the state, religion is necessary ; for morality without dogma is justice without a tribunal. The great multitude needs commands. and therefore an abstract religion without ceremonies does not suffice. One must take religion on faith as the work of God, for all is lost as soon as one sees in it the hand of man. If Christianity has certain peculiar dogmas, these fill out the empty space which is left by the reason.

A significant sign of the times in which the " regeneration of Christianity " was brought about was the device of General Berthier to get the generals into church for the solemn act of Napoleon's coronation: he invited them to breakfast and when the party broke up he arranged to meet the procession as it was going to the church, so that they could not do otherwise than join it.

Such was the salvation of religion, the restitution of the altars, the regeneration of Christianity, in the era which carried Napoleon to victory. Nevertheless the concordat was a mighty triumph for the Church, if by the Church we understand the hierarchy. Only Gallicans, like d'Haussonville and Archbishop Affre, and Protestant idealists have come to a different conclusion. Yet this difference in judgment is no contradiction. For to the latter the Church stood for religion in the spirit of Christ, to the papalists the Church stood for the hierarchy. And hierarchical absolutism has rightly recognised its twin-brother in cæsarian absolutism.

In the ecclesiastical policy of Napoleon we see the origin of the politico-ecclesiastical reaction over the whole of Europe. Wherever the power of the empire extended his initiative was followed. The Italian concordat, the concordats of the states of the Rhine Confederation, the concordats with Bavaria and Würtemberg (whose completion, however, was deferred to a later period), were imitations of the French and date from the time of Napoleon himself. The example which he set of exploiting the most sacred human needs for political purposes proved even at that time exceedingly contagious; and the conquerors of Napoleon had only to follow an established method in order to share with the pope in the exploitation of the popular faith.

They forgot that the final result of the Napoleonic concordat had been the first and severest defeat of Napoleon. Just as little did it occur to them that the course which was alone in accord with the principles of the gospel and of modern times had already been taken by the American Union, and had been crowned with the best success. Whenever anyone pointed to the American principle and its happy results, the republican name of the Union sufficed to cast suspicion upon its liberty of conscience as revolutionary and demagogic.

Napoleon's ill success on the other hand was attributed to the fact that he had deviated from the principles of his concordat and had been disobedient to the divine admonition of the Holy See. The view soon became prevalent which found the first cause of his misfortunes in the papal ban.[1] As long as he stood upon good footing with the pope, he was favoured by fortune. With the papal ban the divine wrath descended upon him. According to this view it is not surprising that after the Restoration his enemies followed his example of using ecclesiastical interests as a means for political ends — with the same result for them all in the end.

But, in order to explain the incredible gains which the Papacy made, we must allow due weight also to the political genius of the Vatican. The priestly politicians have always outwitted secular statesmen, and one day the latter were surprised by a clerical declaration of war. A Consalvi against a Niebuhr had victory assured from the start. It was a part of the far-seeing calculation of the papal secretary, whose eye surveyed the whole broad field in the negotiations for the concordats, to push forward the conventions with the " friendly " governments and retard those with the others. In this way the former became the models for all. In the history of the old popes none of the successors had ever given up a claim which a predecessor had in any instance carried through, and now the decisions of the Spanish and the Sardinian concordats were brought to bear upon France, the French concessions were used against Bavaria, the Bavarian concordat against Naples, the Neapolitan against Prussia, the Prussian bull of circumscription against Hanover and the Church province of the upper Rhine.

[1] The coronation, in which the pope was made to serve the ends of the emperor, was shortly followed by a rupture between the two. On the 10th of June, 1809, the states of the Church were by imperial decree incorporated in the French empire. The pope immediately excommunicated Napoleon.

In the mean time not only did each of the state men think he had obtained more for himself and his government than his colleagues, but they all looked upon the concessions they had made to the Curia as a gift vouchsafed by the latter. None understood that according to the view of the Vatican a concordat was anything but a valid compact between two independent contracting parties, that it was only a concession made for the moment to human ideas of justice, which the Holy Father could take back at any time by virtue of his divine right.

Spain was one of the most " friendly " governments. Immediately after the Restoration, the ecclesiastical decrees of the Cortes of 1812 were suspended and the concordat of 1782 restored. Little Sardinia followed Spain. By the new agreement with Rome not less than ten bishoprics were restored and richly endowed.

In the Neapolitan kingdom, owing to certain long-standing disputes with the Curia, the process was slower; but Consalvi finally obtained his purpose by means of a court intrigue. The old-Catholic Josephine [1] traditions were entirely suppressed by the new concordat; and the Roman Catholic Church was declared the only Church recognised by the law.

In France, the result of the protracted secret negotiations was a concordat concluded in 1817, by which the Napoleonic concordat of 1801 was abolished and the old concordat of 1516 with its pre-Reformation articles was restored. This compact, however, excited decided opposition among the representatives of the state and those of the Gallican traditions, and in a short time had brought forth a considerable body of literature, pro and con. According to the constitution, the project had to receive the sanction of the legislature, to which it was submitted by the ministry as a *projet de loi*. The legislature demanded

---

[1] This refers to the era of the liberal emperor Joseph II. of Austria (1765–1790).

important changes. The pope's answer to these demands was that " the intended changes are impracticable, the whole proceeding inadmissible; for whatever was prescribed by the pope in ecclesiastical affairs, with the sanction of the king, had already the character of a valid legal enactment and could not be submitted to the deliberations of a legislative assembly." The result of this impertinent answer on the part of the pope was that the *projet de loi* was withdrawn. The compact was suspended, and the Napoleonic concordat of 1801 thereby became again valid, and remained so. But the objects of the Vatican were indirectly achieved. And the ultramontanisation of the French Church proceeded energetically, the Curia looking upon the concordat of 1817 as the actually valid agreement. All further conventions were merely provisional.

However great were the acquisitions of the Papacy in the Latin countries, the question here was essentially about the restoration of an ecclesiastical system which had held undisputed sway before the Revolution. The change which the Restoration effected consisted in the increased influence of the Curia upon the inside affairs of the Church. It was quite different in the Germanic countries, especially in Germany, where the destruction of the old empire had entirely altered the ecclesiastico-political conditions. When they undertook to reduce these conditions to order it never occurred to the statesmen of the time to accomplish their object by constituting an independent national Catholic Church; they employed what appeared to them the simplest means: the subjection of the Church to the authority of Rome. Catholics of national proclivities were slighted by those who should have afforded them every possible help, and the Curia understood how to use every favourable moment to fish in troubled waters.

The attitude of the Vatican at this time makes it very evident where the restored Papacy recognised its most dangerous enemy. The revolutionary and destructive principles which at times assumed a threatening attitude towards the Church, yet again and again afforded to the Church the opportunity of presenting itself to the leaders of the state as the most powerful ally against the Revolution. We therefore find the papal diplomacy maintaining close relations with these same revolutionary tendencies in Belgium and the Prussian Rhineland, as well as in Poland and Ireland.

On the other hand the tendency which was opposed with deadly hatred by the papal party and, wherever possible, utterly annihilated, was that ideal of a national Catholicism, full of religious enthusiasm, of moral energy, and of intellectual aspirations, which dated from the pre-revolutionary era and had been preserved through the storms of the Revolution. The opposition to this national tendency is especially manifest in the intrigues set on foot by the Curia against Wessenberg (vicar-general and bishop-elect of the diocese of Constance).[1] The favourable moment for breaking the influence of Wessenberg and his friends had come and was thoroughly used. Catholic Germany was to be ultramontanised, and German Catholic theology, which after the wars of liberation had taken up its task with renewed enthusiasm and which soon raised itself to a level with Protestant theology, was throttled in its infancy.

The history of the German concordat is closely interwoven with the general development of German Catholicism, and must be studied in connection with this general development. Here we shall only briefly refer to the concordats with the other states. It is remarkable that Austria is not among the German governments which at this time formed a compact with Rome. The reason

[1] See page 33, note.

was that in Austria the liberal traditions of the time
of the emperor Joseph long prevailed; and the Curia
gave another illustration of its temporising principles:
it waited for a more favourable time. Russia, however, the ally of Austria, accepted from Pius VII. in
1818 a bull of circumscription for Poland, and Alexander I. richly endowed the Polish Church. For Ireland
also Consalvi won large concessions from the English
government.

The policy of the concordats was nowhere more fatal
than in the United Netherlands, that union soldered
together by the Congress of Vienna. The unnatural
position of the new state — made up of Protestant Holland and Catholic Belgium — was recognised and taken
advantage of from the start by the Curia. Among the
many negotiations which Consalvi carried on in behalf of
the concordats, in which he always succeeded in getting
the better of the state agents, there is none other which
puts his diplomatic skill in so clear a light as the apparently unsuccessful negotiations with the new royal government of the Netherlands. This government was more
bent on winning the clericals by concession than on
remaining true to the glorious traditions of the States-
General, and like all the rest believed that its best support
was in the Roman Curia.

In the year 1817 the ambassador from the Netherlands
in Rome offered the concordat of Napoleon as a basis of
negotiations. The Curia refused to treat upon this basis,
and referred to the recently concluded concordat with
Bavaria as a model. The government asked the Curia
to name the points in which it wished to have the Napoleonic concordat (which was still in force for Belgium)
changed. Consalvi answered that this concordat was
entirely out of the question, and he refused to even
name a basis for new negotiations: " The Holy See
could not take the initiative; rather was it in accordance

with the well-known and unchangeable character of
the general papal laws that the modifications desired
should be indicated by those who desired them."
The government took no account of the popular desire for political liberty, and sacrificed more and more
to clericalism.   The final result was the concordat of
1827, which became one of the prime causes of the revolution of 1830 in Belgium and of the internal disorders in
Holland.

Here too, as everywhere, the path which Consalvi
chose led to the goal—the universal triumph of the papal
principle.   To the era of the concordats are primarily
traced the successes of the papal system in every country, successes which surpassed even those of the first
counter-reformation.   The spell of that wonderful magic
with which Consalvi with his far-sightedness knew how
to captivate the diplomats, for a long time warped even
the judgment of historians.   No less a writer than Ranke
has written a panegyric of Consalvi; and in the preface
to his *History of the Popes* he states emphatically that
" the times when there was any cause of fear are past."
But Ranke's judgment was based upon the despatches of
Niebuhr,[1] the blinded minister of Prussia at the court of
Rome.

[1] A number of references by the author to the great historian of Rome
have been left out in the translation, because calculated more particularly
for German readers.   The author is unsparing in his criticism of Niebuhr.
He was at this time ambassador from Prussia to the Vatican, and although
so keen-sighted in historical matters at a distance, he was entirely blind to
the tendencies of contemporary ecclesiastical forces, and did much to suppress the national aspirations of German Catholicism and to subject the
Church in Germany to the absolute power of the Papacy.

CHAPTER IV

THE STATES OF THE CHURCH UNDER PIUS VII.

IN the eyes of the papal diplomacy there was something
more important even than the restoration of the Order
of Jesus and the new concordats: this was the recovery
of the states of the Church. If this oldest and most
legitimate monarchy, the necessary support for the authority of the Pontifex Maximus, were not rescued from
the Revolution, no other monarch could count upon saving his dynasty: such was the argument among diplomats
who knew nothing of the first principles of independent
statehood. And the Congress of Vienna thought no
more of the fraud and violence which had marked the
foundation and enlargement of the Church state than of
the utter incapacity which its priestly rulers had so often
shown in its government.

It was an old story. And for that very reason, in
order to understand the influence upon the Papacy of
the restoration of the temporal power, we shall have to
glance back to the time when the Papacy first acquired
this power, to the time of the donation of Pepin in
755 A.D.,[1] which Napoleon as the successor of Pepin and
of Charlemagne declared abrogated.

Two centuries of continued conspiracy against imperial

[1] The gift by Pepin of the exarchate of Ravenna, the Pentapolis (Ancona,
Sinigaglia, Fano, Pesaro, Rimini), and the territory of Bologna and Ferrara, was the foundation of the papal states.

rule at Constantinople and of renewed persecutions of the Lombards had gone before this donation. Only then did the Papacy realise its long-cherished hope, by means of the usurpation of the new Carlovingian dynasty in the kingdom of the Franks, the Curia lending its powerful aid to this *coup d'état*. It was the keys sent to Pepin from the sepulchre of St. Peter, the letters written from heaven by St. Peter, and the miracle of the transferred relics, which, together with the lust of conquest on the part of the Franks, gave the death-blow to the Lombard kingdom and brought about the separation from the Byzantine empire in the eighth century. Not until this had taken place could the donation of Pepin and of Charles create a temporal dominion for St. Peter.

The Frankish emperor, as overlord of Rome, reserved to himself certain rights; but even these were forgotten under the weak successors of Charlemagne. Pope Nicholas I., in the middle of the ninth century, supported by the pseudo-Isidorian decretals, was able to set up as independent prince and to dictate his commands to an enervated dynasty as well as to the patriarch of Constantinople and the primate of Gaul.

Upon the ruins of the empire, hastening to decay, the papal monarchy was gradually built up. But what a picture the history of those who followed Nicholas presents in the tenth century! The horrible drama of the trial of the disinterred body of Formosus,[1] the papal pornocracy under Theodora and Marozia,[2] set forth only too clearly the blessings which the temporal power of the popes in its beginning brought upon the people of the papal states.

Looking at the history of Rome with the eyes of a

---

[1] 896 A.D. "The body of the dead Formosus was exhumed, and he was put in state upon the pontifical chair, and tried and condemned by (pope) Stephen, and all his adherents deposed."

[2] Beginning of the 10th century.

Roman, we are not puzzled to understand why such men as Arnold of Brescia and Rienzi found their most faithful adherents in the papal city, and why the history of mediæval Rome is but a series of revolts against the temporal power of the Papacy.

As the immediate subjects of the pope the Romans enjoyed certain advantages, for they chiefly benefited by the large sums of money which flowed into Rome from all countries. But the reverse of the picture was not so pleasing, as Italian patriots well understood. For indolence and aversion to work and want of respect for the law distinguished the people of the Church state from their neighbours. The Pontine marshes, however, and the brigandage are not the worst fruits of ecclesiastical government. Italian patriotism, which sought to build up the longed-for Italian nationality upon the sacred institution of the family, feared above all things the loosening of ethical ties, especially those of matrimony. Among so many thousands of celibate priests, who were infallible in the eyes of their penitents, evil consequences were inevitable. And they were not wanting. As in France the love of French comedy for the adultery cult, and in Belgium the many actions at law on account of rape of children by ecclesiastics, are traceable to this cause, so the Roman cicisbeo is proverbial in all the world. One of the most learned and gifted of the popes — Pius II., as Æneas Sylvius (+ 1464), had given the first example of a licentious adultery novel (*Euryalus and Lucretia*), and it is not surprising that even to this day he has found such imitators as the father of the Countess Lambertini, Cardinal Antonelli. We may not, for good reasons, go into further details; but it would be more than unhistorical to simply ignore these moral results of the papal monarchy. More than twenty-five years ago, long before the inevitable disaster overwhelmed the states of the Church, a highly honoured Italian

5

theologian, the pupil and friend of Passaglia, pointed to this the worst side of the priest-state.

Where the principle is a bad one, its better represent-atives cannot prevent evil consequences. The reforms which the better popes of the eighteenth century, espe-cially Clement XIV., had been able to carry out were short-lived. The storms of the Revolution, therefore, which everywhere played havoc with rotten state insti-tutions, in Germany, Switzerland, and Holland, nowhere did such thorough work in clearing the atmosphere as in the papal possessions. Nowhere did this great judgment of God work better results than here.

After the Revolution, Rome, like all other states, was affected by the new spirit of the times. The first ten years of our century show a marked contrast, as well to the former as to a later period, in the care of general education. The same is true of all other interests. The French system, which came in at the Revolution, put an end to clerical prerogatives, and this effected a number of useful reforms. By opening the offices to laymen public order and safety were secured. Agriculture, commerce, and industry were in every way furthered; and in spite of the evil consequences of the continental blockade there was a marked improvement in the welfare of the people.

All these conditions were changed in a moment when the papal monarchy was restored to its former rights. Nothing else was possible, from the very nature of the Papacy. It is a mistake to suppose that the Zelanti had demanded a return to the old conditions and had stood in the way of the enlightened and progressive Liberali, who wished to retain the reforms of the French period. For it was not till after the return of Consalvi from Vienna that the *Motu Proprio* of the 6th of July, 1816, set up the new administration of the state. The system

as such is independent of personalities. The renewal of
the canon law was the inevitable consequence of the renewal of the Papacy, and the canon law brought confusion into all legal relations under the civil law. For
the source of all right was the grace, *i.e.*, the arbitrary
will, of the pope; and justice became venal.

Ranke in one of his writings praises the administration
of Consalvi and has even a word of excuse for the system
which united the spiritual and temporal government in
the hands of the same officers. His assertions were
refuted by Döllinger in 1861 in his *Church and Churches.*
The very worst of the later abuses are traced to Consalvi's *Motu Proprio* of 1816. The uniformity which
Consalvi professed to retain from the system introduced
by the French was a mere uniformity of destruction, for
it consisted in the suppression of all municipal and provincial institutions and privileges. At the same time all
power was placed in spiritual hands. The states of the
Church became what they had not been even in the Middle
Ages, an absolute bureaucracy after the French model,
only the officers were prelates of the Church. Döllinger
characterised the raw material from which these officials
were taken as that class of Roman ecclesiastics " who
with very insufficient legal and with no economic studies,
more trained than educated, more familiar with Church
ceremonies than with the complexities and the interests
of civil life, place their confidence in the patronage of a
cardinal or a monsignore.''

One of the first measures of the pope after his return
was the renewal of the monasteries and the restoration
of ecclesiastical property. The effects of the French con-
fiscation — whatever its justice may have been — had
passed off and the people had grown used to the new
conditions. Now all the chapters and monasteries received back whatever property had not been alienated
and were indemnified for what had been sold with

five-per-cent. state-bonds.   The state thereby lost considerable income, had to shoulder a heavy debt, and became involved in endless money troubles.

The second step was to restore to ecclesiastics and nobles their antiquated prerogatives.   At the same time the suppression of all provincial and municipal constitutions brought upon the laity the loss of those privileges which they had here and there enjoyed.   Taxes and burdens belonged to the people, revenue and rights to the clergy.

On every hand we find the march of progress arrested and turned back.   Instead of street-lamps and vaccination, which were abolished as revolutionary novelties, the restriction of the Jews in their Ghetto was restored.   The question of closing their quarter every evening was discussed.   This point was yielded, but it was insisted that three hundred Jews should listen to a sermon for their conversion every Saturday.

Social conditions went back even more.   Everything was farmed out, even the victualling of prisoners, and the farmers economised on the fare of these unfortunates (mostly political criminals who failed to acknowledge the benefits of the most legitimate of all monarchies), and so saved themselves from loss.

Regular treaties were made with the brigands, Consalvi having furnished the model.   Robbery and assassination became the order of the day to such an extent that the accounts of these events form a special department of literature in the next ten or twenty years.   And while robbers received annuities and the police left a free field to the bandits, police spies were placed in the service of the politico-ecclesiastical inquisition.

The administration of finance fell into such confusion that in 1816 and 1817 an association of counterfeiters could operate for a considerable time with impunity. Even the funds of benevolent institutions were robbed to a degree which passes belief.   Nowhere did the Bourse

grow into such an upas-tree as here in the paradise of
priests. The famous rich bankers, who received papal
titles as counts and princes, have almost all strange
antecedents.

The feeling among the best people about this sort of
" restoration " soon became evident. There were risings
as early as the years 1816 and 1817. Nor were these due
to the notorious secret associations. The correct papal
doctrine teaches that all the evil in the world comes from
the Carbonari, the Freemasons, and the Protestant sects,
and in the first ten years of the Restoration a number of
books were published about the Carbonari, which the
young diplomats used as true histories. Only these
accounts forgot to state that the first model of a secret
society was that of the Jesuits, and that their own political allies, such as Cardinal Ruffo's Sanfedisti, had learned
the art of conspiracy from the Jesuits. The Carbonari in
their turn got their methods from the Sanfedisti, besides
following them in tracing their origin to remote antiquity.

The secret association of the Carbonari (charcoal-burn-
ers), as far as we can trace it, was founded under Napoleon,
in France, by irreconcilable Republicans, and was then
carried to Naples, when Murat became king in 1810. At
a time when there was a general desire to get rid of foreign rule in Italy it seemed to offer the best means to
that end, and the society spread over the whole kingdom.
The importance of the association was enhanced when
Murat himself, in 1815, entered into alliance with the
conspirators, intending to use their plan for the unification of Italy to further his own interest. The Neapolitan troops carried the association into the states of the
Church. Murat was defeated, dethroned, and executed;
but the association, far from being broken up, spread
over all Italy. It derived its chief importance from its
opposition to the ill-considered measures of the restored

Papacy in the administration of the states of the Church. The anathema hurled at the Carbonari would have been effective only if the abuses had ceased at the same time.

The year 1820 showed the glowing of the embers under the ashes. The revolution broke out in Spain and soon spread to Naples and Piedmont. Fermentation at once began in the states of the Church. It did not come to a public outbreak, because the Austrians soon marched in and put down the rising in Naples and Piedmont. But this forcible restraint of popular feeling was only outwardly effective. Niebuhr's letters of 1820 and 1821 repeatedly express his fear that the states of the Church might be carried away by these movements.

To the great Powers of the Restoration the papal measures of administration appeared so imprudent, that in May, 1821, they issued a common note, which censured certain defects and proposed improvements. These propositions were ignored, as were many that followed; nevertheless, these demands for such reforms as seemed indispensable to the Powers of the Restoration after the movement of 1820 are among the most important signs of the times. All the more because they proceeded from such men as Niebuhr, who, as even his great admirer, Mrs. von Bunsen, says, could find no other cause for the revolution in Naples than the influence of the Jacobite spirit of destruction. This, he thought, could be suppressed only by force.

The diplomats in Rome needed no special powers of observation to discover the heel of Achilles of the Papacy, which even in the days of Boccaccio and Machiavelli had been very evident. But this appreciation of the temporal power as the Papacy's vulnerable point led them to wrong conclusions, and their expectations that the inevitable loss of secular dominion would carry with it the forfeiture of the Papacy's commanding position in the spiritual sphere were doomed to disappointment.

CHAPTER V

POPE LEO XII. (1823–1829)

THE nature and consequences of the principles which governed the actions of Pius VII. became more and more evident under the reign of his successor. Upon the death of Pius (August 21, 1823), the Cardinal Annibale della Genga was chosen, and assumed the name of Leo XII. As nuncio in Lucerne and Cologne, Munich and Paris, he had made himself known as an expert and astute diplomat; in Paris he had, after a sharp personal conflict, yielded to the jealousy of Consalvi. After the Restoration of 1814, therefore, he at once joined the Zelanti as the enemy of Consalvi. His election in the conclave was a victory for this party. No sooner, however, was he initiated into Consalvi's plans than he recognised in the latter his master, and continued to follow with energy the paths he had marked out.

It was a remarkable lesson which the new pope received from the secretary of his predecessor. In a lecture of several hours' duration, whose gist is known to us through Consalvi's own communication to the French ambassador, the duke of Laval, he gave to his present chief a survey of all the various countries and the connections which he had formed in them. From France, Spain, England, and Austria, to Russia and the South American republics, he opened up perspectives of the future, and filled his former opponent with such admiration, that Leo afterwards pronounced his predecessor fortunate in

having had such a minister. Everywhere was shown prudent consideration of existing circumstances, consistent
" dissimulation " of antagonistic principles, at the same
time everywhere magnificent expectations. Giving equal
consideration to Bourbons and Bonapartes, outwardly
yielding towards the Spanish court, but at the same time
making advances towards the insurgent colonies of South
and Central America, in Poland adding fuel to the ecclesiastical opposition, and counting upon the good will of
Austria, which had " never yet proved obstinate,"—such
was Consalvi's own representation of his political principles, while at the same time he pointed to the successes
which were expected in England, and as a new means of
agitation advised the proclamation of a year of jubilee.

Out of gratitude for this view of the future which he
had opened up, Leo XII. appointed Consalvi prefect of
the Propaganda. Though the latter died soon after
(January, 1824), the principles of his policy remained.
The accession to the throne of the candidate of the Zelanti was marked only by a more decided emphasising of
the lines drawn under Pius VII.

A circumstance characteristic of the accelerated reaction under the present reign was the permission given
by Leo XII. for the publication of two writings, whose
issue Consalvi, from motives of political prudence, had
prohibited. One, by the Dominican Philippo Anfossi,
declared the restitution of spiritual property necessary
for the salvation of those who had obtained such property
without the sanction of the holy see. The other, by
Carolo Fea (superintendent of the Capitoline Museum
and the Chigi Library), maintained the supremacy of the
papal see over temporal princes and in temporal things.
Before this he had only been allowed to prove the dogmatic infallibility of the pope.

Not only were others permitted, under the new pontificate, to express such views; Leo himself acted in the

same spirit. As cardinal, he had been considered no friend of the Jesuits. As pope he showed them more favour than his predecessor. Soon after his accession the Collegium Romanum was restored to the Jesuits, on which occasion their sacred customs and their great learning were extolled; and the various memoirs of these times tell of the continued increase of their possessions in Rome during the following years.

The new encyclical of Leo XII. (May 5, 1824) condemned, under the name of tolerantism, liberty of faith and of conscience, and anathematised the Bible societies. The spread of the Bible in the language of the people was called a fatal practice, a godless invention, which, by means of perverted interpretation, was making of the Bible a gospel of the devil. The condemnation of dissenters was more specifically emphasised in the brief of the 2d of July, 1826, to the clergy of Poitiers: " Everyone who separates himself from the Roman Catholic Church, however otherwise blameless his manner of life, has on account of this one crime, because he is excluded from the unity of Christ, no part in the eternal life; God's wrath hangs over him."

Following the advice of Consalvi, Leo ordered a jubilee for the year 1825—to the praise of God for the victory over the Revolution. Special indulgences were proclaimed for prayers in behalf of the extirpation of heresy. With the jubilee was connected the beatification of the Spanish minorite Julianus. The accounts of the miracles upon which his claims were based, and which were pictorially represented in St. Peter's Church, were so audacious as to fairly challenge modern ethics and modern culture. One of the three miracles required for the beatification pretended that the new saint had caused half-roasted birds to fly away from the spit.[1]

[1] The Romans thought a saint who should reverse the process deserved the preference (Nielsen).

The pomp of the processions during the year of jubilee was extraordinary. The Propaganda boasted that during this time 150 Protestant and Jewish souls had been rescued from damnation. The duke of Angoulême [1] received the holy sword. Frederick the Great, in his time, had laughed at this sword, when his enemy, the Austrian general, Daun, received it (after the battle of Hochkirchen, 1758). Now it gave a new glory to the man who put down the Spanish revolution and restored Ferdinand VII. (1823). The widowed queen of Sardinia received the golden rose.

The populace in Rome expressed its opinion of the successes of this year of jubilee by setting up a large bottle (*fiasco* [2]); and behind a pious exterior was concealed the worst kind of immorality. But to the world without the jubilee had placed the Papacy in a glowing light. And to follow up the advantage, the indulgences were extended to other countries for the first half of the year 1826, the year following the jubilee.

The reign of Leo XII. is also marked by acquisitions of a more substantial nature, the fruits of the prudent policy of Consalvi. A number of new concordats were negotiated: among these was the concordat with Hanover, which had held out for some time, but now was obliged to take shelter under the bull of circumscription for Prussia (1827). Of great importance for the papal policy was the reorganisation of the ecclesiastical province of the Upper Rhine. This included the dissolution of the see of Constance and the definitive removal of Wessenberg. [3]

---

[1] Commander of the French forces which invaded Spain in 1823 and suppressed the revolution.

[2] A bottle (*fiasco*) was found cut in the wall of St. Peter's close by the door by which on the previous day the pope had entered in solemn procession to open the year of jubilee.

[3] See note 1, page 33.

A further victory was inaugurated by the brief concerning the newly founded see of Basle. The conference of the state diocese was able to oppose only a theoretical claim of independent state-rights to the papal pretensions which this brief contained. The same is true of the concordat with the Netherlands, which paralysed the last remnant of governmental authority in the revolution-loving provinces.

Besides the European concordats, there were those with the South American republics, which, with their newly awakened love of political freedom, had begun to aspire to ecclesiastical independence. They now became sons of the Vatican, more obedient even than their brothers in the mother-country of Spain. In these more than half-barbarous lands it was possible to introduce once more the unadulterated principles of the Curia, especially its intolerance towards dissenters. The same countries were afterwards held up by the reactionaries of Europe as the ideal of the true liberty of the Church.

Thus was the Church newly established on both sides of the ocean and everywhere the vacant bishoprics restored; and all along the line we see the victory of the papal principle over the old rights of the national churches.

These triumphs of the papal policy all appear as the ripened fruits of the seed sown by Consalvi. Leo's secretary of state, the aged Sommaglia, did not equal his predecessor in diplomatic skill; but the pope found a satisfactory substitute in Bernetti. The latter had inherited from Consalvi the art of appearing liberal towards the politicians, and thereby making the guileless phraseology of the Curia current among these very politicians. Scarcely less important were the services now rendered by Monsignore Capaccini, also a pupil of Consalvi, whom the latter had drawn from a mathematical professorship into the diplomatic service. Bunsen, in spite of later disappointments, continued to preserve a kind remembrance of him, and in 1828 he warmly recommended him to the English nobility.   Capaccini, on this same journey to England, sought to persuade the old Catholic archbishop of Utrecht that it was his first duty as a Christian to do violence to his own convictions and render a blind obedience to the pope.   In England he undertook to quiet the fears of statesmen in regard to the policy of the Curia.   At the same time the Irish bishops, with the assent of the papal legate, declared officially that the theory of papal infallibility was not in accordance with Catholic Church doctrine.   The so-called emancipation of the Catholics (1829), founded upon this declaration, was one of the first events of the following papal reign; to Leo XII. belongs the merit of having prepared the way for it.

All these successes would not have been possible had not the spirit of the times now, as before, been favourable.   For the action of the several governments, which after the suppression of the revolutions in Naples and Spain (1820–23) made the muzzling of popular aspirations their first concern, was greatly to the advantage of the Papacy; and with this factor we must couple another, equally favourable to the Papacy,—the prevailing tendency in the still fashionable French literature.

Lamennais' celebrated journey to Rome took place before the year of jubilee, 1825.   He was everywhere hailed as conqueror.   His fervent propagandism in behalf of the conception of liberty, which Gregory VII. and Boniface VIII. had represented in opposition to the temporal rulers, prepared a welcome for him in Rome such as a simple author had never yet received from the wearer of the tiara.   The pope hung Lamennais' picture in his bedroom.   He offered him the cardinal's hat, and made him rich presents.   Besides several audiences, he invited him to an intimate conversation. The pope himself ordered apartments for him in the Roman college, later he was offered rooms in the Vatican. Cardinals and prelates vied in their efforts to make his acquaintance. Among all these honours, Lamennais thought much of the fact that several Jesuits visited and expressed their agreement with him. In later times Wiseman said of Lamennais' journey to Rome: " He stood at this time at the summit of his fame, and was considered one of the most highly gifted representatives, not only of the faith but also of the strictest Roman principles."

The significance of Lamennais and of the ideas for which he stood represents an important chapter in the history of French and Belgic Catholicism. Even before his journey to Rome he had exercised an increasing influence in favour of the papal system, by a whole series of writings as reckless as they were brilliant. The journey to Rome gave the highest authorisation to his activity. After his return from Rome he began his war of extermination against Gallicanism, a war which became fatal in its influence upon the history of France; and the blessing of Leo XII., as well as of his successor, accompanied him in this work. But the Lamennais of the first period can only be understood as the representative of a general and growing tendency, whose after-effects meet us in all lands, and are not at all confined to the Church.[1]

While thus the power of the Papacy as a spiritual institution was being strengthened, the temper of the population of the Church-state was becoming from year to year more hostile to the papal monarchy. The reign of Leo XII. shows in this respect a remarkable change in comparison with that of Pius VII. There is no doubt that the personalities of the two popes made a great

[1] Lamennais died a most determined opponent of the Church of Rome (1854).

difference. Pius VII., the persecuted martyr, the mild and amiable man, had formed many personal friendships even among the enemies of the papal policy. His monument, for which Consalvi had left a considerable sum, was executed by the Danish Protestant, Thorwaldsen. The lines of his face bear a mild and soft expression. Gregorovius tells us, in his masterly work on the sepulchral monuments of the popes, that the princes of the Church of the time of the Thirty Years' War appear so thoroughly typical of this warlike period that they would be in place in the camp of Tilly or of Wallenstein; the monument of Pius VII., on the other hand, reminds one of the sufferings of the Revolutionary era, which won so much sympathy for the pope.

These personal sympathies were wanting to Leo XII. His earlier and later life had shown contrasts somewhat too highly coloured. As nuncio in Germany and in France della Genga was known to be the father of a large family of illegitimate children. So much the greater was the outward appearance of piety which Leo XII. as pope assumed, more especially in his precepts for others. Priests were forbidden round hats, short coats, and worldly neckties. Special prescriptions were given for the dress of women. Attendance upon church was forced upon the Jews more strictly than under Pius VII., their ghetti were surrounded by walls, all mercantile contracts between them and Christians were declared invalid. Theatres, even private ones, were placed under strict censorship; also the products of science. The scientific standard of the censors under Leo XII. may be judged by the fact that one of them confiscated the writings of Galvani (the discoverer of " galvanism "), confounding them with the works of Calvin.

With such a spirit animating the government it is not a matter of surprise that the disposition towards it of the population, especially that part which expected something more from the state than *panem et circenses*, was not favourable. The ill will of the Romans increased every year after the *fiasco* of the year of jubilee. The pope was obliged, in the year 1826, to enlarge the prisons of the Inquisition; at the same time he hurled renewed anathemas against Carbonari and Freemasons. The effect was the same as before.

Valuable light is thrown upon the reign of Leo XII. by Döllinger in his *Church and Churches* (published in 1861); and since the events of 1870 there is an added interest in comparing the conclusions which the author lays down in this work with the subsequent course of events. The book is the most brilliant and most enthusiastic pleading for the primacy of the Papacy, the most acute and able polemic against the churches separated from the Papacy. Nevertheless, it cost the author the irreconcilable resentment of the papal party.

The explanation of the apparent contradiction lies in the historical portraits which he draws of the popes. Nothing which could be said to the credit of any of them is forgotten. Of Leo XII. he says (p. 555) not only that " the sick, weakly pope worked indefatigably," but we learn that he was animated by the best purpose, that he felt how unbearable the present conditions and institutions were, and only deceived himself as to the choice of means and in his effort to put new life into what was dead. What, then, was the result of his reign? The restoration of the Inquisition, the institution of a widely ramified system of espionage for watching over officials and the morals of the people. Besides this, the surrender of the entire system of education into the hands of the clergy, the reintroduction of the Latin language in the legal processes of several tribunals, and prohibition of vaccination. This is Döllinger's summing up: " Leo's administration became the most unpopular of any for the past hundred years." The sources upon which this judgment is founded are the annals of Coppi, the highly esteemed Roman prelate, who was himself frequently consulted in state affairs, and the official reports of the French ambassador, Chateaubriand.

Not only did native Romans become, under the second of the Restoration popes, more inimical to the papal power than under his predecessor; keen-sighted foreign observers also, even when they came to Rome full of sympathy for the fight that the Papacy in its stronghold waged against modern infidelity, found themselves bitterly disappointed. As second chaplain attached to the Prussian embassy, young Richard Rothe [1] was called to Rome at the time of the change of popes. During his university studies at Heidelberg he had fallen under the influence of a strongly "catholicising" conception of the Church. He began to admire Gregory VII., and became enamoured of a character like that of François de Sales. In this mood he came to Rome. Here he soon received a very different idea of the Papacy and its satellites. He became, indeed, more imbued with the noble magnificence of the Catholic Church-ideal, but he now learned to make a clear distinction between Papalism and Catholicism.

After a short stay in Rome (a few months before the accession of Leo XII.) Rothe writes that it is impossible for him to describe how the Roman cult disgusts him. In speaking of the first " circular letter " of the new pope, he characterises " the incredibly impudent tone " as most offensive. His letters give vivid but melancholy pictures of the *Anno santo* and the new saints. The year of jubilee moves him to complain that the Church in Rome has become a perfect institution for excise. As the foundation of the whole Roman system he recognises complete religious infidelity. He entered into controversy with a

[1] The celebrated German theologian, author of *Theological Ethics*.

Jesuit father, but found his opponent too far beneath any possible intellectual standard. The sum and substance of his judgment of what he learned in Rome is given in the following words:

The Catholic Church in this place has no conception of the spiritual life which since the Reformation has developed in European Christendom. One becomes here more and more convinced that the Reformation gave birth to a really new spiritual world. What would have become of Europe, not only as regards religion, but also in science, art, and politics, without the Reformation?

The desperate struggle of the Curia against Protestantism appeared to him in Rome so entirely hopeless that he says: " In order to become indifferent to all machinations of Catholicism against Protestantism, and to lose all fear of the former, one needs only come to Rome."

The death of Leo XII. (February 12, 1829) occurred under such striking circumstances that even the Swiss guard on duty spoke of poisoning, and Massimo d'Azeglio expressed the same suspicion. Hase says: " He made himself generally hated in Rome; from prince to beggar, nobody was his friend." In a letter written by Bunsen's wife, published in his biography, she says:

The simultaneous deaths of the pope and the banker Torlonia have brought out the most striking contrast in the public opinion; the death of Torlonia was universally lamented, while that of the pope was received with indecent joy. The time of the year in which it took place (that is, the interference which it caused with the carnival) was the only circumstance connected with it which was not welcome to the populace of Rome.

Bunsen recognised more clearly than most of his contemporaries the spirit of the restored Papacy. But it was only in sleepless nights that he thought of the danger which it threatened to the modern state or the Protestant Church.

6

CHAPTER VI

PIUS VIII. (1829–1830), AND THE REVOLUTION OF 1830

LEO XII. was succeeded by the aged and sickly Pius VIII., who died within a year. So short a reign could produce no important changes; its historical character consists in carrying forward the principles of the Restoration.

Only diplomats who have no real understanding for ecclesiastical questions speak of liberal or illiberal popes. The fact is that all individuals, no matter what their differences, have to yield to the machinery of the Curia. Pius VIII. in some aspects of his character may remind us of Pius VII., and Pius IX. resembled both in that the first phase of his reign was characterised by greater mildness. On the other hand, the sharp, rugged, ungenial nature of Leo XII. seemed to be renewed in Gregory XVI., and then to a greater degree in Leo XIII. But the course of the papal policy has remained invariably the same under the government of one and all. It is this unchangeableness of policy which has found its mystical expression in the dogma of infallibility.

Pope Pius VIII., formerly Cardinal Castiglioni, has been pictured as a man of mild spirit. Like the former pope whose name he adopted, he had suffered under the persecution of Napoleon. The process of his election was inaugurated in the conclave by an enthusiastic speech

82

which Chateaubriand delivered, who as French ambassador in Rome delighted the society of the nobility, but
who was unable to change the course of politics.

It was said to the credit of the new pope that he was
freer from nepotism than his predecessor. But his first
circular letter made it unmistakably evident that from
the moment of the " ador: tion " the individual was lost
in the system. His salutation to Christian society consisted in the customary series of anathemas against liberty
of conscience under the name of indifferentism, against
the Bible-societies, and against national development as
represented by the aspirations of Carbonari and Freemasons.

The renewed anathemas had the usual effect. Even
under the short reign of Pius VIII. there were disturbances in the Romagna. It was during this reign that
Cardinal Rivarola, sent to quiet these movements, condemned at one stroke 509 persons (among them 30 noblemen, 156 owners of estates or merchants, 74 officials, and
38 soldiers). It was considered a sign of special leniency
that the sentences of death were commuted to other
punishments. But neither strictness nor leniency could
improve untenable conditions. Hardly had Pius VIII.
been laid in his grave when open revolution broke out in
the state of the Church itself.

But, however weak in its own home, even this short
reign chronicles triumphs in foreign politics. A few
weeks after the accession of Pius VIII. the emancipation
of Catholics in England, for which preparations had long
been made, became law (April, 1829). Wellington's Tory
ministry, in their desire to outdo the Whigs, carried the
emancipation through in a manner which did not stop
with satisfying the just demands of the times, but tore
down bulwarks indispensable for the protection of the
state. At the same time the defections to the Church of

Rome, which had already begun, made increasingly rapid progress among the upper ten thousand.

In the same year, 1829, the order of the Jesuits received in the person of the Belgian Roothaan one of its most capable generals. The Company had spread to such an extent that assistants had to be given to the general for the four provinces—France, Spain, Italy, and Germany.

In France, the well-wishers of the order had come to consider its triumph assured for all time. The opposition to the order had indeed grown so powerful during the last period of Leo XII. that, in spite of the personal antipathies of Charles X., it brought about the liberal ministry of Martignac (1828). This ministry did attack the root of the evil: by the ordinance of June 16, 1828, it forbade the members of prohibited congregations to perform their offices in the smaller seminaries. But for this very reason it had soon to yield to the intrigues of the court. In its place the ministry of Polignac was called (1829), the very incarnation of clericalism. Its work was the July ordinances of 1830.[1] With these the bottom was knocked out of the barrel: the July revolution was effected with hardly any serious conflict, and the most popular war-cry of the opposition was, " À bas les Jesuites."

The fall of the friend of the Jesuits in France, Charles X., however otherwise unwelcome, gave to the Papacy an opportunity of showing itself as the guardian of legitimacy against the revolution. Charles had done more service in the pope's cause than anyone, and might surely calculate upon the solidarity of conservative interests so often appealed to by the Curia. But the pope was by no means of that mind now. The papal policy

[1] These ordinances of July 26, 1830, by which the elections recently held were declared illegal, the electoral system changed so as to restrict the suffrage to the rich landowners, and the publication of newspapers and pamphlets without the royal consent was prohibited, were the immediate cause of the revolution of 1830.

did not for a moment hesitate to sacrifice the royal tool, just as, by the concordat with Napoleon, it had sacrificed the legitimate pre-Revolutionary bishops of France; just as in after times it was to sacrifice the German bishops who had compromised themselves in the papal interests.

Charles X. had been more papal than the pope himself. Consalvi, in his time, had not concealed his personal contempt for this prince, who was a blind devotee of the system of the Restoration. In the programme which he drew up for Leo XII. he said expressly that it would cost the pope some effort to induce Louis XVIII. to forget the journey of Pius VII. to Paris for the coronation of Napoleon, but that the king's brother (Charles X.) had never heard of this journey, or had at least forgotten it. But Pius VIII. did not even content himself with leaving Charles X. in the lurch; shortly before his death he expressly made it the duty of the French clergy to subject themselves without resistance to the new order of things, to pray for the new ruler, and to show him fidelity and obedience.

This relation of the Papacy to the July revolution in France exhibits the connection, which we observe elsewhere on a much larger scale, between the Papacy and the revolutionary movements [1] of this time. Lamennais

[1] The author's contention that the Church of Rome has regularly sought and obtained profit from revolutionary movements is confirmed by a competent witness in regard to the recent riots in Milan. Dr. Nevin, rector of St. Paul's Church, Rome, writes under date of July 7, 1898, in a communication to *The Churchman*, as follows: " There is no doubt about it, that the clerical authorities in North Italy, for some time since, did all in their power to stir up sedition against the existing government. Any tools they could find—socialistic or anarchical—they have been not slow to turn against their country. And the country had a close call last May." In the same letter Dr. Nevin adds this interesting information: " Within this month six Roman priests have applied to me here to be received into the Church as a refuge from the impossible evils of the Papacy, and I have little doubt but that a movement for Catholic reform will soon arise in Rome itself."

is again the storm-bird of the general revolution; he enjoyed the blessing of Pius VIII. as well as that of Leo XII. After his brilliant reception in Rome by Leo XII. he had entered into the second phase of his activity. His first beginning had been as the pupil of de Maistre in the struggle against political revolution; now, in the name of the Church, standing as it does above the state, he had become himself the leader of the revolutionary movement.

In the year 1829 appeared his work, *Concerning the Progress of the Revolution and of the War against the Church.* The subjection of the state to the infallible pope was here preached, quite in accord with the bull, *Unam Sanctam*, of Boniface VIII.[1] Gregory VII. was represented as the great patriarch of European liberty. But the living pope as well had it in his power—so Lamennais declared—to reduce this doctrine to a present fact and to depose disobedient princes; for it is the Church alone that defends liberty. The rapid spread of this work surpassed that of all his other writings. In the course of the year 1829 four editions appeared in Belgium alone.

Immediately after the July revolution Lamennais founded the *Avenir*. This journal soon found its chief task in adding fuel to the insurrection in Belgium (1830).[2] At the same time he laid down with masterly skill the principles intended to regulate the clerical use of the press, which through him became a factor in papal politics. A " general agency for the defence of religious liberty " was likewise founded by his associates, and spread its ramifications over the whole of Europe.

Lamennais not long after experienced the same fate as

---

[1] 1302 A.D. : " Subesse Romano Pontifici, omni humanæ creaturæ declaramus—omnino esse de necessitate salutis."

[2] The most serious consequences of the French July revolution of 1830 were the revolutions in the United Netherlands (Holland and Belgium, united by the Congress of Vienna) and in Poland.

Charles X. As soon as he had done his duty he was dismissed. But as long as Pius VIII. reigned, whatever Lamennais did found favour with the Curia. The constitution of Belgium, with its mixture of liberal and clerical phrases, bears the stamp of his thought. The leaders of the revolution in Poland (1830), like Lamennais, preached liberty in the sense of Gregory VII. O'Connell, the leader of the repeal agitation in Ireland, with all his oratorical gifts, was intellectually the pupil of Lamennais.

The influence of the ideas represented by Lamennais was very effective towards the increase of the papal power. And this proves anew that the restored Papacy, as well as the greatest of its predecessors,— Gregory I., Nicholas I., Gregory VII., and Innocent III.,—knew well how to draw the vital ideas of the time into its service. For Lamennais is to be understood only as the incarnation of modern ideas. The last period of his life proved unequivocally that to satisfy the longings and strivings of the nations was the sacred object of his endeavour.

The prudent use, however, which the Papacy made of his ideas reveals to us only in part the Curia's attitude towards the revolutionary movements. To fully understand this attitude, we must not confine our survey to the ideal enthusiasm of Lamennais and his friends; we must also take into view the more remote causes of the revolution in each separate state.

To begin with Belgium: the events of the year 1830 throw light upon the nature of the liberty which the clerical party there demanded. The complaints against the ruling house of Orange were not different from those which at the close of the last century had been made against Joseph II. of Austria. The first grievance urged in the pastoral letters of the bishops against the administration of the United Netherlands was that equal rights were given to the various forms of worship; what, above all, they demanded was the suppression of dissenters, by the restoration of the ancient prerogatives of the hierarchy.   In Belgium as well as in Austria under Joseph, spiritual lust of power concealed itself behind the mask of liberty.

We find the same abuse of liberty as a popular watchword in Poland and in Ireland.   The constitution, which Czar Alexander I. had granted to the Poles in 1815,[1] while he denied it to the Russians, promised the healing of old wounds, and held out the prospect of a better future to the oppressed estates.   The historian Gervinus, himself a true liberal, recognises the first cause of the Polish revolution in the fact that the improvements which had been effected in the social condition made the demagogues of the hierarchy anxious lest the people should gradually become accustomed to the new order of things.   Even during the reign of Alexander I. the clergy and the nobility had laid their mines for a violent outbreak.   If Nicholas (1825) drew the reins tighter, the reason lay in the extent to which the revolutionary parties had gained ground. It was not, however, until the revolution of 1830 to 1832 had done its work that the unhappy Poles lost all that was left them of their bright prospects.   But the word liberty, in the mouth of Roman Polonism, retained in these new struggles the same meaning it had in the

[1] The new kingdom of Poland was created by the Congress of Vienna in 1815.   Alexander I. of Russia, who was made king of Poland, maintained the independent existence of the state of Poland, and the latter was joined to Russia by mere personal union.   The kingdom of Poland kept all its institutions, its Roman Catholic Church, its schools conducted in the Polish language, its currency, postal system, etc.   "At this period of absolutism no other people of central Europe had as much political liberty as the Poles" (Seignobos).   Nevertheless agitation was immediately begun in Poland against the Russian government, ending in the insurrection and war of 1830 to 1832.   The defeat of the Poles was followed by the complete wiping out of Polish independence and the Russification of Poland.

past.   It meant the annihilation of every other form of
belief.

In Ireland the course of events was no different.   Catholic emancipation had taken place a year before the July
revolution of 1830; and Catholic emancipation gave the
impulse to the movement for the repeal of the Union.
Not until after the emancipation did O'Connell find the
time ripe for his demagogic activity.   So-called liberty
of conscience served in Ireland as well as elsewhere to
fan the flames of religious and race hatred.

It was mainly in the Roman Catholic countries, Belgium, Poland, and Ireland, that the French July revolution of 1830 led to a violent overthrow.   But the same
year witnessed for the first time—though even now only
sporadically—similar outbreaks upon Protestant ground.
The so-called revolutions in Switzerland do not come
under this category.   But the temper of the spirits in
Germany presents a striking phenomenon, for in the disturbances of 1830 we observe essentially the same tendencies which eighteen years later won a temporary
victory; and these tendencies brought forth new movements and gave to the history of the times an entirely
new aspect, presenting a decided contrast to the entire
previous development of the reformed countries.

The reason of this contrast between the past and the
present demands impartial examination.   But where else
can we look for this reason except in the prevailing spirit
of the Restoration period, in its diametrical opposition to
the ideals of the Reformation and to the principles of
the eighteenth century, and its disappointment of the
just expectations of the wars of liberation ?

The last word of the policy of Metternich was its international hatred of the Reformation.   This policy was
transmitted to the other courts of Europe.   Everywhere
national aspirations were forcibly suppressed in favour of

the arbitrary creations of diplomacy; all spiritual life was equally suppressed in favour of a hierarchy which the rulers forced upon the people. In short, we find again the same principles active that had been victorious in the counter-reformation of old.

Where there was such a heaping of inflammable material, it was unavoidable that the sparks, borne with lightning speed from France over the various countries, should kindle a flame. The policy of the rulers was once more successful in suppressing the political movement. But the irritation of the popular mind found vent in other spheres: in the poetry of "young Germany," in the dissolution, by Strauss and Feuerbach, of the foundations of faith, in the undermining of the national authority among the growing generation.

To this gradual impairment of the ethical foundations of the national life are also to be traced the triumphs which the Vatican won over the state in the revolutionary disorders of the following times. But events were happening, under the inspiration of the anti-revolutionary spirit, with its centre in the Curia, which even at this early date paved the way still more directly for these triumphs. Great importance belongs to the reign of Pius VIII. in this respect, for it prepared the way for the first Prussian ecclesiastical conflict and provided the means for stirring up the population of the upper Rhine against the laws of the state. Both these movements belong to the history of German Catholicism. But the cause of both, which lay in the policy of the Papacy itself, calls for our attention in connection with the reign of that pope who played the chief part in the business.

The concessions which the Prussian state had made when the concordat was passed—concessions which Pius VII. characterised as *mirifica*—were accepted by the Curia, but no concessions were made in return. The one thing which the state required, in order to guarantee the equality of the churches, and which was quite rightly placed at the head of the demands for an honest compact between Church and State, equal matrimonial rights, had been declared by the Curia and its henchman Niebuhr to be inadmissible for discussion. The consequences soon appeared. Not only did the Evangelical part of the community find itself oppressed; the state itself, up to its highest tribunal, was reduced *ad absurdum.*

In order to appreciate the later conflict we must here enter into some local details. The striking helplessness of the state against clerical tactics appears very clearly in the events previous to the negotiations with Pius VIII. Cases had multiplied from year to year where Roman Catholic clergymen, before the marriage between two parties of different faith, exacted the promise that all prospective issue without regard to sex should be trained in the Roman Catholic faith, and professed themselves unable to perform the marriage without this promise. In vain had an order of the cabinet of 1825 insisted that the demand of such a promise could not be permitted either to the Evangelical or the Catholic clergy. In the two following years violations of this principle of equality only increased in number.

The following case, which can be substantiated by the official papers of the Prussian ministry of public worship, is one of the most singular. It happened in the little town of Bocholt in the diocese of Münster. The Roman clergyman in this place had refused to marry a Protestant dyer and a Catholic woman without the aforesaid promise. The law in Prussia orders that where the parents have not otherwise decided, the children should follow the faith of the father. The man sought to obtain from the magistrates the relief which according to law they were bound to give. Upon their advice, he went to the bishop with a petition for relief. The bishop refused. There followed a complaint, which through the several lower

tribunals was taken before the president of the province
of the Rhine.   He, unable to give relief, made a personal
report to the king.   A communication from the cabinet
was issued to the president, destined for the eyes of the
bishop.   The bishop took refuge behind the clergyman,
and the latter refused to yield.   There followed renewed
correspondence between the president and the bishop,
again without result.   Finally, the man was advised by
the state authorities to have his marriage performed by
the Protestant clergyman.   He did so.   Then the Catholic priest refused the woman absolution.   The husband's
domestic tribulations now began, and in a few months he
declared that if he got no relief by the end of the year
he would give the promise and have the ceremony repeated according to the Catholic form.   The priest was
then called upon to state his reasons for refusing absolution.   He took refuge behind the sanctity of the confessional.   In the end, the president could only demand
that " the priest should be called upon to declare under
oath that the Catholic wife was not excluded from the
Communion in consequence of the husband's refusal to
give the promise, but for other causes connected with the
state of the woman's soul, which he as confessor was not
at liberty to divulge."

It was the natural consequence of the politics of the
Restoration and of the concordats that the state was
absolutely unable to protect the equality of the different
churches.   Bunsen had succeeded Niebuhr as Prussian
ambassador in Rome.   The latter's view still prevailed,
according to which the bishops were to be " kept in
order by the pope."   The question of mixed marriages
was the critical one.   Negotiations were carried on for
a year with Leo XII.   He had given a verbal promise
and an understanding seemed almost reached, when **Leo**
died.

Negotiations were resumed with Pius VIII. A proposition was made by a number of cardinals to disallow all mixed marriages without a papal dispensation: the bishops were to insist upon the conversion of the non-Catholic party before marriage; and the draft of an encyclical in this sense was laid before the pope. This proposition was not carried into effect, but the pope took the opportunity of impressing upon the Prussian bishops that "the most certain dogma of our religion is that, outside of the true Catholic faith, no one can be saved."

After long waiting for a decision of the vexed question, the king of Prussia finally lost patience and declared that if the papal court did not within six months adopt measures of relief, the matter would be settled by the authorities of the state. Shortly before the end of this time-limit there appeared the brief of Pius VIII. of March 25, 1830.

But what a masterpiece of Jesuitical tactics this brief was, with its purposely ambiguous expressions, capable of the most diverse interpretations! Under Archbishop Spiegel of Cologne it was interpreted as allowing the claims of the state; under his successor it was made to mean the opposite. In later times the clerical press declared that the brief never permitted a priest to celebrate a mixed marriage.

The ambiguous contents of the brief only increased the difficulties of the situation. King Frederick William III., not satisfied with its vagueness, long urged a change of the brief. But its author, Cardinal Capellari, himself succeeded to the papal throne as Gregory XVI. As pope he insisted upon the literal reading of the brief, and so he succeeded in bringing to an open rupture the conflict which had been long preparing and in inflicting the first decided defeat upon the hated modern state which claimed equal rights for all the churches.

We have to record also a measure taken in the short

reign of Pius VIII., whose effect was to undermine the loyal and peace-loving spirit of the Catholics of South Germany. His predecessor had paralysed the influence of Wessenberg by the dissolution of the see of Constance. Still the South German governments preserved something of Wessenberg's spirit. They agreed (January 30, 1830) that only a German, who had a record of particular excellence in the cure of souls and in the office of teaching, should be made bishop, and that any bishop thus elected was bound before consecration to render the oath of allegiance to the head of the state. The papal brief of Pius VIII. of June 30, 1830, condemned these " erroneous doctrines," and called upon the bishops to instruct the faithful concerning the objectionable character of these principles of the government.

On his death-bed Pius VIII. lamented that it had not been possible for him to canonise Alfonso da Liguori. But he did accomplish the erection of an opposition patriarchate to the orthodox patriarchate of Constantinople.

CHAPTER VII

THE REIGN OF GREGORY XVI. (1831–1846)

IF we measure the advance of the modern Papacy along the line of the three tendencies named at the close of the first chapter, the reign of Gregory XVI. records the most rapid progress. No other pope has taken his stand in the same spirit of enmity against the demands and the wants of our modern world; none has by his consistent energy achieved so great triumphs in the struggle against the inconsequence and the incapacity of the temporal powers. At the same time, the process of corruption and decay within the soil in which the Papacy itself is rooted now reached its climax. In our review of these events we begin where the reign of Gregory itself begins, with the revolution against the papal authority which broke out openly in the states of the Church.

Hardly anywhere was the French July revolution greeted with so much joy as in the papal states, and almost on the same day, the 2d of February, 1831, on which Gregory was chosen pope, the long-smouldering dissatisfaction broke out in the insurrection of Bologna. The movement spread quickly through the other provinces and cities; and not only did native Carbonari take part in it, but some came from foreign countries, as the two sons of Queen Hortense, of whom the older perished in the struggle; the younger (afterwards the Emperor Napoleon III.) was saved in a most romantic manner.

Even the holy father in Rome was for a time in such peril that preparations were made in Civita Vecchia for his embarkation; but an open revolt in the capital was finally prevented.

The occurrences at Bologna were highly significant. Representatives from all those parts of the states of the Church which had thrown off the temporal rule of the pope came together, February 26, 1831, for the purpose of forming a legislative assembly. This assembly at once adopted unanimously a resolution that the rule of the Curia in the districts represented by the congress had ceased. A union for a common government was effected, and a committee formed the draft of a new constitution. This triumph was of short duration; Austrian troops soon moved in and put down the insurrection.

But the ministers of the great Powers in Rome united, as they had done in the year 1820 (just as was afterwards done with Turkey), to urge upon the holy father a reform of the abuses which, to the everlasting disgrace of his administration, had now become matters of common notoriety. The memorandum of May 31, 1831, which emphasised the necessity of radical reforms, was composed by Bunsen at the request of the other ministers.[1] It showed the sympathy for the legitimate rule of the popes which Bunsen had inherited from Niebuhr. This sympathy, however, did not at a later time prevent the party inimical to reform, interested in the continuance of the abuses, from pursuing the author with its particular hatred.

In reply to this memorandum, there appeared soon after (July 5, 1831) a declaration of the papal secretary of state, Bernetti, which announced a transformation of the whole system of administration in the papal states. Bernetti followed in the steps of Consalvi in making liberal concessions with reference to the administration

---

[1] Bunsen had succeeded Niebuhr as Prussian minister at Rome in 1827.

of justice and finance and the participation of the laity in the government. On the other hand, the two most essential reform proposals — the right of voting for the municipal and provincial councils and the appointment of a council of state from the laity — were ignored; moreover, the promised reforms in the administration and in the finances were, with few exceptions, never carried out. This papal declaration, however, appeared so satisfactory to the diplomats that immediately afterwards the foreign troops evacuated the territory of the pope.

But the inhabitants of the ecclesiastical provinces were not so easily satisfied. The city of Bologna made a solemn protest and sent a memorial to the ministers of the Pentarchy of great Powers.[1] This memorial explained the shortcomings of the administration, and pointed out that even an administration undertaken with honest intentions would afford no sufficient remedy, so long as the cause of all the evil was not removed and the temporal and spiritual government entirely divorced. This desire, everywhere freely expressed, was not fulfilled. The dissatisfaction continued, and the Austrians had no sooner departed when, in January, 1832, new disorders broke out in the Marches.

The papal troops, gathered from the dregs of the population like the notorious soldiers of the keys of former times, were incapable of restoring order. At the same time they were guilty of such outrageous acts of violence that the irritation rapidly increased, and the tottering papal chair was obliged once more to call Austrian bayonets to its aid. Their second entry into Bologna, however, excited the jealousy of France, and suddenly a French fleet appeared at Ancona (February, 1832).

In the papal states and in all Italy this occupation of

[1] Austria, France, Great Britain, Prussia, and Russia: the five chief negotiators at the Congress of Vienna.

Ancona excited great hopes ; for the government of Louis Philippe still preserved an appearance of liberality. The citizens of Ancona were so exuberant in their joy that the pope excommunicated them. But the French expedition had quite other objects than those which the Italian patriots hoped for. Instead of helping the Italians they restored the papal administration, and after this there was no more mention of the improvements announced in the preceding year. As long as Ancona and Bologna were occupied, the peace of the state was not disturbed. But how little had been gained in behalf of a real peace, how the fire continued to smoulder under the ashes, how the influence of the secret societies was not in the least broken, became evident when the occupation ceased in 1838; a few years later, new risings, murders, and disorders of all kinds showed that public order had not been secured.

In 1843 and 1844 there was bloody guerilla warfare when an attempt was made to put down the disturbances. In 1845 an insurrection of greater magnitude broke out in Rimini. All these attempts were suppressed by the Swiss regiments and the rough bands of papal volunteers, and were punished with imprisonment, exile, and executions. But—as Döllinger affirmed in 1861—the government seemed to have no conception of " the intense bitterness produced by the consciousness that heavy tribute was exacted for the payment of foreign mercenaries, which were used to hold the people in subjection and to enable the power of the state to refuse all popular demands."

Bernetti had been succeeded in 1836 by Lambruschini as secretary of state (the same who as papal nuncio in Paris had persuaded Charles X. to publish the famous July ordinances of 1830), and popular dissatisfaction, which had been steadily increasing, assumed much larger dimensions under the latter. Nothing now stood in the way of Gregory's desire to restore everything to the mediæval standard. But to what purpose was it that, in pursuance of this policy, the larger part of the educated youth of Rome languished in imprisonment or in exile ? To what purpose was it that continued arbitrary absolutism made it appear as if there were no further cause for fear ? To what purpose was it that railroads and learned conventions were prohibited, access to the Vatican library made more difficult, and the entire system of education placed in the hands of the Jesuits ? All this did not make the social condition of the papal state any better.

In the fifteen years of Gregory's reign the debt of the state increased from twenty to forty million scudi; several items of income had to be mortgaged for a number of years, and yet there was a yearly deficit of two to three millions. More than once the necessities of the lower classes increased to actual famine. The number of political prisoners had reached six thousand; and the best part of the ambitious youth of the land remained in exile, where it became thoroughly imbued with the ideas of Mazzini, who had been already active during the revolution of 1830.

But nothing so much showed how completely demoralising the policy of Gregory had been as the absolute necessity which was felt at his death of choosing a successor who represented different ideas. There was the feeling that it was simply an impossibility to continue the government along the same lines; this decided the choice of Pius IX., and this prompted the latter to make his celebrated reforms.

Gregory assumed towards the whole civilised world and the needs of our modern era the same attitude as he did in the government of the Church-state. He maintained the old papal inflexibility, he insisted on all the former claims, opposing himself to all modern ideas. As a young ecclesiastic in 1799, he had written an essay to celebrate the " triumph of the Holy See " brought about by the reaction against the Revolution. As pope he exhibited an enmity towards modern culture such as one would think proper in a Camaldulite monk. His edict on the subject of studies, of September 12, 1831, is full of the most timid and intolerant restrictions. But his most celebrated document, as a disavowal of all that is dear and precious to the present generation, is the encyclical by which he announced to the episcopacy his accession to the papal throne; which, however, was delayed by the revolution in the states of the Church, and did not appear till after the suppression of the disturbances, August 15, 1832. In this encyclical the pope declares implacable war upon the freedom of science and learning and upon all really liberal views, in politics as well as in the Church.

The cause of the existing wide-spread unbelief and of the revolt against the exclusively valid dogmas of the Church is a false science. Academies and schools are shockingly full of new abominable teachings, by which the Catholic faith is not only secretly and hiddenly opposed, but by which it is openly attacked in merciless warfare. Through instruction and example on the part of teachers the minds of the youth are corrupted, the vast subversion of religion and the shocking decay of morals is effected. Therefore, in order to keep such novelties from the Church, we must insist upon it that to the pope alone belongs the right of judging concerning doctrine and the government of the whole Church; the bishops must therefore cling to the Roman See, and the priests be obedient to the bishops. The discipline which has received the approval of the Church may not be disapproved or subjected to the power of the state. It is absurd to speak of a regeneration of the Church, it is abominable to attack the law of celibacy and to doubt the indissoluble nature of the matrimonial bond. But especially are we to fight against indifferentism, or the illusion that one may be saved in any faith; from this is derived the insane idea that every man has a claim to liberty of conscience. This pernicious error is promoted by the immoderate liberty of opinion which prevails to the destruction of the Church and the State. Thence come changes of opinions, the corruption of youth, the contempt of religion and of its laws among the people, and the ruin which threatens the commonwealth. The sources of all these revolutionary movements, which subvert all the rights of magistrates and bring slavery to the people under the appearance of liberty, are above all the criminal and insane tendencies of the Waldenses, Beghards, Wiclifites, and other similar sons of Belial. And for no other cause do the present innovators exert their powers but in order to boast with Luther that they are free from all laws; and the sooner to attain this end they do not shrink from the most infamous crimes. Herewith is connected the injurious and thoroughly detestable freedom of the press, in consequence of which the most absurd and insipid doctrines and errors spread themselves with ease; and it is foolish to assert that the effects of the bad writings are destroyed by written refutations. Therefore the Roman Index is a beneficent institution, and it is a grievous error to deny to the Church the right of the prohibition of books.

In the end, the bishops are exhorted to constancy in opposing all innovations, and princes are called upon to give them their aid because the peace of the state depends upon the welfare of the Church. " The favour of the blessed Virgin Mary, who alone suppresses all heresies, will bless these efforts."

This encyclical has since become the type of all following papal allocutions, especially in its proficiency in damning and scolding. It has been surpassed as the strongest manifesto of the Papacy only by the Syllabus-encyclical of 1864. All of Gregory's official acts are, moreover, in agreement with it. Only a few of the principal ones need here be named. The year 1839 saw five new canonisations, accompanied by many miracles, among them that of Liguori. The year 1841 witnessed a special threat of excommunication against all who failed to inform concerning those whom they knew to have broken the rules of fasting; this measure placed a premium upon denunciations of servants against their masters. In the year 1844 was published a more explicit condemnation of the Bible societies, with the command to deliver copies of the forbidden book to the bishops. At the same time the old rules for the treatment of heretics were made more stringent; Catholic theologians pursuing independent researches were condemned, and the opposition to the governments which sought to preserve the rights of states was continued.

But all these actions of the pope were no longer isolated phenomena, manifestations of personal antagonism to a hostile world. On the contrary, they indicate a general policy; for we now meet with a number of literary productions which give evidence of the existence and the spread of a papal " school " in Rome. The increased importance of this " school " is distinctly traceable in the Gregorian era. It does not, of course, imply the production of works of unbiassed scientific research, but we cannot deny to this new school a high degree of learning. Names such as Mezzofanti [1] and Angelo Mai [2] gave to the college of cardinals the reputation of a learned congregation. Perrone issued edition upon edition of his *Prælectiones Theologicæ*, combining the defence of the curialistic system with the most disgusting vilification of the Reformation. Cantu wrote his *Universal History* in the spirit of an " orthodox " historian; it was translated into all the principal languages. Rosmini elaborated a

[1] A linguistic genius. He understood more than fifty languages.

[2] Papal librarian, learned in classical and patristic literature. He discovered the palimpsests.

philosophical system, in which numerous modern ideas were incorporated in the defence of ancient tradition, and for a long time enjoyed protection in high quarters against charges brought before the Congregation of the Index. Among learned astronomers the name of the Jesuit Father Secchi began to enjoy a growing reputation. The colleges of the restored Company, constantly increasing in number, began to rival the old order in the effort to train eminent specialists. And now the *Doctores Romani*, in the service of the Jesuits, began to spread themselves over the several national churches. The consequence was the rise of a special papalistic literature.

In proportion as the influence of the Society of Jesus increased in its opposition to the conciliatory tendencies which had been dominant since the days of Clement XIV., each country which was subjected to its influence found itself more and more confronted with its own "Jesuit problem." During the period between the revolutions of 1830 and 1848 this problem comes into view in several places. In one country the pious fathers created the revolution, in another they provoked it. The acute crisis was again in France; the great question here was, What attitude shall the new government take towards the Jesuit problem?

The answer to this question shows us the vacillating character of Louis Philippe's system. So long as popularity was pursued as the great object, we find great alacrity in instituting proceedings against the hated order. The year 1831 brought the abolition of the ordinance of 1816, which had permitted the preaching of mission sermons, and the confirmation of the ordinance of 1828 against the appointment of Jesuits in the seminaries. But so soon as the government showed a desire to win over the clergy, and when the bishops raised the cry of " freedom of instruction " (from every other supervision but their own), the Jesuits knew at once how to make use of the favourable turn to further their own interests. With that masterly ability which the order has always shown of choosing the right man for every position, they now used the pulpit orator Ravignan,— who delighted the Parisian *haute volée*,—to smooth their path. After Ravignan had gained sufficient popularity, he openly acknowledged himself a Jesuit, and in his book, *De l'existence et de l'institut des Jesuites*, he asserted that, in spite of the law,[1] there were more than two hundred Jesuits in Paris (1844). It was officially stated that the order possessed forty-three houses in France, among them the large mother-house in the Rue des Postes in Paris, and that the number of the professed was three times as large as had been given out. At the same time it was revealed through testimony given in a suit at law that they had resumed their mercantile activity; just as had happened in 1764, when the same thing was shown in the course of a legal investigation which brought about the overthrow of the old order in France.

The government, however, did nothing, in spite of the open defiance of the law. But the mind of the people made itself distinctly known. Michelet and Quinet in their lectures in the College of France brought this lawlessness to the light. Cousin put the question of its toleration in the House of Peers, Thiers in the House of Deputies. At the same time, the great excitement produced by Eugène Sue's *Juif Errant* proved how general was the belief in the immoral tendencies of the order. Finally the government laid before the chambers a bill concerning secondary instruction, in which it was ordered that all teachers should give assurance of belonging to no prohibited congregation.

But when it came to carrying out the law that had been passed by the chambers, the ministry was obliged

---

[1] The Jesuits had been expelled from France in 1831.

to negotiate with Rome. The end of the matter was that the government declared officially that their proposals had been accepted at Rome. The general of the Jesuits, for appearance sake, temporarily closed a few of their institutions; in reality, however, the condition of affairs remained as it had been. And soon after this Guizot openly took sides with the Jesuits when he interfered in the affairs of the Swiss Sonderbund.

In Switzerland the order had established itself in Fribourg, and during the reign of Gregory it succeeded in gaining a foothold in Schwyz (1835). In 1839 a motion was made in Lucerne to call the Jesuits to the public school of the canton; this, however, was not carried out until the liberal government had been overthrown in 1841. The clerical attempt at insurrection in Aargau failed, and its only consequence was the dissolution of the monasteries in which the insurrection had centred. On the other hand, in Wallis the liberal party was again defeated (1840), and their attempt to regain the ascendancy frustrated at the expense of some bloodshed.

These isolated instances were only the precursors of more determined action. Soon after, those cantons that favoured the Jesuits, including the three original cantons together with Lucerne, Fribourg, Wallis, and Zug, combined to form the rebellious Sonderbund (separate federation). In opposition to this revolutionary measure, whose instigators the Jesuits were known to be, all the rest of Switzerland was united in holding that the peace of the country called for the banishment of the order. A motion to this effect was made in the Diet, but was lost; and in 1844 Lucerne showed its contempt for this measure by officially giving to the Jesuits the administration of the system of education. The liberals were persecuted, and the Jesuits installed with great solemnity. The motion for the dissolution of the Sonderbund failed of a majority in the Diet (April, 1846), and at the death of Gregory, two months later, the party of the Jesuits seemed dominant in Switzerland.

In proportion as the order of Jesuits succeeded in identifying itself with the Church was the opposition increased to those tendencies in Catholic theology that were not in sympathy with the order. ·In this respect, as in others, the reign of Gregory is remarkable.   Up to this time, the war against national-Catholic aspirations had been waged indirectly by means of the concordats.   Now the time seemed to have come for making a direct attack upon the much-dreaded freedom of learning.   The condemnation of the teachings of Hermes,[1] which showed both ignorance on the part of his opponents and lack of scrupulousness in the use of means on the part of the Vatican, forms an epoch in Catholic theology; it was the first act of the great drama in which from this time on all conscientious and honest investigators became the victims of Rome's enmity.   The disavowal of Lamennais assumed a similar significance for the development of French Catholicism.

Few indeed as yet foresaw the full consequences of the system pursued at Rome.   The followers of Hermes on the one side and the friends of Lamennais on the other submitted.   In the glowing enthusiasm for the Catholic Church-ideal which both shared, their leaders remained now, as before, the most powerful champions of the Church in its struggle with the state.   Montalembert and Baltzer outdid one another in the same championship.   But it is a striking fact that both were obliged before their death to acknowledge that they had fought for an " idol."

---

[1] An eminent Roman Catholic scholar, professor in the university of Bonn, the leader of German liberal theologians.   His work, *Introduction to Christian Catholic Theology*, was condemned by the pope.

The movement which philosophy and science had inaugurated throughout the intellectual world received the consideration of Gregory only so far as he was enabled to hurl his anathema against it. It was especially the university according to the German ideal, which from this time on became the object of particular hatred in Rome. The representatives of these universities saw as yet no danger in Rome's anathemas, while the masses, under the heel of the hierarchy, rendered willing obedience to the papal mandate.

Gregory's disputes with the temporal powers show very clearly how successful had been the disciplining of the masses whom the politicians of the concordats had delivered into the hands of the Papacy. For in this field his stubborn, consistent policy achieved its greatest triumphs. Even those changes which brought large momentary losses in the end led to the triumph of the papal policy. Thus it was with the wars of the Carlist revolution in Spain.[1] The pope gave indirect aid to the pretender. The party of the queen-mother Christina more than once resorted to measures of retaliation, such as the dissolution of the monasteries, a measure which greatly affected the material possessions of the Church in Spain. The Curia, on the other hand, did not hesitate to use extreme measures. The allocution of February 1, 1836, refused recognition to the queen, Isabella; the allocution of March 1, 1841, even ordered general public prayers for the country of Loyola. And yet, in spite of this opposition, no sooner had Isabella become independent sovereign than concession upon concession was made to the Vatican.

[1] Upon the death of Ferdinand VII. in 1833, his brother, Don Carlos, refused to acknowledge the female succession and claimed the throne. Christina, the widow of Ferdinand, assumed the title of governing queen until her infant daughter, Isabella II., should attain her majority. This is the origin of the two parties, the *Carlists* and the *Christinos*.

But the victory over deeply fallen Spain was not to be compared in moral significance to the triumph over the modern state of Prussia. In pursuance of what has been said in the preceding chapter concerning the measures of Pius VIII., we may here describe briefly the preparations which were made by the Curia for its battle in Germany, the great Church war of Cologne.[1]

Pius VIII. had, on the 25th of March, 1830, issued a brief on the subject of mixed marriages.[2] The obscure and ambiguous expressions of this brief had been found unsatisfactory by the Prussian government. After a prolonged correspondence, an order of the cabinet of the 27th of February, 1831, decided upon the return of the brief with the express declaration that the Prussian government entertained no desire that the pope should sanction anything that was opposed to the general principles of the Catholic Church, but that it was only a question of expunging such expressions as would necessarily lead to dispute. The demand which the Church made of the exclusive right to the education of the children of mixed marriages carried dissension into countless families. To prevent this, to preserve equal rights for all: this was to the state an obligation it could not shirk.

The Prussian government, although in returning the brief it was conscious of performing its duty toward its own subjects, showed little knowledge of the state of affairs in Rome and their slippery ways. The new pope had been, in his former position, the chief author of the brief, and understood better than anyone the purpose of the ambiguous expressions. While the French minister had been instructed in the most decided terms that

---

[1] The "Church war of Cologne," with which this and the following paragraphs deal, turned upon a difference on the subject of mixed marriages between the ministers of the state and the Roman Catholic authorities of the diocese of Cologne, and ended in a compromise in 1840.

[2] Page 93.

mixed marriages would not be tolerated, and a brief to
the Bavarian bishops of May 27, 1832, had been couched
in unmistakable language, Prussia, with whom the Vatican could not deal in the same autocratic manner, was
treated to ambiguous expressions, and only those who
read between the lines of the brief could understand the
real wishes of the pope.

At the same time we observe that the Vatican, in its
intercourse with the states, began more and more to look
for help to the revolutionary spirit which was active in
undermining the authority of governments. An official
report of the Prussian minister during these negotiations
contains the following account in reference to this subject:

It is undeniable that the revolution in Belgium and the
prevalent opinion, which is steadily gaining adherents among
the most opposite parties, concerning the freedom of the
Church from the state, has given to the Roman court a less
compliant disposition towards the temporal power and especially towards Protestant governments.

The longer the determination of the question of mixed
marriages was postponed, the more did the difficulties
of the situation increase, aggravated as they were by the
general condition of ecclesiastical affairs. As we look
back upon the activity of Archbishop Spiegel of Cologne,
we see how almost incredibly difficult was the situation
of this pious and patriotic prince of the Church. At
every step he was hindered in his noble endeavours by
the ill-will of Councillor Schmedding of the Prussian
ministry. This man, the superior of the archbishop by
virtue of his office in the state, was a useful tool in the
hands of the papal policy, which was systematically bent
upon undermining the religious peace.

The archbishop of Cologne, in answer to a question of
the ministry, handed in an opinion which, with a thorough
knowledge of the policy of the Curia, proved how upon

the basis of former determinations of the canon law the
papal brief might be reconciled with the just demands of
the state.   Therewith was presented the means for a
satisfactory solution of the question.   But Schmedding's
report of the negotiations ignored the archbishop's proposals.

Under these circumstances Bunsen was appealed to for
aid, and he was recalled from Rome.   He proposed a
direct negotiation with the archbishop.   Count Spiegel
came for this purpose to Berlin, and the result was the
convention of June 9, 1834.   Loyally carried out, it
would have led to mutual peace among the churches and
to the strengthening of the state; but thereby it would
have achieved the opposite of that which the Curia pur-
posed.

As long as Archbishop Spiegel lived (died 1835) religious peace was preserved.   But no sooner had he closed
his eyes than systematic attempts were begun to inflame
the passions of the Catholic population.   The first measure in this direction was the papal brief against Hermes
(see note 1, page 106), which escaped the injunction of the
royal placet by being smuggled into the Rhineland from
Belgium.   The government itself came to the aid of the
Curia by the choice of Baron von Droste as the successor
of Count Spiegel in Cologne.   In the new archbishop the
Vatican gained a useful tool for furthering its own policy,
and the note of the secretary of state, Lambruschini, of
March 15, 1836, at once formally opened the war.

This note, together with the short-sighted policy of
Niebuhr and the brief of Pius VIII., is the source to
which is to be traced the conflict which soon came to a
violent outbreak.   At the time that this note was issued
the Curia announced the intention of sending a nuncio
to Berlin.   At the express command of the king this
offer was rejected as " an innovation in every way objectionable, under whatever form it might be made," and

this refusal was meant " not only for the present case, but generally once for all, without any ambiguity and definitely, with such degree of decision that any future repetition of this attempt should thereby be obviated." When the Curia made the same attempt the following year in St. Petersburg, the king of Prussia at once took measures looking to an agreement of both governments in their policy touching this matter. But what the nuncio could not directly accomplish was brought about indirectly by Archbishop Droste. And thus, in the policy pursued by the Vatican, we recognise the immediate cause which brought about the Church war of Cologne, in which the triumphs achieved by Gregory XVI. were as great as the wounds inflicted upon the religious peace of Germany.

The accession of Frederick William IV. (1840) was followed by the embassy of Count Brühl to Rome, and the nomination of Schmedding to the newly established " Catholic " department of the ministry of public worship. The opposition on the part of the German Catholics to this appointment was so effectually put down by means of the bureaucracy that the Curia was relieved of the necessity of taking any direct steps in the matter, and was able to ascribe to the government the odium of the inquisitorial measures.

The papal histories of the reign of Gregory XVI. make the triumphs of the Curia in its disputes with Spain and Prussia secondary to the moral triumph of the Papacy over the Russian emperor. When Nicholas I. visited Rome in 1845 he had the courtesy to pay a visit to the pope. From this " audience " (to use the clerical language of the visits of reigning sovereigns to the pope-king) he is said to have returned quite pale and under great emotion. Gregory himself is reported by the same authority to have said afterwards to his intimate friends that he had told the emperor the truth. There is no trace of any direct consequences of this conversation, as far as we are concerned with the future actions of the emperor. But the entire later development has proved that the " papistical " policy has always shown itself superior to the " cæsaro-papistical."

On all sides did Gregory XVI. win success except in the ecclesiastical state itself. Leo was little loved, but Gregory XVI. died under the glowing hatred of the Roman population. In spite of increasing financial straits, the expenses of his Swiss guard were constantly increased. One of his last decrees had freed his family from the inheritance taxes. He ennobled his barber. At the baptism of the latter's son, thirty-one patriarchs, archbishops, and bishops stood sponsors.

CHAPTER VIII

THE FIRST "LIBERAL" PERIOD OF THE REIGN OF PIUS IX. (1846–1850)

THE history of no pope is so full of change and so rich in events as that of Pius IX. We find in his pontificate a curious interweaving of all the separate threads which we have followed in the history of the modern Papacy; the various tendencies which began with the Restoration seem to have approached more closely their goal.

The first thing which strikes the student of history is the remarkable series of reforms with which Pius began his reign. These are, however, but the natural reaction from the Gregorian extreme, and their effect could be none other than to show the impossibility of a reconciliation between the progress of the age and the Papacy. The final overthrow of the temporal dominion of the Papacy was founded in its own unnaturalness.

If politically Pius made the attempt to reconcile himself with the liberal tendencies of his time, ecclesiastically he never had any such intention. Even his last acts, which threw the world into such commotion, had their origin much earlier than in the days of his exile at Gaeta (1848 to 1850). They were the direct consequences of all the former steps of the restored Papacy, and are not explained by personal embitterment or mystical religiosity. Only in crudeness of expression did the last productions of Pius IX. surpass everything that went before.

8

But whatever were Pius' principles, political and ecclesiastical, his pontificate shows a marvellous series of triumphs for the papal system, triumphs which were achieved in spite of the antagonism of this system to the spirit of the times. No former year had been so favourable in its results to the policy of the Roman Church as the year of revolution, 1848, with the era of reaction which immediately followed. We shall have to note in almost all countries a considerable intensification of the ultramontane tendencies, crowds of conversions, concordats more favourable than ever, " Catholic " factions holding closely together, and, above all, a closer connection of the national churches with Rome. Especially in the second period of the pontificate of Pius IX., from his return to Rome to the Italian war, did fortune smile upon him. But even his later years, following the Council of the Vatican, though they brought apparent reverses, only prepared the way for the triumphs of his successor.

So long a reign as that of Pius IX. would have been of great importance apart from the many crises which fill it. By its connection with the general history of the times, this reign divides itself naturally into four periods: the first (1846 to 1850) shows the irreconcilability of the Papacy with modern ideas; the second (1850 to 1859) brings before us the triumphs which it achieved in spite of this fact; the third (1859 to 1870) shows, in connection with the Italian and the Austrian-Prussian war, that on both sides of the Alps people had begun to grasp the idea that the conflicts with Rome represent a decisive battle for some of those things which humanity holds most dear, while at the same time the Curia was sharpening new weapons for this battle; finally, in the fourth period (1870 to 1878) we have before us the great war, whose battle-field is the world, which began with the Vatican Council.

When, to the great joy of the Romans, Gregory XVI. died, on the 1st of June, 1846, the choice of his successor vacillated for a short time between Gregory's secretary of state, the like-minded Lambruschini, and the fifty-four years' old Count Mastai Ferretti from Sinigaglia; in two days the conclave elected the latter (June 16th). A man now ascended the throne of St. Peter whose personal amiability and agreeable appearance could not but win sympathy; the Roman people in particular greeted the choice of this genial and popular cardinal with extra-ordinary enthusiasm. The high degree of his theological ignorance, coupled with a still higher degree of vanity, was known to but a few of the initiated.

Persuaded of the necessity of discarding the system of Gregory and of not disappointing the Romans in the reforms they expected of him, Pius began his reign with an attack upon the numerous abuses, and with the retrenchment of avoidable expenses. A month later appeared the decree of amnesty, which restored many political prisoners to life and to their friends. Like an electrical current the glad tidings of this act ran through the hot-blooded populace, and from Rome loud jubilation spread over all Italy.

An opposition was indeed immediately formed against the reform-loving pope. The governments began to express doubts; the so-called *setta Gregoriana*, the adherents of Gregory and his policy, made demonstrations. But Pius was not frightened; his further actions gave evidence that he was convinced of the necessity of far-reaching reforms, and that he was determined that no obstacle should frustrate his purpose. When the council of state protested, he formed a new council from the younger prelates, and nominated the liberal Cardinal Gizzi as secretary of state.

There followed (April to July, 1847) a new Roman municipal constitution (whereby there was formed an

assembly of a hundred members with a senator at the head
and eight conservators); a council of state (consisting of
the deputies of the provinces as a diet for counsel and
debate), and the institution of a *guardia civica* (citizens'
guard).   Measures of similar tendency were the permission of greater freedom to the press, the sanction of railroads, the admission of the laity to the offices of state,
the taxation of monasteries, personal investigation of
monasteries and hospitals, circulars to the generals of
orders, and the dismissal of the Swiss soldiers.

When finally Pius protested against the occupation of
Ferrara by the Austrians,[1] he became the hero of all
Italy and appeared to be at the head of the Italian
national movement.   At the anniversary of his accession Rome was brilliantly illuminated (June 16, 1847);
the manifestations of joy and emotion continued until the beginning of 1848.   The pope was celebrated
as the prince whose chief care it was to moderate the
expressions of joy on the part of his subjects.

The hopes which the younger Italy placed in Pius are
shown by the letter of Mazzini of September, 1847:
" There are two kinds of men, the superstitious and the
hypocrites; but humanity cannot live without faith and
religion.   The pope should therefore place himself at the
head of a new religion of humanity.   His chief duty
however is to bring about the unity of Italy."   In Protestant countries the glorification of the liberal pope was
hardly less than in Catholic.   Princes with arbitrary
tendencies were referred to his example.   Public opinion
proclaimed everywhere the praise of his name.

But the same pope, who began with political reforms,
gave even then distinct evidence that in every other respect he was the genuine representative of the unchange-

[1] Austria had occupied the castle of Ferrara with her troops, claiming the
authority of an article in the decrees of the Congress of Vienna.

able Papacy; this he did by his encyclical of November 9, 1846, in his letter to the archbishop of Cologne of July 3, 1847, and in the bull concerning the oriental question of July 23, 1847. Soon followed the most unequivocal document, the allocution of December 17, 1847 (containing the pope's negative to the demand of Mazzini). Over the existing political excitement, these ecclesiastical acts were at the time little regarded; in the eyes of the historian reviewing the past great significance attaches to them.

The encyclical at his accession was composed in the same tenor as Gregory's pastoral letters. It is full of bitter lamentations over the times,

in which the most violent and dreadful war is inflamed against the interests of Catholicism by those who, united in infamous associations, alienated from sound doctrine, and turning the ear from the truth, are bent upon bringing forth out of darkness all sorts of monstrous opinions and spreading them among the people. This is done, not only by the deniers and blasphemers of God, but also by those who dare to interpret God's word by their own judgment, according to their own reason, while God Himself has established a living authority which teaches the true meaning of his heavenly revelations and composes all disputes in matters of faith and of morality by an infallible judgment.

The Bible societies are again condemned,

which, repeating the device of the ancient heretics, contrary to the rules of the Church, translate the books of the sacred Scriptures into every vulgar tongue, accompany them with perverse interpretations, distribute them free in immense numbers and at great expense to all individuals of both sexes, even to the uneducated, and have no hesitation in teaching the people that everyone may reject tradition and the authority of the Church and interpret the words of the Lord and pervert their meaning according to his private judgment.

Under the same anathema fall

the perverse instruction in philosophical studies, the abominable system of religious indifferentism, the detestable attacks upon the holy state of priestly celibacy, which are favoured even by ecclesiastics, who allow themselves to be overcome by flatteries and the allurements of sensual pleasure, and the doctrines of communism, which are opposed even by the rights of nature.

Good and bad are damned in promiscuous variety; alternating condemnations and lamentations make up the accustomed greeting of the vicar of Christ.

In like manner, the letter to the archbishop of Cologne renewed the condemnation of the teachings of Hermes [1] which Gregory XVI. had pronounced, with the same ignorance of the German system that the first condemnation had shown. The bull issued at the same time for the oriental Church was meant to show to the oriental Christians that as schismatics they had just as little rights as the Protestant heretics; without the slightest consideration of the Greek patriarch or of the English-Prussian bishop, " the exercise of the jurisdiction of the Latin patriarch was restored " in Jerusalem.

It was especially the allocution of December, 1847, in which Pius guarded himself against all conclusions that might be drawn from his political in reference to his ecclesiastical position. ˙ Solemnly he protests against the idea " that it should ever enter into his mind to permit the slightest diminution of the authority of the Holy See or of received laws, or to cherish other traditions than those of the Church." He expresses grievous sorrow

that so many of the enemies of the Catholic truth should have allowed themselves to place the most absurd opinions on an equality or to mingle them with the teachings of Christ, and

[1] See page 106, note 1.

to spread the godless system of religious indifference ; that some have even done him the abominable injury of pretending that he was as it were the partaker of their folly ; that especially from some of his ordinances for advancing the civil welfare of the ecclesiastical state, which surely contained nothing contrary to religion, as well as from the amnesty granted at the beginning of his pontificate, they concluded that he was of such benevolent spirit towards the whole human race as to believe that one could be saved outside of the Catholic Church. Thereby they have inflicted upon him so great an injury that he is not able in words to express his detestation of it.

Politically, Pius would be liberal; ecclesiastically, reactionary. The inner contradiction in this position was made evident with surprising rapidity in the developments which immediately followed. Soon the liberal party, encouraged by himself, went beyond him, and the old Italian national ideas proved stronger than the so-called rock of Peter. At the very beginning of the year 1848, one after another of the Italian states became the scene of insurrections. In Lombardy there was the greatest fermentation against the foreign dominion. In Sardinia Charles Albert made preparations to take the sword of Italy into his hands.[1] The events in Naples[2] carried the Romans away in enthusiastic sympathy. And into this powder-cask, which the pope himself was accused of opening, fell the spark of the Paris February revolution of 1848.

It was the pope himself who more than any other had started the movement to which the throne of the French citizen-king fell a sacrifice, and which in rapid succession

[1] The war between Sardinia and Austria in 1848 and 1849. The Sardinians were defeated by Radetzki at Custozza and Novara. Charles Albert abdicated in favour of his son, Victor Emmanuel.

[2] Ferdinand II., king of the two Sicilies (including Naples), was obliged, in consequence of the disturbances in his kingdom, to grant a constitution and appoint a liberal ministry.

led to risings in Vienna and Berlin.   He had at first rejoiced and not concealed his joy that the son of Philipp
Égalité had been overthrown and that the state of the
godless Joseph II. was shaken to its foundations.   But
it lay in the nature of the revolution itself that, once
started, it should turn against the sovereignty of the pope
himself.   A foretaste of this had been given in the year
1847.

When Gregory XVI. died, the reactionary party of the
Sonderbund in Switzerland, favoured alike by Guizot,
Metternich, and Frederick William IV. of Prussia, seemed
in a position to make light of its enemies.[1]   But a few
months later there had taken place in Berne and Geneva,
in Zurich and in Waadt, a change in the government, by
which the democratic tendencies of 1830 were carried a
step further.   This change also secured a majority in the
Diet against those who favoured the Jesuits.   In July,
1847, the dissolution of the unconstitutional Sonderbund
was pronounced; in September it was resolved to carry
out this dissolution by force of arms.

The rebellion was disappointed of the help which had
been promised, and a rapid campaign of a few weeks
dissolved the Sonderbund.   The victors, the noble General Dufour at their head, made every effort to draw the
bonds of federation closer than ever with those whom
they had conquered.   But upon one point they insisted.
The perpetual banishment of the Jesuits was pronounced
to be the fundamental law of the federation.   While
therefore in the neighbouring states everything was in
confusion, Switzerland adopted the new constitution,
which became a source of strength outwardly and inwardly, and which acted as a bar to the desire of intervention in the following era of reaction.

This expulsion of the Jesuits from Switzerland is not
to be understood, as it would have been a few years later,

[1] See page 105.

as a measure of hostility to the Papacy itself. Pius IX. was then considered rather as an opponent than as a friend of the order. The reports of his nuncio, Luquet, from Switzerland (published in Lucerne, 1861) are very compromising to the pious fathers. But the further course of events only too soon made the order of Loyola and the Papacy appear as synonymous terms.

On the other hand, the most significant symptom of those days is found in the unanimity with which the popular voice, wherever it found expression, turned against the order. In February, 1848, the Jesuits were driven from Sardinia and from Lombardy. Naples and Sicily followed the example of their North Italian brethren. In the same February (before the revolution had swept over Austria and Prussia) the Bavarian Jesuit college in Altötting was closed. And before long, even in the ecclesiastical states, the Society was dissolved and its goods confiscated.

Not only had Pius IX. started the revolutionary conflagration in Europe; he was soon obliged to experience it in his own land. When every day brought new accounts to Rome of the progress of liberal principles in neighbouring states, the impatience of the Romans over the half-measures of the Papacy could no longer be restrained. Pius, until then adored as a god, was now impetuously urged to further concessions. He was obliged to yield. On the 14th of March, 1848, appeared the Roman constitution, and at the same time a reform ministry was appointed containing only two clerical members. Alongside of the college of cardinals, to which belonged the functions of a senate, there were instituted two chambers to which was given the right to grant taxes and to approve of all laws.

In spite of these concessions, the news of the revolutions in Vienna and in Milan created new disturbances.

The Austrian minister was insulted, volunteers from Rome went to the aid of the Lombards, and the ill will of the people vented itself particularly against the Jesuits. Before the end of March they were obliged to leave Rome and the ecclesiastical states.

In vain was the appeal for moderation which, on the 31st of March, 1848, Pius addressed to the Italian people. In vain did he go so far as to declare that he

recognised in the events of the last months more than the work of man, even the voice of God; that he, as one to whom was given the voice to interpret the silent eloquence of the works of God, was moved to rejoice over so much that appeared religious and noble in the storms raging around them.

More was demanded; people wanted the ecclesiastical state to take part in the war against Austria. The ministry of Mamiani and the Chamber of Deputies gave loud voice to this demand. The commander of the papal troops, without the authority of the pope, crossed the Po. Tumult followed tumult in Rome.

Once more the pope raised his voice in warning, in the allocution of April 29, 1848:

As the successor of Peter, who embraces in love all peoples, every war is to him an abomination; but he is filled with horror at the idea that they wished to place him at the head of an Italian republic. He had not been able to calm the fiery zeal of those of his subjects who wished to participate in the events in upper Italy. But in this he had had the same experience as other and far mightier princes; he himself had sent his troops to the borders of the Church-state only for its protection. As the father of all the faithful he can take no part in political factions and can wish for nothing but the peace of the whole world, especially of Italy.

He made the same declaration in answer to every new urging.

The enthusiasm for the pope cooled with astonishing rapidity, and soon was turned into coldness and hatred. One event followed on the heels of another: the dismissal of the Mamiani ministry, the failure of several other attempted ministerial combinations, the nomination of Count Rossi to the presidency of the ministry and to the ministry of the interior, his attempts to re-establish quiet and order, his assassination on the steps of the chamber of deputies (November 14, 1848), the tumultuous deputations to the pope (in favour of a democratic ministry, recognition of Italian nationality, the continuation of the war against Austria, and the calling of a constituent assembly).

Then came the approval by Pius, under coercion, of all demands made upon him, while the bullets penetrated into his rooms; the flight of most of the cardinals; finally the celebrated flight of the pope himself to Gaeta in the carriage of the Bavarian ambassador (in the night of November 24, 1848). The rupture between the Papacy and Italian freedom was thereby for ever decided. Pius himself, as a neutral and well disposed historian says, was " evidently less of a prophet than of a reed which is shaken to and fro by the wind."

From Gaeta the pope protested before all the world against the ministry that had been forced upon him, and declared all the measures that proceeded from it to be wanting in legal sanction and invalid. In Rome a provisional junta was formed and the ministry Corsini-Camerata-Galetti called a constituent assembly.

Again, and more decidedly, Pius protested on the 1st of January, 1849,

against this call of a so-called national assembly as a detestable sacrilegious crime against his independence, which deserves the punishment pronounced against it by divine and human laws. According to the decrees of the Council of Trent the major excommunication is to be passed upon all who in any way call in question the sovereignty of the pope. It is a matter of conscience and duty for him to preserve and defend the sacred pledge of the patrimony of the bride of Christ. Still he will not forget that he is the vicar of Him who exercises not only justice but also mercy. He therefore prays day and night for the conversion and salvation of those who have been led astray and hopes fervently that they will soon return into the fold of the Church.

The Romans felt no inclination to return to the fold; they laughed at the anathema. The only effect of the pope's manifesto was to bring to full expression the ill will which had long been cherished against the *régime* of the priests. All classes of people agreed in the energetic desire to rescue the temporal sceptre from the spiritual power; in the union of both they recognised the ultimate source of all corruption and of the general decline. The constituent assembly which was opened on February 5, 1849, on the 9th of the same month solemnly decreed the deposition of the pope as temporal prince, and proclaimed the Roman republic. There followed, on the 18th of February, the law which confiscated all property of the dead hand as belonging to the state, with the expressly declared intention that the eradication of every remnant of the clerical system was a necessity in order to further the cause of religion and to offer the best proof of the purity and the sacredness of the work of the republic.

Political history informs us that at the same time the second war between Sardinia and Austria broke out in Upper Italy.[1] Charles Albert of Sardinia drew once more the sword of Italy, and Toscana was liberated by Guerazzi; but the decisive victory of Radetzki at Novara (March 23, 1849) completely destroyed the high hopes of the Italian patriots.

[1] There had been a truce from August, 1848, to March, 1849.

The effect upon the Romans was that the constituent assembly now nominated a dictatorial triumvirate, with Mazzini at its head. This triumvirate appealed to the people with a solemn proclamation:

Our programme is our mandate. Preservation of the republic, protection against dangers within and without, a worthy representation in the war for liberation: this is our duty and we shall perform it. The very victories which oblige the enemy to thin out his army by expansion may sooner or later lead to his defeat. Your forefathers were always victorious because they declared him to be a traitor who yielded to danger, and you will not be unworthy of these forefathers, not unworthy of the banners which we have brought from the graves of our ancestors for the hope of Italy and the admiration of Europe.

The pope again protested against these steps; at the same time he called for the intervention of the Catholic Powers. The French republic under the presidency of Napoleon accepted the call to destroy the sister-republic. But although the French landed at Civita Vecchia in April, 1849, in overwhelming numbers, the resistance of the Romans under the leadership of Garibaldi was so heroic that they did not complete the conquest until the end of June.[1]

The pope still remained outside. September 12, 1849, he published at Gaeta a *motu proprio* promising reforms in the finances and the administration. September 18, 1849, there followed a decree of amnesty with almost more exceptions than concessions. It was not till April, 1850, that he returned. The Romans remained coldly silent; his only support was the French bayonets. The capital of Christendom did not thereby become more churchly-minded.

[1] From this time the Papacy was upheld in Rome by the French, in the Legations by the Austrians. The French occupation of Rome lasted until 1870.

CHAPTER IX

PIUS IX. AT THE HEAD OF THE EUROPEAN REACTION [1]
(1850–1859)

THE measures with which Pius began his reign had
been in effect a protest against the principles of
Gregory; in April, 1850, the pope returned to Rome to
follow from henceforth in the steps of his predecessor.
All his subsequent measures have a decidedly Jesuitical
stamp. No pope had yielded to the wishes of the Jesuits
to the same extent as did the penitent Pius. His relations to his own subjects became more and more strained,
until finally there came the inevitable reaction. Nevertheless, the external triumphs of this period were almost
greater than those which Pius VII. achieved after the
restoration of the Papacy.

During the same year, 1848, in which the pope, after
having been idolised, became a hated exile, the power of
the Papacy was in almost all countries extraordinarily
increased. A number of very dissimilar causes co-operated towards this result, the mistakes of opponents
no less than the efforts of friends. The governments
above all, seduced by the magic formula of the " solidarity of conservative interests," increased the favour formerly shown to the Curia as the " oldest conservative
power." So-called " orthodox " Protestants coquetted
with Roman ecclesiasticism; in all Protestant churches

[1] See the division of the pontificate of Pius into four periods, page 114.

the crypto-papal tendencies gained in influence and partially succeeded in capturing the ecclesiastical authorities.
Even more effective were the operations of the revolutionary party, which, blind to the true significance of
religion, tended to strengthen the influence of the priesthood. The public elections often showed that the cities
were outvoted by the people of the country under the
leadership of the priests; unbelief, as always, brought
superstition in its wake.

All external conditions were shaping themselves favourably to the Papacy; Protestantism was powerless, or else
its representatives gave open aid to the enemy; and all
the while the compact force of Curialism, working with
immense and magnificent energy, knew how to use the
right moment to fish in troubled waters. The general
demand of those days for the destruction of absolutism
in the state was exploited in the interests of ecclesiastical
absolutism, and the revolution for which the Vatican was
chiefly responsible was made use of to get rid of unfavourable influences.

The rushing waters of the revolution were led into the
bed of clerical societies; there was formed a whole
series of German " Catholic " associations, the deposit of
revolutionary fermentation. Alongside of the open societies were the secret congregations and fraternities, and
in the track of both came the Jesuit missions. All these
separate apparently scattered forces were not split up, but
were made to operate toward the same common end:
not only to make the Church into a state within a state,
but also to subject to it the whole spiritual life of the
people, in the school, in matrimony, and in the press;
and this end was achieved by the wise policy of the episcopate, which from the first moment made it the object
of their efforts to exploit the triumphs of the revolution
in their own interests. To all this are to be added the
tactics of the Vatican itself, turning all circumstances to

immediate advantage.   Thus it was enabled, by its direction of the army of auxiliaries, to convert the year of its
adversity into a year of triumph.

Among the acts of the pope which belong to this period
we consider first those of a religious character.   All these,
whether they had to do with the canonisations of individuals or with questions of dogma, show him to be
entirely in the hands of the Jesuits.   After these, we
shall consider his political measures, in allocutions and
concordats.

The series of beatifications was opened immediately
after his return from Gaeta, July 16, 1850, with the
Jesuit, Peter Claver.   Other members of the Company
of Jesus were John de Britto (beatified May 18, 1852)
and Andrew Bobola (July 5, 1853), and later the well-
known German Jesuit, Peter Canisius (August 2, 1864).
Among the other orders, only the order of the Brothers
of Mercy received an accession to the beatified, in John
Grande (October 1, 1852); besides these, two founders of
new congregations, Paul vom Kreuze (October 1, 1852)
and John Leonardi (July 9, 1861), and three virgins were
received into the same class.   The biographies of these
worthies are full of unnatural asceticism and unnatural
miracles.

The pope did not yet, at this period, undertake any
canonisations.   The twenty-six Japanese martyrs had to
wait until the convention of bishops in the year 1867.
But as early as the year 1854 we hear of a new miracle-
working effigy of Mary and an indulgence of the papal
vicar-general in connection with it; and not less than
three jubilees were crowded into the years between 1851
and 1857.

All these are, however, events of secondary importance,
such as happen under every pope.   But this period of
Pius IX. has made itself ever memorable by another

unparalleled event, the definition of a new dogma,—that of the Immaculate Conception of the Virgin Mary. A writer who enjoyed the approval of the pope expresses himself (some years before the papal infallibility was made the order of the day) in the following manner concerning this event, in a pamphlet published in Vienna, 1865, entitled *Pius IX. as Pope and as King:*

This is an event peculiar to the pontificate of Pius IX., such as no former pontificate has to show; for the pope has defined this dogma independently, in the plenitude of his own authority, without the co-operation of a council; and this independent definition of a dogma includes, though not expressly and formally, nevertheless without a doubt and actually, another dogmatic decision : namely, the decision of the question whether the pope in matters of faith is infallible in his own person, or whether he can claim this infallibility only at the head of a council. Pius IX. did not, by his action of December 8, 1854, theoretically define, but he did practically claim, the infallibility of the pope.

That is to say, the newly conceived idea of ultramontanism, rejected by the ancient councils, has received the papal sanction. Herein, and not in the dogmatic question, lies the historical significance of this event.

How much the pope had at heart this favourite doctrine of the Jesuits, which had been rejected by the most eminent representatives of the mediæval Church, was shown by the fact that the first public act of his exile in Gaeta, the encyclical of February 2, 1849, announced to the bishops the creation of a commission for the decision of this question, and commanded them to express their views upon it. Pius in this letter said " that from childhood nothing had been so near his heart as to adore the most blessed Virgin Mary with especial piety and devotion and with the most sincere heartfelt love, and to accomplish all that would serve to the greater honour of this

9

Virgin and to the furtherance of her glory and worship."
He furthermore expressed his hope that " the most blessed
Virgin, who had ever saved Christian people from all evil,
would, in her merciful love as mother, turn from him his
adversities and sorrows and change his grief into joy."
After his return to Rome, which according to this view
he owed to the intercession of Mary, the matter, always
dear to his heart, became still more important, and all
hesitation and difficulties were overcome by the revelations of hysterical women and the appearances of Madon-
nas to children.   The miracles of La Salette and the
newly added miracles of Lourdes finally turned the scale.

The commission created for taking counsel concerning
the new dogma rendered in December, 1853, by the
mouth of Passaglia, this decision, " that to the Virgin
Mary, on account of her sanctity and grace, surpassing
that of human nature, which could not be explained on
natural grounds, was to be ascribed, on the basis of
Scripture, of tradition, and of the existing cult, a conception untainted by hereditary sin."   Passaglia furnished
more extensive proof in a work of three volumes.

The answers of the bishops to the request for their
views were not quite so unanimous.   None of them, indeed, opposed the dogma; but thirty-two declared themselves against the opportuneness and four against the
competence of the proposed convention; and among
these voices in opposition were that of Sibour in Paris,
Diepenbrock in Breslau, and Schwarzenberg in Salzburg.
Four hundred and forty prelates yielded to the desire of
the pope.

On the 1st of August, 1854, Pius published the call for
a council in Rome; at the same time he called for the
prayers of the faithful, and proclaimed the indulgence of
a jubilee.   The intended council, when it met, was nothing
more than an episcopal conference of 192 prelates, which
held its first session on November 20th in the Vatican,

and on December 4th assented nearly unanimously to the proposition of the pope. On the 8th of December Pius celebrated a solemn high mass in the Sistine Chapel, placed upon the effigy of the Virgin a diadem of diamonds, and proclaimed the celebrated bull, *Ineffabilis Deus*. In this bull he declared

by virtue of the authority of Jesus Christ, that of the apostles Peter and Paul, and of his own: that the doctrine, which maintains that Mary in the first moment of her conception was by special grace and special privilege of God preserved from all stain of hereditary sin, had been revealed by God and was therefore to be believed firmly and constantly by all the faithful.

The allocution of the following day gave expression to the papal joy and pictured the errors and the evils of the time, the war with which was placed under the protection of the immaculate mother of God.

The far-reaching nature of the revolution which had taken place in the development of Catholicism from the former episcopal aristocracy, predominant even at Trent, to a direct papal absolutism was made evident by the very slight opposition manifested to an event unheard of in the history of the Catholic Church. The whole modern world appeared to care for it just about as much as for a dogmatic decision of the Dalai Lama of Thibet or of the Mikado of Japan; even the representatives of the Catholic episcopate were silent at the evident flouting of their rights. The wish of Frederick William IV. to put into effect a common protest of the Evangelical churches against the " unbiblical " doctrine failed by virtue of the absence of any common authority.

The few voices which made themselves heard in opposition were isolated. In Italy four priests appealed to the ancient doctrine of the Church against the new decision; they were excommunicated. The same fate overtook a priest, Braun, from the bishopric of Passau in Bavaria, who had likewise used his knowledge of the middle ages to his own injury.   Nevertheless there were occurrences which proved that under a smooth surface all was not so quiet as it seemed: such were the tragical assassination of Archbishop Sibour of Paris (1857), with the exclamation of the ecclesiastical murderer, "Down with goddesses" ("*à bas les déesses*"), the attitude of opposition maintained by the Chamber of Deputies and the government in Portugal, the public ridicule of the dogma in Brussels, finally the pastoral letter of the old-Catholic bishops in Holland.

This last document is, from the Catholic point of view, undoubtedly the most important.   The letter of the bishops to the pope accompanying it proceeds upon the assumption that " their duty of watching over the purity of the Catholic faith forbids their keeping silence, forasmuch as the new dogma is entirely novel in its teaching." They furthermore protest against the slight cast upon the episcopal office in the treatment of its representatives by the papal see, and finally appeal from the decision of the pope to a future general council.   The pastoral itself contains a conclusive refutation of all the arguments cited in the papal decree in favour of the new dogma.   In regular order, with literal citations from the Scriptures, the Church fathers, the papal constitutions, and other official writings, it is shown:

that the dogma in question is taught neither by the sacred Scriptures nor by tradition; that it had its origin in the fourteenth century and even after this time expressed only the sense of a party; that the wonderful consensus of Catholic pastors and believers, which the pope asserted, has never existed; that the old papal constitutions concerning this dogma were only intended to allay the disputes to which it had given occasion, without deciding for or against it; finally, that, forasmuch as the immaculate conception had not been believed either everywhere or at all times or by all, it could not constitute an article of faith.

The decrees of the Council of Trent are more particularly examined; the dispute of the Scotists and the Thomists in the fourteenth century, also the battle fought in Spain after the Council of Trent between Dominicans and Jesuits, are exhaustively treated; and from the decisions of former popes it is clearly proved that none of them dared to settle so uncertain a matter by his own arbitrary decision.

But, however convincing this polemic was to the veterans of ancient Catholicism, Jesuitism had already gained the victory in the Catholic Church. The dogma of Mary, more than anything else, indisputably proves this fact; it did not require the erection of monuments to Mary in Rome, Cologne, Aix-la-Chapelle, and elsewhere. In the allocution already referred to on the day after the proclamation of the dogma, the pope in consistory declared with triumphant joy: " We know the feeling of admiration which has been awakened in the hearts of men for the Catholic religion, which like the light of the sun shines before the eyes of all." What was meant by the term " Catholic religion " had been long before explained by the paraphrase of Boniface VIII., to the effect that it " was necessary for all human creatures to obey the pope of Rome under pain of loss of salvation."

The growing strength of the Papacy in the new epoch manifests itself in the bulls by which the hierarchy was " restored " in England and in Holland, the former on September 29, 1850, the latter on March 4, 1853. The agitation which these measures produced in both countries was only too much justified by the conduct of the Curia in those nationalities where a longer rule made more decided measures possible. Thus the new concordat with

Spain, of the year 1851, expressly prohibited the toleration of any other than the papal Church, likewise the
compacts with several South American states. The
ecclesiastical dispute in the upper Rhinelands, which
reached its climax in 1854, was intended to establish the
rule of the Curia where the denominations were equally
divided. The Austrian concordat of August 18, 1855,
had buried the last remnant of Josephine ideas and made
the imperial state once more the paradise of the hierarchy;
and after prolonged futile negotiations the smaller states
succumbed to the pressure of Austria. The conventions
with Würtemberg and Baden, the compromises with
Hesse-Darmstadt and Nassau, were worthy offshoots of
the Austrian concordat. Everywhere we see again the
immutable policy of the Curia gaining ground in the
struggle against the modern state.

The time had come—so the Vatican thought—when it
might with impunity set the whole civilised world at
naught. The abduction of the eight-year-old Jewish
boy, Mortara, in Bologna, under the pretence that two
years before he had received private baptism from his
Christian nurse, was, in spite of all protests, sustained
(July, 1859).[1] The mediæval superiority of the pope to
every human law seemed to have returned. The divine
retribution was soon to follow.

[1] Edgar Mortara was seized by order of the archbishop of Bologna. The
French government interfered to obtain his release, and Sir Moses Monte-
fiore went to Rome for the same purpose. A protest against the seizure was
signed by the archbishop of Canterbury, by bishops, noblemen, and gentlemen of England.

CHAPTER X

THE PAPACY DURING THE RECONSTRUCTION OF ITALY [1]
AND GERMANY (1859-1870)

IN the beginning of January, 1859, the French *Moniteur* published a series of letters from Rome, by Edmond About, which made a startling disclosure of the corrupt *régime* prevalent in the ecclesiastical states. Among other things we read this:

The Roman Church comprehends, not counting the Jewish boy Mortara, 139 millions of souls. It is governed by seventy cardinals or princes of the Church, as it first was by twelve apostles. The cardinals are nominated by the pope, the pope by the cardinals. From the day of his election the pope becomes infallible—at least according to the view of de Maistre and the best Catholics of our time. Bossuet did not believe this, but the popes have always believed it. If the head of the Church declares that the Virgin Mary was born without taint of hereditary sin, the 139 millions of Catholics are obliged to take his word for it. This discipline of the spirits is much to the credit of the nineteenth century, and posterity will be grateful to us for it. It will acknowledge that we, instead of breaking our necks over theological disputes, have

[1] " The process [the union of Italy] occupied eleven years and was made in five successive annexations : Lombardy, 1859 ; Tuscany, Modena and Parma, Romagna, January, 1860 ; Kingdom of Naples, the Marches, and Umbria, at the end of 1860 ; Venetia, 1866 ; Rome, 1870. The first three operations formed a continuous series which ended in the creation of the Kingdom of Italy."—Seignobos.

devoted ourselves to the building of railroads and telegraphs, and to the construction of steam-engines, without entering into quarrels about the infallibility of a man. But even a generation so busy as this may feel itself obliged for once to turn its attention from its own business and to apply it to the spark which for years has been secretly smouldering in the ecclesiastical state, which within twenty-four hours may set all Europe in a blaze.

There follows a description of the wretched condition of affairs in the ecclesiastical state, given with that mastery of style which is the special gift of the French. But it was not so much the literary excellence which gave to these letters their importance; the most significant fact was that they appeared in the *Moniteur*, and that, after it had been inhibited, they were sold without hindrance all over France.

Soon followed the war of 1859, in which France and Sardinia were united against Austria.[1] The offer of the pope to give up the foreign garrisons was made too late, nor could the intervention of England prevent the war. The brave Austrian army was defeated at Magenta and Solferino, more in consequence of the incapacity of its leaders than of the bravery of its enemies. Again the destiny of Rome was decided in the fields of upper Italy. As soon as the Austrians had evacuated the papal provinces (they left Bologna June 13, 1859), the provinces rose in insurrection against the pope. The bloody conquest of Perugia by the papal troops only increased the bitterness of feeling, and at the end of June the whole of the Romagna was freed from the rule of the pope.

Then came the unexpected peace of Villafranca (July 11, 1859) between France and Austria. This peace promised the restoration to their sovereigns of Tuscany,

---

[1] Napoleon and Cavour had formed an alliance, whose object was the expulsion of the Austrians from Italy.

Modena, and Parma,[1] and the papal states were to be restored to the pope, but only in case this were possible without armed intervention. There was, however, not the least expectation of a peaceful restoration on the part of the inhabitants of the Romagna, and the encyclical of June 18th concerning the necessity of the temporal power, as well as that of September 26th concerning the spoliation of the Romagna, were ineffectual to accomplish the purpose.

The year 1859 was not to expire without making the dangers of the future appear even more threatening than the losses of the present. The pamphlet, *The Pope and the Congress*, issued anonymously from Paris, and calling forth within a few weeks more than a hundred other writings *pro* and *con*, made the problem of the temporal power of the pope a burning question of the day. This pamphlet not only raised the question as to how the head of a Church which excommunicates heretics could at the same time be the head of the state which protects liberty of conscience; it made the direct demand upon the pope to sacrifice his temporal power to the love of peace, the welfare of his subjects, the general good and the peace of Europe; he was to be indemnified by other sources of income, and was to keep Rome as his capital. This plan (which in its essence Napoleon I. had favoured) was repeated, somewhat modified, in the letter which Napoleon III. addressed to the pope, December 31, 1859, in which he demanded renunciation of the lost provinces, and promised the guarantee of the Catholic Powers for the rest of the papal territory. The pope was to acknowledge the king of Italy as his vicar over the Romagna;

---

[1] The duke of Modena, the duchess of Parma, and the grand duke of Tuscany had been obliged to take refuge in Austria and Switzerland. Provisional governments had been formed and the union of these duchies with Sardinia proclaimed.

the Catholic Powers were to provide an army corps for
the preservation of order in Rome.

The above-mentioned pamphlet was generally ascribed
to the counsellor of state, La Gueronnière.   The allocution of January 1, 1860, characterised it as a network of
hypocrisy and contradictions.   The encyclical of January
19th, in answer to Napoleon's demand, contained the first
instance of the *Non possumus,* which later became so
celebrated: " The pope cannot give up what belongs not
to him, but to all Catholics; by such renunciation he
would violate his oath, his dignity, and his rights, en-
courage insurrection in the remaining provinces, and
injure the rights of all Christian princes."   In answer
to all further proposals Pius, by the mouth of Antonelli,
persevered in this refusal.

At the same time all the means of which papal Rome
had the disposition were put into motion.   The episcopacy of all countries entered a protest against " an act
of violence, by which an attack is made upon the most
ancient of all possessions, and by which all ideas of right
and all legal relations are brought into question."   Bishop
Dupanloup of Orleans was pre-eminent in the general
chorus by the most violent invectives; the Prussian
bishops, expressing their opinion in a joint manifesto,
would have reduced their Protestant prince [1] to the position of a servant of the pope-king.   Innumerable were the
demonstrations by which the Catholic nations were stirred
up, the addresses, assemblies, sermons, associations for
prayer, etc.

The greatest actual profit was derived from the Peter's
pence which was everywhere called for; but even the
costliest gifts were totally consumed in the fitting out of
a papal army " which consisted of sundry knights of the
faith, of drunken Irishmen, of vagabonds from all nations,
and Austrian soldiers on furlough."   As leader of this

---

[1] Frederick William IV., 1840–1861.

army, the old African hero, Lamoricière, aspired to the fame of a modern Don Quixote.

To these worldly weapons was added the once-dreaded excommunication. After the vote taken in the annexed countries [1] excommunication was on the 26th of March, 1860, solemnly pronounced upon all those

who had been guilty of rebellion, invasion, usurpation, and any of the other outrages named in the allocution; all instigators, helpers, counsellors, and adherents of such, all those who had facilitated the execution of these deeds of violence or had executed them; finally all those who, themselves sons of the Church, had reached such a degree of impudence that, while continually protesting their reverence for and devotion to the Church, they attacked her temporal power and despised her authority.

No names were given, but the indications as to who were meant were clear enough.

But the existence of the states of the Church was so much opposed to the most essential needs of the Italian people, that little heed was given to its claims.[2] In fact, the effect was rather the opposite of that intended. The clerical agitation and the papal preparations for war after Garibaldi had undertaken his celebrated expedition to Sicily and had crossed to the mainland (1860), served as a pretext for demanding the dissolution of the papal army of foreign mercenaries, and for the entrance of Italian troops into Umbria and the Marches. The engagement of Castelfidardo (September 18, 1860),

[1] By a vote taken in March, 1860, Tuscany, Modena, and Parma pronounced for union with Sardinia.

[2] The following events in Italy must here be recalled : Garibaldi conquered Sicily and Naples from Francis II. in 1860. In the same year the Sardinian troops entered the papal states and defeated the troops of the pope at Castelfidardo in the Marches. Naples and Sicily voted to join the kingdom of Sardinia. The whole of Italy except Venice and the Campagna was now united, and in February, 1861, the first Parliament of united Italy was opened by Cavour.

in which the papal troops were defeated by the Piedmontese, left to the Curia only the cheap consolation of de-
corating the fallen with martyr crowns.   The conquest
of Ancona took away the last stronghold except the actual
patrimony of St. Peter.   Umbria and the Marches became, like Naples, the booty of the " Piedmontese beast
of prey," and after the conquest of Gaeta the first Italian
Parliament was able to greet the first king of Italy (February, 1861).

The end of the open war only changed the scene of the
struggle; and the war of opposing principles became all
the more embittered.   While the pope is being supported
by the episcopate and foreign nations rival one another
in demonstrations of devotion, two addresses are issued
from Rome, in May, 1861, with ten thousand signatures,
for the liberation of the capital of Italy.   A series of new
pamphlets,— *Pope and Emperor — Rome and the French
Bishops — France, Rome, and Italy,*— was published in
Paris.   Cardinals such as Liverani and d'Andrea, popular preachers such as Gavazzi, scholars such as Passaglia,
however much they differed among each other, were
united in their opposition to the papal rule, and an overwhelming majority of the lower Italian clergy ranged
themselves with them on the side of the nation.

The party of Passaglia, representing the so-called Pas-
saglism, formed a sign of the times whose significance is
inferior to none.   Whether Passaglia was right or wrong,
whether his voice commanded attention in Rome or not,
—not in the result of this movement lay its chief importance, but in the fact that it existed at all, and that an
exceedingly large part of the lower clergy enthusiastically
adopted these views.   Terribly incisive were the representations of this Italian, priest and Jesuit:

Who is so blind, so short-sighted, as not to see that the Italian
people is running into the danger of forsaking the paradise of

the Church ? that this danger is not far off but near, not small but very great ? A large number of Italians have already openly or in secret separated themselves from this mother and thus she is robbed of a multitude of chosen children; a large part of the clergy are in dispute with the majority of the laity; almost all the pastors are separated from their flocks, and the pastor of pastors himself, the successor of St. Peter, the august vicar of Christ upon earth, hurls censures and excommunication against the Italian kingdom and against Italian society. Better it were to consider whether in the present disposition of the Italians the excommunication hurled against them may not awaken more of bitterness than of improvement, may not rather mortally wound than cauterise the wound.

That this representation was not exaggerated was proved by the immense approbation which Garibaldi found in all Italy, even when he declared that " he professed the religion of Christ, not the religion of the pope and the cardinals, the enemies of Italy," and when he called upon the people to " cut the cancer of the Papacy out of Italy." Even in the German Rome, in Munich, where, according to repeated rumours, the exiled pope would most likely have sought a refuge, Döllinger, the provost of the Collegiate Church, delivered in April, 1861, his lectures on the states of the Church, those lectures which created so much excitement and whose real significance only few guessed at the time.

The diplomatic fencing which began in 1861 and continued almost during the entire decade, especially between Rome and Paris, may well be passed over in an account of ecclesiastical history. The policy of the Vatican is illustrated by the assembly of European bishops that took place in Rome upon occasion of the canonisation of the Japanese martyrs (1567), with the address of submission signed by 21 cardinals, 4 patriarchs, 53 archbishops, and 187 bishops, which advocated the necessity of the temporal dominion of the pope (June 8, 1862), and the allocution of the latter on the following day. Italian popular sentiment is shown in the addresses of the lower clergy, published by Passaglia, whose signatures soon reached to beyond 10,000, as well as in the enthusiastic address in which, in answer to the vituperations of the foreign bishops, the Italian Parliament gathered round its king (June 18th).

Garibaldi's expedition to the capital, with the watchword, " Rome or death," suffered shipwreck at Aspromonte (August 29, 1862)[1]; but the suppression of this insurrection by the government secured the recognition of Italy by the great Powers. The convention between France and Italy of September, 1864, which made Florence the capital instead of Turin and promised the withdrawal of the French troops, soon proved to be simply another provisional arrangement.

In the pope's answer to this movement he changed his base from the political to the ecclesiastical ground. This answer was given in the encyclical of December 8, 1864. The Syllabus which accompanies this encyclical, treating of the errors to be avoided by papists, comprehends about everything on earth that is subject to the papal anathema, and places itself in opposition to all the best elements of modern civilisation just as much as to revolution and to infidelity.

The chief enemy whom Pius attacks in his Syllabus receives the name of Naturalism, as the comprehensive designation of all those errors that oppose themselves to the influence of the Church upon individuals and upon nations. All the consequences, as well, of this naturalistic view of things are individually condemned: so the " damnable pernicious errors " of freedom of religion and of

---

[1] The Italian government was obliged to interfere in this attempt of Garibaldi, and sent troops against him, by whom he was wounded and captured at Aspromonte.

worship, of the independence of the temporal from the spiritual power, the theory of popular sovereignty, and the errors of socialism and communism. Through the influence of all these monstrous principles human society has become endangered; it can only be saved by the restitution of all rights belonging to the Church over princes and peoples. For while the pope, in his own opinion, may bring all worldly affairs before his tribunal, princes may not, upon any pretext, interfere in matters of religion. The Catholic religion is alone entitled to the public exercise of worship, every other form of worship is to be suppressed, and the crime of heresy is to be punished.

The Syllabus of eighty errors, cited by name, divides itself into ten chapters: naturalism and absolute rationalism, moderate rationalism, indifferentism, socialism together with secret associations and Bible societies, errors concerning the Church, concerning civil society, concerning morals, concerning matrimony, concerning the temporal power of the popes, finally the errors of modern liberalism. The last-cited error, which really comprehends all others, is this, that the pope can and must reconcile himself with progress, liberalism, and with modern civilisation.

In spite of the unambiguous anathemas of the Syllabus, a good deal of ingenuity was spent, especially in France and Germany, to soften and change the meaning of some expressions. Even Curci [1] attempted to show, in 1881, that all the sentences of the Syllabus could not have the same binding power as articles of faith, because they originated in different kinds of *acta Pontificis*, in briefs, encyclicals, allocutions, etc., and that not one of them was taken from an actual dogmatic bull. But quite irrespective of the fact that this only suggests again the

[1] See page 25, note 1.

well-known question, When does the pope really speak
ex cathedra ? the extension of infallibility to the anathemas of the Syllabus has been expressly decided by Leo
XIII. (April 21, 1878).

More memorable, however, than the arts of interpretation by which the majority of learned Catholics thought
to reconcile themselves to the Syllabus, was the indifference which the Protestant world once more showed towards these renewed papal pretensions.   Most scholars
looked upon the Syllabus as a rusted sword.   The historian Sybel has declared that the frivolity or the ignorance
with which the statesmen disregarded this frank declaration of papal sovereignty has few parallels in history.

The Curia did not conceal its purposes, neither did its
Jesuit press.   To all attempts at a mutual approach which
the kingdom of Italy made (such was the mission of
Vegezzi in 1865 [1] and many others which did not become
known to the public), the papal secretary of state answered with the now proverbial *Non possumus.*

In the relations to other states also the old irreconcilable spirit was inclining to more drastic modes of expression than ever before.   This statement applies to the
school dispute in Baden, to the insurrection of the Poles
against Russia (1860–63), so full of horrors, to the Sisy-
phus-like attempts of the poor Emperor Maximilian of
Mexico to satisfy the insatiable demands of the clerical
party.   A like intensification in the language of the
Curia is shown in the brief of September, 1865, against
" that abandoned society generally called Freemasons."
The fact that the king of Prussia was the head of the

---

[1] This mission was for the purpose of an agreement with the pope about
the bishoprics which remained unfilled.   The Italian government wished
to have the number of bishops reduced.   If there had been 59 instead of
230, there would still have been a bishop to every 250,000 souls, a third of
the number in the Belgian dioceses.   The pope would not hear of this, and
the negotiations were broken off.

national lodge gave to this papal declaration of love a peculiarly piquant flavour.

The Curia has always been accustomed to mingle spiritual pretensions with political intrigue. And its hopes were, after the issue of the Syllabus, founded upon the increasing confusion of the political situation, especially upon the growing tension between Prussia and Austria. From the centres of the anti-Prussian agitation the emissaries of the Jesuits understood how to lay far and wide their network of wires. The grand duchy of Baden was undermined by the agitations. Ranke's disclosures of the religious background to the preparations for the Seven Years' War find in no small degree their parallel in the events leading up to the war of 1866 between Austria and Prussia. That in the eyes and in the sense of the Curia it was a religious war is attested by the expression of Antonelli when the news was brought to him of the battle of Sadowa: "*Casca il mondo.*" In perfect agreement with this view, Windhorst afterwards traced to this battle-field the origin of the *Kulturkampf* in Prussia. The policy of Prussia towards the Curia, which was at that time very compliant, cannot well be charged with being the cause of this conflict. The simple truth is that the papal principle stood in irreconcilable opposition to the modern state as represented by Prussia: the clerical journals of the time leave no doubt of that fact.

The war of 1866 added the Venetian territory to the Italian state (Lombardy had been won in 1859). And now the national demand, which would be satisfied with nothing else but Rome for the capital, became all the more urgent. The national hero, who during the official war had been forced into the background, thought to cut with the sword the Gordian knot of double-tongued policy.[1] But hardly had Garibaldi with his little band

---

[1] In October, 1867, Garibaldi renewed his cry, "Rome or death," and gathered about eight thousand followers. The Italian government, which,

started for Rome, when the French emperor ordered the return into the ecclesiastical state of the troops that had been withdrawn the year before.   At Mentana—so says the official report of the French general—the chassepots performed miracles.   Once more was Rome kept out of the hands of her children by a foreign occupation.

The nature of the hopes which the Curia cherished, and to which these miracles of Mentana gave fresh impetus, was made manifest at the so-called centenary of Peter, June 20, 1867.   The pompous assembly of bishops gave to the pope-kingship a dogmatic consecration.   The bishops declared solemnly:

The see of St. Peter has remained for eighteen centuries immovable and inviolate as the organ of truth, the centre of unity, the foundation and bulwark of freedom, while kingdoms and empires have been perpetually rising and falling.   Therefore they offer to the pope the well-merited testimonial of their reverence and give public expression to their wishes for the preservation of his temporal power and for the sacred cause of religion and of justice which he defends.   It is the dearest and most sacred object of their hearts to believe and to teach what the pope believes and teaches, to reject the errors that he rejects, to march under his leadership, to fight at his side, prepared with him to meet all dangers, all visitations, and all trials.

The pope's answer to this episcopal address and his public allocutions breathed an intensified war spirit and a hope " to break through the ranks of his enemies."

A teacher of religion in a Prussian gymnasium proved the temporal possessions of the popes to be the special work of divine Providence, and exemplified it by the

in 1864, had engaged to protect the possessions of the pope, could not give him aid.   Garibaldi persevered and fought at Mentana, near Rome.   He had beaten back the papal troops, when the French advanced and began to shoot down Garibaldi's men by hundreds with their chassepots.

unhappy end of the Hohenstaufen emperors. Archbishop Manning and Bishop Martin issued pastoral letters to prepare for the completion of the work by the general council which the pope had in view.

But even the most pronounced devotees of the Papacy were surpassed by Pius IX. himself in total disregard and unconcealed contempt for liberty of conscience. The canonisation of Pedro Arbues, which he performed, was the exaltation of the Inquisition in the person of one of its most detestable executioners. By placing the so-called " martyrs of Gorkum " [1] upon the Roman calendar, judgment was pronounced upon the war for the liberation of the Netherlands. Whether the canonisation of Balthasar Gerards (the murderer of William the Silent), which had been proposed in the college of cardinals at the time of the first counter-reformation, came again under consideration is not known.

Alzog, an orthodox writer of "correct " opinions, has himself testified of Pius IX. that " he performed more beatifications and canonisations than any of his predecessors." Upon the same occasion he refers to the decree of December 10, 1863, by which doubts concerning the genuineness of relics, especially the little bottles of blood, were rebuked " to avoid giving offence to the faithful." It is remarkable that Alzog in this connection allows himself the observation that " this decree is not sufficient in view of the frequent reappearance of renewed doubts." Such rebellion against a papal decision, which surely was delivered *ex cathedra*, will probably have to be cancelled in the next edition.

Hardly a year passed without all sorts of spectacles and demonstrations, in which not only was the Papacy identified with Christianity, but the pope himself personally put in the place of Christ. The year 1869 was distinguished

[1] The nineteen priests and friars who were put to death by William de la Marck when he captured Gorkum for the United Provinces in 1572.

by the semi-centennial jubilee of the pope's priesthood. It was celebrated with great pomp not only in Rome, but in the smallest parishes. In Germany there was much sung on this occasion the so-called " Pius hymn," which addresses the pope explicitly as sinless:

> Pius, the priest, in humble admiration
> We look to thee, a sinful generation ;
>   No sin in thee we see ;
> Thou wonderful flower of the altar,
> Of our nature the highest exalter—
>   We point with pride to thee.

CHAPTER XI

THE FIRST VATICAN COUNCIL

THE inner organic connection between the encyclical of December 8, 1864 [The Syllabus encyclical], and the ecumenical council called by His Holiness Pope Pius IX., which is to be opened this year, is self-evident. The plans which were there initiated are here to be extended, completed, and by the most solemn act at the disposition of the Church to be made the most common and lasting possible property of the Church.

With these words the German organ of the Jesuits, the *Voices from Maria-Laach*, introduced its readers into the business of the council before it had met. At the same time (February 6, 1869), the Roman organ, the *Civiltà Cattolica*, created a sensation by publishing an article in which the proclamation of the personal infallibility of the pope was expressly defined as the means to the dogmatisation of the Syllabus. Louis Veuillot seconded this proposal in the *Univers* in an article full of the coarsest vilification of all possible opponents.

The papal bull of convocation, *Æterni Patris* (June 29, 1868), had given no clue to the questions which it was proposed to submit to the council. According to this bull, the purpose was simply the salvation of the Church and of society from threatening calamities, the extirpation of modern error, and the destruction of the enemies of the Church. The memorable letters, which soon fol-

lowed, addressed to the oriental bishops (September 8,
1868) and to the Protestants (September 13, 1868), made
use of the occasion for urging their subjection. Even
the measures of preparation for the council itself gave no
clue as to whether the expectations of the Jesuit papers
were authorised or not.

At the same time, the character of those in whose hands
these preparations had been placed was very significant.
Count Reisach was first made president, after his death
Cardinal de Angelis took his place. Bishop Fessler was
chosen official secretary. In the seven special commissions appointed before the sitting of the council, there
was a decided predominance of the element to whose influence the proclamation of the Syllabus is traceable.
Bilio, the chief author of the Syllabus, and Perrone, the
violent and foul-mouthed controversialist against Protestantism, played an important part. Other Italian
theologians of the same tendency were Spada, Cordoni,
Bertolini. On a par with these was the Frenchman
Freppel and the Belgian Deschamps, who made themselves equally prominent by their immoderate zeal. The
English convert Manning and his countryman Talbot
had also long been known as violent infallibilists. Among
German theologians, only the Jesuit father, Schrader,
and the two Würzburgers, Hergenröther and Hettinger,
occupied positions of any prominence. The most eminent theologians of Catholic Germany were at first entirely
left out. Later some of them were called in, but, as if in
mockery, were given the most trivial questions of form
to occupy themselves with: Hefele and Alzog with
costumes and ceremonial, Haneberg with the rites of
oriental monasteries.

The questions to be submitted to the council were made
known only in the most general outlines. The seven
commissions, at the head of each a cardinal, divided
among themselves the order of business, the ceremonial,

matters of ecclesiastical politics, missions, the orders, dogmatics, and discipline. The counsellors whom they called in were by a special oath obligated to silence concerning the transactions. No knowledge whatever of these preliminaries was given to the foreign bishops. On the other hand, everything was done to add to the outer splendour of an event which was to surpass all former spectacles. To this purpose there was even proclaimed the indulgence of a jubilee (April 11, 1869).

The language proceeding from the Jesuit press, coupled with the official silence and the painful feeling of uncertainty about what was imminent, called forth a decided movement among Catholics, especially those of the more advanced countries. The character of this movement is explained by a Church historian of orthodox submissiveness, who says that " in Germany, even among the most faithful and highly esteemed Catholic laymen, apprehensions made themselves felt, which they considered themselves obliged in a most respectful address to lay before their bishops."

The German bishops thereupon issued the first pastoral from Fulda, which was intended to allay these apprehensions. For,

nevermore will or can a general council declare a new doctrine which is not contained in the sacred Scriptures or the apostolical traditions. Nevermore will a general council proclaim doctrines which are in opposition to the rights of the state and of its magistrates, which without necessity set themselves at variance with the existing conditions and the needs of the present time. The purpose of the council rather can be no other than to place the ancient and primitive truth in a more clear light. Just as unfounded and unjust is the suspicion that freedom of deliberation will be curtailed at the council.

With no less decision did the most highly esteemed leaders of the French episcopacy declare themselves,

Darboy of Paris and Dupanloup of Orleans at their head. They were joined by Gratry, Maret, Montalembert, in learned expressions of opinion full of deep feeling. In a literary production of the first order " Janus " placed the claims of the Papacy in the light of its own history. The work of " Janus " was by indirect indications attributed to Döllinger; another writing, *Considerations for the Bishops of the Council Concerning the Question of Papal Infallibility*, was with more certainty attributed to him.

The *Voices from the Catholic Church*, which appeared during the year of the council, had their centre in Munich. Bonn and Breslau, Tübingen and Fribourg were well known as faculties of old-Catholic views. Even the leader of the ultramontane party in Switzerland, Philipp Anton von Segesser, protested, "on the eve of the council," energetically against the " so-called papal system, which in reality is nothing but the translation of the Byzantine theory of sovereignty into the ecclesiastical sphere, and against the effort arising from this theory to transfer the doctrine of the infallibility of the Church in matters of faith to the person of the pope." " For this consecration of monarchical absolutism in the sphere of the Church must bring the Church into complete antagonism with the whole political formation of the present and place the relations between Church and State upon the basis of a mutual war of extermination."

Neither statesmen nor Protestants could therefore complain of any lack of warning voices on the part of the most competent judges in Catholic circles. The president of the Bavarian ministry, Prince Hohenlohe, brother of the cardinal, made himself the organ of those earnest Catholics who recognised the inevitable danger to the state and to liberty of conscience; he was supported by the votes of the theological and law faculty in Munich. But his suggestion of common measures for prevention (in the circular of April 9, 1869) was everywhere considered inopportune. Bismarck and Beust [1] were in remarkable accord in the answers they gave. The enlightened liberals met Hohenlohe's pessimistic views with derision. Not long after, as a reward for his German patriotism, he was overthrown by the Bavarian patriot party. The latter was warmly seconded in this work of piety by the chief of the Lutheran Church of Bavaria, Herr von Harless. In Paris and Rome the removal of Hohenlohe encouraged the opposite party to advance with increasing boldness.

Diplomacy, which by this time had become inquisitive, was quieted with the assurance given by Antonelli that the holy see would not " propose " its own infallibility. The pope did, indeed, not propose it, he only caused it to be proposed. But in the application of the means, which Pius personally used for the intimidation of opponents, nothing was left unattempted, from friendly persuasion to angry threat and brutal force. Those that hesitated he scolded as sectarian enemies of the Church and of the apostolic see, among whom the only difference was that some might be more the slaves of princes, some more ignorant, and some more cowardly. The so-called liberal Catholics of France especially gave him cause for renewed outbreaks of anger. The gentle prince of peace did not even hesitate to prohibit the mass for the repose of the soul of Count Montalembert, who died during the council.

About the same time, the German *Voices from the Catholic Church* were placed upon the Index. More and more manifest became the decisive influence of the Society of Jesus. Their accustomed arts of refined craftiness and cunning intrigue were perhaps never exercised in the same degree. Ample experience had taught the prudent fathers to understand the spirit of the times. They knew that a momentary excitement would not last

[1] Chancellor of the Austrian empire.

long (this had been the experience in England and Holland at the institution of the new hierarchy, and everywhere at the publication of the Syllabus); that wise statesmen would soon weary of ecclesiastical affairs. A no less clear observer, Döllinger, came in the year 1869 to the same conclusion, namely, that there would be no sudden great apostasy, no open revolt on a large scale; all would remain placid, only too placid.

After the council had been opened on Pius' favourite day, the 8th of December (1869), there came to light, one by one, the studied measures of preparation by which the predetermined end was to be brought about. Behind the scenes all had been set in order, while of the fathers of the council themselves those that were not among the initiated groped in the dark. The very vessels in which the Holy Ghost was to dwell were distributed in the most remarkable manner. There were 767 members entitled to a vote. Out of these, the whole of Germany was represented by fourteen votes, and among these were Martin of Paderborn and Senestrey of Regensburg, almost the most passionate advocates of the papal theory. Of Italian votes, which were at the certain disposition of the pope, there were 276. The thirty generals of orders had, contrary to all usage, received the right of voting. Besides these, there were 119 bishops *in partibus* and missionary bishops, who almost all lived in Rome at the expense of the pope. For, as Alzog said, " Pope Pius IX. had, with his accustomed considerate attention, provided suitable lodgings and decent sustentation for the prelates of small means coming from far." Of their theological knowledge the most incredible stories were soon in circulation on good authority. In like manner the literary status of the eighty Spanish and South American bishops excited much derision.

But even among the minority, although it far out-

balanced the majority in moral, theological, and official
weight, there soon appeared serious defects of knowledge
and greater weakness of character.   Besides, their position was from the beginning weakened by the servile submission to the pope which prompted them to call in
question less the truth than the opportuneness of the
Jesuit dogma.   Still we must be just.   The poor bishops
repeatedly applied to their governments demanding
whether, in case of continued opposition, they might
count upon governmental support.   They were left without answer.   This is asserted especially in the case of
Bishop von Ketteler of Mayence.

To intensify the disproportion in numerical strength
between the two parties, the order of business (proclaimed
by the bull, *Multiplices inter,* of November 27, 1869) was
especially designed by the dispositions it made to prevent
the opposition from asserting itself.   The machinery
did the service required of it; one cannot help feeling that
the whole thing was a farce.   No proposition was admitted unless it had the sanction of a deputation appointed by the pope.   The distribution of the members
of the commissions was such that Alzog naïvely complains: " The constitution of the dogmatic commissions
is the most questionable proceeding in the human activity of the council."   The presidents of the special congregations (committees) were nominated by the pope.
In the general congregations the right of speech might
be refused to any member.   In the public sessions all
discussion was excluded, members could only vote *placet*
or *non placet*.

The rule of unanimity, which had formerly prevailed
where dogma was to be determined, was abrogated, and
a simple majority was required.   The acoustic arrangements in the hall where the sessions were held were as bad
as they could be.   The demand of another hall was refused.   Even the use of the stenographers' reports was

denied the fathers of the council.   When one of them (in
the first general congregation of December 10th) complained of the proceedings as a manifest contravention of
the Tridentine decisions, he was called to order by the
president with the assertion that this matter had been decided by the pope and was not submitted to the council.
On the 14th of December another papal law was communicated, which took the discussion of the question of
censorship out of the hands of the council.   But, worst
of all, the propositions themselves (the *schemata*) were
distributed only singly and piecemeal, so that no general
survey of their number or of their contents was possible.

The complaints and the protests of the fathers against
these arbitrary proceedings had no other effect than the
change of some unessential details.   These very changes
proved in the end to be rather injurious than advantageous; in place of *viva-voce* addresses, written presentations
were now demanded, which could, without attracting attention, be consigned to the waste-paper basket.

In short, the same bishops who in their own homes
stood above the officers of the state were in Rome treated
as papal lackeys.   One of them complained that more
decency was preserved in an assembly of cobblers than in
the council.   But even this expression appears mild compared with the official protest of the bishops of the
minority:

We consider it no longer compatible with our episcopal dignity, with our official position in the council, and with the
rights which belong to us as members of the council, to prefer
any requests, after our experience has fully taught us that
not only are our requests not considered, but that they are
not even thought worthy of an answer.   There is nothing left
us but to raise our protest against a proceeding which appears
to us equally injurious to the Church and to the apostolic see,
that in so doing we may repudiate the responsibility for any
possible evil consequences as well before men as before the

judgment of God. To this end may this declaration be for
ever a witness.

Not until the machinery had been put fairly in motion
was the purpose of the whole proceeding, hitherto kept
a secret, gradually made known. The first two public
sessions were consumed with formalities; the first with
the opening ceremonies, the second with the confession
of the faith (January 6, 1870). Immediately after this,
however (beginning of January, 1870), a proposition for
the proclamation of the infallibility was set in circulation
and signatures to it collected. At the same time agitation was begun in the press (the *Civiltà* and *Unità Cattolica* in Rome, *Univers* and *Monde* in Paris, *Tablet* in
London, etc.). Pius IX. presently issued briefs in
praise of the agitators (f. i., to Guèranger, the abbot of
Solesmes).

The minority in opposition were now roused to activity.
And however fruitless their efforts were, historical interest
in the proceedings of the council will always turn atten-
tively to these as the most important witnesses for
Catholicism against Papalism.

In opposition to an address which issued from the College of Jesuits in favour of the dogma, a counter-address
was set in motion which implored the pope not to listen
to the former. The most eminent bishops of Germany,
Austria, and France, whose dioceses in number of souls
far surpassed those of the infallibilists, had placed themselves at the head of this movement. These were the
very men who in their own countries were known as the
first champions of clerical pretensions. After the council
they all made " the sacrifice of the reason," as one of
them called it, and forced their subordinate clergy to
render obedience to the now divinely revealed dogma.

The following were leaders of the opposition in the
council: Rauscher (Vienna) and Schwarzenberg (Prague),

Melchers (Cologne) and Förster (Breslau), Ketteler (Mayence) and Scherr (Munich), Darboy (Paris) and Dupanloup (Orleans).   The most learned opponent of the new
dogma, who knew it to be irreconcilable with the history
of the Papacy, was Bishop Hefele of Rottenburg, in
Würtemberg; for no man understood better than he the
question of the heretical pope, Honorius I.[1]   The most
open and pugnacious enemy was the bishop of Croatia,
Strossmayer.

The greatest surprise, however, was occasioned by the
opposition of the bishop of Mayence, whom his diocese
knew above all as the enthusiastic patron of the Jesuits.
In Rome, Bishop Ketteler had circulated a special pamphlet against the dogma.   After all other attempts to
move the pope had proved futile, he went so far in an
audience on July 15, 1870, as to go down on his knees three
times before the pope and to entreat him not to throw the
Church into such danger.   Pius declared to him at the
time that the matter had gone too far to allow of any
change being made.   This happened on the same day
on which there was incorporated in the language of the
formula of infallibility the passage which has given to it
its thoroughly revolutionary meaning.

The disposition prevailing among the bishops of the
opposition forms one of the most interesting phases in
the history of the council.   Long they refused to believe
the incredible.   Then we see them wandering to and fro
like a flock of sheep which feel the nearness of the wolf.
They cherish now this, now that hope.   And all the
while the Jesuit machinery was going its undisturbed
course; all necessary measures had been taken.

The pope, who when he was plain Abbot Ferretti had
believed in the infallibility, was now penetrated with the
idea.   He met a reference to ancient tradition with the

[1] Died 638, anathematised by name as a Monothelite heretic by the Council of Constantinople in 680.

answer: "*La tradizione son' io*" (" I am the tradition "). In return for the loss of their former independence toward the pope, the bishops were promised so much more power in their jurisdiction over the lower clergy. This object was accomplished by the *schema* concerning the life and official duties of the lower clergy, which contained surprising information concerning the morality of the latter. Such were the bribes which were offered to the bishops; it was an intensification of absolutism from grade to grade.

The course of affairs was predetermined, and the only question was concerning the manner in which the new dogma should be introduced into the ancient doctrine of the Church. The second of the so-called dogmatic *schemata* gave the opportunity. The *schemata* of discipline, laid before the council together with the others, treated of practical ecclesiastical questions (among them, the question of a new uniform catechism). The first dogmatic *schema* was devoted to a condemnation of " Rationalism." The second dogmatic *schema* treated in fifteen chapters of the Church of Christ. The second part of this *schema* was devoted to the primacy of the pope; in the original document, however, it contained no word about his infallibility.

The fathers of the council were given but the shortest time to sanction this *schema*, which was not communicated to them until they had arrived in Rome. For the first ten chapters they were allowed ten days (till March 4th). And yet in this time 120 written proposals concerning these chapters were handed in.

When, on the 6th of March, the second part, concerning the primacy of the pope, was to be taken up, it was found that there had been inserted between the eleventh and twelfth chapters the sentence: " Romanum pontificem in rebus fidei et morum definiendis errare non posse."

This newly proposed all-important question was given ten days for consideration, and it was only through a determined effort that the limit was extended to the 25th of March. In spite of the short space of time, some 150 written remonstrances were handed in.

The bishops of the opposition also brought before the council new considerations of great importance, in which (besides the numerous dogmatic objections) special reference was made to the change in the relation to the state which would follow from the dogma, in which attention was also called to the declaration made by the Irish bishops before the Catholic emancipation.[1] But all these efforts were without effect. A majority had been secured for the dogma, and the pope followed the principle that majority makes authority.

Thus was inaugurated the so-called general debate upon the fundamentally altered second part of the dogmatic *schema*, entitled " Constitutio dogmatica de ecclesia Christi." It lasted from May 14th to June 3d, in fourteen general congregations.[2] Then, although forty announced speakers had had no opportunity of speaking, a motion was made to close the general debate. Again it was to no purpose that eighty-one bishops protested; they were simply voted down, and on the 6th of June the council proceeded to the special debate.

The first three of the chapters now under debate (of the institution of the apostolical primacy in St. Peter, of its continuance in the Roman popes, of the nature and

---

[1] The Irish bishops had declared that the infallibility of the pope was not in harmony with Catholic doctrine. This declaration made possible the passing of the Catholic emancipation bill by the English Parliament in 1829.

[2] All propositions were first considered in one of the standing committees ; then in a " general congregation " where they were discussed in " general " and " special " debate. If accepted, they were proclaimed in a public assembly. After the reading of the decree in the public assembly, the last vote was taken. The pope might then either give or refuse his sanction.

character of the primacy of the Roman pope) consumed the time until the 14th of June.

The special debate on the fourth and last chapter, concerning the infallibility, lasted from June 15th to July 4th. The speakers in opposition were during its course frequently interrupted and forced to silence by loud expressions of displeasure and impatience.

After hurried consultation in commission, the council proceeded on the 13th of July to the vote. There were present 601 fathers of the council. Of these, 88 voted *non placet*, 62 *placet juxta modum* (conditionally), 451 *placet*. Once more, apparently out of consideration for the scruples of the middle group, the question was referred to the commission. On the 16th of July their report was made.

It was not until this stage of the proceedings that the additional clause, spoken of above, was inserted, which has given to the dogma its revolutionary significance: " Romani pontificis definitiones esse ex sese, non autem ex consensu ecclesiæ, irreformabiles." Not only in and by themselves, but with explicit exclusion of the agreement of the Church, the papal decrees became thereby " incapable of reform." The majority did not refuse to accept even this.[1]

In such manner, immediately before the fourth public session of July 18th, was the vessel brought into port.

[1] The infallibility is decreed in these words : " Sacro approbante Concilio docemus et divinitus revelatum dogma esse definimus : Romanum Pontificem, cum ex cathedra loquitur, id est, cum omnium Christianorum Pastoris et doctoris munere fungens pro suprema sua apostolica autoritate doctrinam de fide vel moribus ab universa Ecclesia tenendam definit, per assistentiam divinam, ipsi in beato Petro promissam, ea infallibilitate pollere, qua divinus Redemptor Ecclesiam suam in definienda doctrina de fide vel moribus instructam esse voluit ; ideoque ejusmodo Romani pontificis definitiones esse ex sese, non autem ex consensu ecclesiæ, irreformabiles. Si quis autem huic nostræ definitioni contradicere, quod deus avertat, præsumpserit—anathema sit."

11

This public session itself had no other than formal significance.   But the bishops of the minority did not even
attend it.   By a written representation of the day before,
they confirmed and renewed the expression of opinion
given in the general congregation; but at the same time
they declared that their filial piety and devotion towards
the holy father did not permit them, in a matter that
touched his person so closely, publicly and in his presence
to vote *non placet*.   And so there were only 635 voting
members present, of whom only two voted No.[1]   And
without fear of further opposition Pius IX. could proclaim the bull, *Pastor æternus*.   A violent storm at the
time shook the cupola of St. Peter's.   On the following
day came the declaration of war by France against
Prussia.

[1] These two were the American bishop Fitzgerald of Little Rock, Arkansas, and the Sicilian bishop Riccio.

CHAPTER XII

PIUS IX. IN THE INTERNATIONAL "KULTURKAMPF"

THE ecclesiastico-political plans of the Jesuits had been long prepared, and the pope was more and more dominated by the order. The 18th and 19th of July, 1870, witnessed the realisation of these plans. The proclamation of the new dogma was to coincide with the victory of Roman Catholic France, in order to establish the Papacy in the full possession of its new autocracy. So the Jesuits calculated, and no such comprehensive plans had ever been made except when Philip II. of Spain, the emperor Ferdinand II., and Louis XIV. of France undertook to establish uniformity of belief.

The influences which prompted the Empress Eugenie, in spite of the hesitation of her sick husband, to fan the flames of war ("her little war," as she called it) are noticed even in the work of the Prussian general staff, which otherwise, in all questions of a non-military nature, preserves the utmost reticence. The Jesuit keepers of the empress's conscience received their directions from the same Jesuit college at Rome in which the addresses in favour of the new dogma had been set up and the further acts of the council comedy had been prepared. As soon as the last difficulties which had stood in the way of the proclamation of papal absolutism had been set aside, Benedetti, the French ambassador, received the order for the insulting demand upon the king of Prussia which he made at Ems.

But, however masterly the manner in which the threads had been spun, the unexpected issue of the great war was destined once more to upset the calculations of the pious fathers, just as had been the case with other revolutions in which they had played an active part,—that of Don Carlos in Spain and of Don Miguel in Portugal, the Swiss war of the Sonderbund, and the seven days' campaign of 1866. The bravery and the discipline of the German army, for the first time feeling itself united, tore in pieces the network woven with so much astuteness.

Indeed, the result of the war, so frivolously set on foot, was not only the unification of Germany and the overthrow of the Napoleonic empire, but also the liberation of Rome from priestly misrule. On the 3d of September, 1870, at Sedan, were fulfilled the most daring predictions of German seers. On the 20th of September the Italians at last entered their capital, amid the acclamations of the people. When the pope again hurled his savage anathemas against a united people, he was simply reminded that the truth of the old story of the fall of man had been once more confirmed. It was said among the Italians that the holy father had yielded to the voice of the tempter to make himself equal to God; but on the very day that he had eaten of the forbidden fruit his papal monarchy had fallen a prey to death. The declaration of war, connected as it was with the dogma of infallibility, was immediately followed by the withdrawal of the French troops from the states of the Church, and as soon as foreign bayonets ceased to be at their disposition the rule of the priests was doomed to an ignominious collapse.

Although the political consequences were the reverse of what the papal Curia had hoped, their expectations were fully realised in the ecclesiastical sphere. Here they had wisely calculated that amid the storms and horrors of war the new dogma would make its way unnoticed; and they reaped the fruits of their calculations. The shrunken council was adjourned on the 20th of October, 1870, without bringing to an issue the questions of discipline or the catechism. But what interest was there in these secondary questions, when the main object, the overthrow of the ancient constitution of the Church, had been carried against all opposition?

It now appeared very clearly how untenable had been the position of the bishops of the opposition. They were not satisfied with a speedy subjection for themselves; but, where their subordinates were not capable of the same feat of instantly reversing their convictions, they sought to bring them to it by force. As concerns the prelates of France: the fact that their patriotism interfered with their opposition to the new dogma may be attributed to the distress of their humiliated country; their leader, Darboy, was soon enough to meet the same end as his immediate predecessors, Sibour and Affre. But this excuse is wanting to the German bishops, who, in August, 1870, again met in Fulda and issued from the grave of St. Boniface a second pastoral letter, which stood in the most pronounced contrast to the former epistle.[1]

The *Breach of faith and lack of veracity of the German Bishops* is not only inscribed on the title-page of a contemporary pamphlet, but is deeply engraven on the hearts of the people. The same gentlemen who before had given the assurance that the council would proclaim no new dogma now declared that all true Catholics were bound for the salvation of their souls to submit themselves unconditionally to the unanimous decrees of the council, which were in no wise impaired by the differences of opinion that had appeared during the deliberations.

Even more contemptible seem to us the devices by

[1] See page 151.

means of which the dogma of the infallibility (as a few years before was done with the Syllabus) was construed to yield a meaning foreign to its intention. These mis-interpretations were, moreover, contrary to the express personal declarations of the pope.

Not one of all the bishops who in the council opposed the dogma remained true to his convictions. To be sure, they had the same excuse then as for their vacillating conduct during the council: they not only lacked all support from their governments, but the latter even urged them to submission. The *sacrificio dell' intelletto* of Bishop Hefele is traceable directly to the intervention of the court of Würtemberg.

In some places formal steps were taken against the proclamation of the dogma. Austria suspended the concordat, Bavaria refused the *placet* to the papal bull, several of the smaller states declared themselves unable to sanction the ecclesiastical innovation. But nothing was gained with these formalities. Although the other governments did not with the same brutal frankness constitute themselves the beadle of the Curia as did the ministry of von Mühler in Prussia, which gave its aid to Archbishop Melchers for the expulsion from his parish of pastor Tangermann, who opposed the dogma, yet nowhere was there a suggestion of any common consistent action.

In the meantime the wisdom of liberal journalism made fun of the dogma, but the patrician circles as well as the lowest classes of the populace were better disciplined, and the numerous clerical associations and corporations proved more powerful than the conscientious scruples of the learned.

While the German troops were in the field against the foreign enemy, the bishops, submissive to the pope, pronounced excommunication upon those who remained true to their ancient faith. Like rocks in the raging sea they stood at their isolated posts ; foremost among them, Döllinger. The sacrifice which these enthusiastic representatives of the Catholic Church ideal made for their faith has never been appreciated at its full value by Protestants.

The case of the Bavarian congregation of Mering, with its brave pastor Renftle, is proof that, if the Catholic congregations had had other leaders, a large majority would have remained faithful to the old Catholicism. But an isolated parish like this in Bavaria had so much to suffer from the fanatics that surrounded it, that only a firm and well-defined attitude on the part of the state would have availed to assure its existence. The states, however, did not take up the battle which was forced upon them until it was too late, and even then they opposed to the unyielding and consistent attitude of the Curia the inadequate sophistical arts of advocates. The long series of disorders which are comprehended under the name *Kulturkampf* cannot be too clearly distinguished from the religious opposition to a dogma which stood in direct contradiction to the essence of all religion.

We shall in the following pages attempt to represent the connection between these conflicts as we trace them in the several countries, and their common centre. A detailed account would exceed the limits of this work. Not, indeed, for the reason often given, that the development in whose midst we stand is not ripe for historical representation. Behind this argument there too frequently lurks a certain prudence, or rather moral cowardice, which fears to give offence to those in power. The independent historian is bound to keep himself free from such considerations, as well as from any consideration of service to sect or party. But a full history of the *Kulturkampf* would call for first-hand testimony from both sides, and this task does not come within the sphere

of this work.   We can only expect to draw correctly the
lines which mark the more and more intensified struggle
between Catholicism and Papalism.   To this end it will
be necessary to call attention to certain events of the last
period of Pius IX. and to the inheritance which he be-
queathed to his successor.

The sum and substance of these events and this inheritance may be expressed in one word : it was war against
modern society.   The absolutistic *coup d'état* which overthrew the constitution of the Church changed the relation
of the state to the Church into a condition of perpetual
war, which might be interrupted by a shorter or a longer
period of truce, but which must necessarily break out
again and again.

The accustomed predilection of politicians for allowing
themselves to be deluded by the Curia has not been
lessened since the Vatican Council, and it only required a
few diplomatic courtesies from the successor of Pius IX.
to throw into oblivion even the infallible bull, *Unam
Sanctam*,[1] with its consequences as they affect the state.
But Pius did not descend to courtesies, and the remainder
of his reign was taken up with anathemas against modern
unbelief, which refused to subject itself to the infallible
oracle of the Vatican, and with abuse of the leaders of
the state and of popular representation in the several
states.   No single state was spared in this war against all.

The most irreconcilable of these struggles, although apparently it was not connected with religious affairs, was
that of the Curia with the Italian people.   On the 20th
of September, 1870, the Italian troops had entered Rome,[2]
greeted this time with the unmistakable acclamations of
the populace.   The result of the popular vote in the city
of Rome for annexation to Italy was over 40,000 Yeas to

---

[1] The bull which marks the height of the papal pretensions, A.D. 1302.
See page 86, note 1.

[2] In consequence of the withdrawal of the French troops.

something more than 40 Noes, and the relative proportion was the same in the rest of the hitherto papal territory. Thereupon King Victor Emmanuel issued the decree of the incorporation of Rome with the national state. Garibaldi's wish was fulfilled: Rome was the capital of a united Italy.

Although this was the end of the temporal sovereignty of the pope, the Italian government presently gave the clearest proof that it intended no diminution of his spiritual claims, rather that it would in every way protect and increase them. The guarantee laws of 1871 gave the pope not only for all time the rights and honours of a sovereign and a dotation which surpassed the amount of his former income, but offered at the same time full liberty for the exercise of his ecclesiastical sovereignty and entire renunciation on the part of the state of the royal *placet* and of any claim to co-operation in the investiture of bishoprics and of benefices. Cavour's watchword of " a free Church in a free State " was thus realised, and indeed the state suffered the most decided limitations in its own proper sphere. At the same time the pope was so much more protected than formerly in his struggles with foreign powers, that nobody could now get at him to do him harm, so that very soon the official German press accused the Italian guarantee laws of making the pope impossible of attack by means of these defences. But not long after the same official press maintained the defence of the pope against Italy; this was in payment for the help which had been given in putting through the law for the monopoly of tobacco in Germany.

The oppositions and jealousies of the several states were in fact much more advantageous to the Papacy now that it was no longer tied down by its own temporal sovereignty. The pope was sure of French sympathy in his war with Germany, and of German sympathy in his war with France. For the moral power of future popes no moment was indeed more favourable than that in which the Italian soldiers entered through the breach in the Porta Pia, and thereby sundered the fetters by which the universal spiritual dominion was bound to the local temporal sovereignty. But no man recognised this less than did Pius IX. The Jesuit father, Curci, showed a clearer sight, but he received for it an ill reward.

Pius declared the incorporation of Rome with Italy to be a robbing of God Himself. The Italian government he would call nothing but the " subalpine government." No year passed without protests against its evil deeds. The guarantee laws were spurned as a fraud, a deceit, as an insult to the holy apostles Peter and Paul.

Among numerous similar demonstrations we notice especially the elevation of the holy " foster-father " Joseph to the position of patron-saint of the Church and the solemn consecration of the whole world to the Sacred Heart of Jesus. The pompous celebration at the twenty-fifth jubilee of the pope's accession and the fiftieth of his consecration as bishop, and those on his birthdays were used for similar agitations. In place of the dotation, which year by year was refused, there were collected in all countries uncounted millions in the shape of Peter's pence for the poor captive in the Vatican. His fictitious captivity was compared with the sufferings of Him who had not where to lay His head. The several events of the passion even were applied to the Christ, who was again crucified in the person of the pope. Noble Parisian ladies gave the pope a golden crown of thorns, which he graciously accepted. In Belgium there were sold, among the poor, wisps of straw from his prison, and photographs in which the pope appeared imprisoned behind iron bars.

But the passionate struggle which Pius waged against his own people was surpassed in importance by the war against the young German empire. In Italy, in spite of all

the bitterness of opposing principles, there were not wanting ecclesiastics who identified themselves with the interests of the people. The northern barbarians, on the
other hand, had not only to contend with the grasping
ambition of a Gregory VII., but the story of the mediæval
Papacy in its opposition to the Salic, the Hohenstaufen,
and the Bavarian dynasties was repeated. The Church
became the enemy of the state, and the wedge of internal
self-dismemberment was driven into the nation which had
only just been externally united.

The far-sighted policy of the Jesuits, by which the proclamation of the new dogma and the breaking out of the
war with France were to take place at the same moment,
has approved itself especially with regard to Germany.
The war drew the attention of the governments and of
the people from what was happening in the Church.
Prince Bismarck is known to have said that after the
French war he was surprised by the mobilisation of the
clerical party. The Prussian state officials had given
almost no thought to the dogma and its significance.
The warnings of Prince Hohenlohe [1] were coolly repudiated in Berlin, and had no other consequence than the
fall of the clear-sighted Bavarian minister. When Count
Harry Arnim, the Prussian ambassador in Rome, having
been converted from his former disparagement of the
inner-Catholic movement, pointed out the consequences
of the dogma as it affected the state, he found the politics of Berlin occupied with quite different cares. But
the unexpected victories of the German army brought in
their train the liberation of Rome from the papal yoke.
Thereupon deputations, first of the bishops, then of the
laity, demanded at Versailles the interference of the
German empire in behalf of the restoration of the temporal power of the pope—that is, war against Italy in
addition to that against France. It was the negative

[1] See page 152.

answer to this demand that led to the formation of the
party of the Centre, the centre namely of all parties opposed to the German empire newly born on the 18th of
January, 1871.

The contradictory principles, whose operation determined the future political and ecclesiastical history of the
new empire, now stood clearly defined one against the
other.   The war between State and Church was inaugurated.   But while on the clerical side both object and
means were clearly understood, the state took hold of the
affair at the wrong end, and the means applied all bear
the character of incompetence and impracticability.   In
order to understand the future triumphs of the papal
policy, we must here recall the principal mistakes of its
opponents.

If we compare the so-called *Kulturkampf* in Germany
with the former ecclesiastico-political struggles of the
century, we can draw only one conclusion: all the teachings of history concerning the purposes and the means of
the curialistic policy were utterly neglected.   The Prussian successes in the field were due above all to the fact
that the enemy was never undervalued, that every step
made by the opposing army was carefully watched, and
every precaution taken to meet each emergency.   For
the great ecclesiastical struggle there was lacking all
knowledge of the enemy as well as all preparation in the
home camp.   The futile struggle of Napoleon with the
Church, after he himself had raised it out of the dust,
should have suggested a careful calculation of the forces
before the breaking out of the war.   This first struggle
between emperor and pope had ended in the success of
the Curia, and so had all similar contests since.   Only
quite recently, the so-called restoration of the Catholic
hierarchy in England and Holland had shown clearly
enough how little power there was in any sudden excitement of the popular mind as compared with tactics which

count not by years, but by decades and by centuries, which take all such momentary outbreaks previously into calculation.

Nor was it necessary to go to foreign countries to learn the lesson; for the severe defeats and losses which the Prussian state had suffered since the ecclesiastical conflict in Cologne should have pointed out the necessity of not living from hand to mouth in ecclesiastical politics. But instead of learning from the principles put into practice in the campaigns of 1866 and 1870, Prussia went into the war just as blind and just as ignorant of the enemy as in the year 1806.

The causes, therefore, which brought about the clerical triumph over the ecclesiastical policy of Bismarck are not far to seek. The very qualities which make the statesman who deals with material forces powerful render him less fit for a correct judgment of things which are not of this world. All judging of religious-ecclesiastical affairs from the political-military point of view is doomed to disappointment. The question here is not of armies which are reviewed on parade, but of apparently trifling, even invisible forces. Napoleon ridiculed the ideologists; he suffered bitter punishment for his contempt of ideas. The German policy in the *Kulturkampf* met with the same fate.

The papal account of Church history in the nineteenth century even now begins, not without reason, with the victory over the first French emperor and concludes with the triumph over the first German imperial chancellor. Posterity, more unprejudiced and better informed than the present generation, will hardly be able to pronounce any other judgment than that the German statesman who of all possessed the greatest mind failed in almost every instance in which he dealt with ecclesiastical questions. The confusion of political and ecclesiastical party divisions was by his action greatly intensified.

Although this issue of the ecclesiastical policy of a statesman whose work lay in an entirely different direction is easily explained from the nature of things, we must not overlook the hindrances which from the beginning stood in the way of success. The influence which the Jesuit associates *en robe courte* exerted during this century at the various courts reminds one of the shrewdest and most successful operations of the seventeenth century. This is true almost more of Protestant than of Catholic courts. In the former, the opinion prevailed that one could never go too far in toleration, with the result that many channels were opened for the worst forms of intolerance. Nowhere was this more true than in the society of the Berlin nobility. The influence of the family Radziwill, related to the royal house, worked hand in hand with that of a large and compact circle of lower, higher, and highest dependents of the court.

The so-called Catholic circles in the closest neighbourhood of the court were at the same time in every conceivable manner seconded by those Protestant court chaplains who were secretly undermining the normal development of the Evangelical Church of Prussia. This is especially true of that specifically clerical tendency whose character is defined in the phrases: " throne, bayonet, and catechism " and " *connubium imperii et sacerdotii*," which looked upon the papal cohort as an enviable pattern and a most desirable ally in the guardianship of the popular faith. It was the underground machinations of the " Protestant Jesuits " that prepared the way for the papal triumph over the state and over the Evangelical Church.

At the time of the clerical mobilisation, Herr von Mühler, the predecessor of Falk, was minister of public instruction. It was during his administration that the president in chief of the Rhine province offered his

official aid to Archbishop Melchers of Cologne in carrying
out the violent measures, alluded to above, against the
honoured pastor Tangermann in Unkel. Driven from
his parish (one of royal patronage) on account of his opposition to the new dogma, Tangermann remained true
to his conviction. Whoever is at all familiar with the
disposition of the Catholic clergy at that time knows how
many hundreds of men with less courage of their faith
were restrained from following their convictions by the
attitude of the Prussian government in this case.

Not till after the end of the German-French war was
there recognised the necessity of taking a stand against
the clerical intrigues. Even then it was a long time before it became clear to the authorities what was at issue.
Many were the mistakes made by the Falk ministry;
but they were one and all connected with the false system
which at Berlin was made the basis of all proceedings.
While in the enemy's camp the most approved instruments always worked in the most fitting places, on the
part of the state men were called to the direction of the
struggle—overnight recognised as necessary—whose life-
work had hitherto been entirely different. The chief of
the new ministry, Falk, had in all former positions distinguished himself by legal acumen and human warmth
of character. But not only did he himself enter into an
entirely new field, he was obliged largely to depend upon
coworkers who systematically opposed him. Of the
men whom he himself called to his assistance, the most
influential (ministerial director Förster) was an official of
high character and a man of clear legal head, and he
rivalled his chief in the power of work; but he lacked
all knowledge of Catholic popular life and of the forces
which conditioned it.

In the ministerial " general staff," as Windhorst de-
risively called it, there prevailed a spirit of clever
ambition, which was very little burdened with religious

convictions, and attached itself to every political faction that promised advantage for its own career. The ministry, as such, in spite of the warning given a generation ago by Bunsen to separate worship from education, still combined the most heterogeneous tasks. There was not the remotest idea of any such concentration of forces as obtained in Rome.

The first and purely defensive measure against the growing danger of treachery in the home camp, the dissolution of the so-called Catholic department, falls into the time of the administration of Mühler (July 8, 1871). The other measure of the same year, the so-called pulpit paragraph against the misuse of the pulpit for political incendiary addresses, was proposed by the Bavarian minister, Lutz, and accepted by the German Reichstag (December 10, 1871). It was not until the beginning of 1872 that the law concerning the superintendence of schools was enacted as the first positive measure of the Falk ministry (February).

That there was in Berlin no desire for a war with the Church was proved soon after by the proposition which Prince Bismarck made in Rome to accredit one of the cardinals (Hohenlohe) as Prussian ambassador to the Curia. With a lack of consideration unheard of in the annals of diplomacy, the pope refused this proposition (May 2, 1872). In spite of this personal insult, the imperial chancellor declared repeatedly that he would not give up the hope of a peaceful agreement, if not with the present, with the succeeding pope. The German empire now, however, adopted, with the enthusiastic approval of the public, the example given by free Switzerland of the exclusion of the disturbers of the peace, the order of Jesuits (July 4, 1872); but by this step no change was made in the direct relations between Church and State.

In the same month, Pius IX. had, in his reply to the address sent him by the German " readers' association," predicted the destruction of the great image by the little stone coming down from the heights (according to Daniel ii., 34). His Christmas allocution described the proceedings of the German emperor as *impudentia ;* and in general he missed no opportunity by writing and by speech to infuse personal venom into the struggle of principles. Against all this the state was so defenceless that certain articles of the Prussian constitution had to be changed (April 5, 1873) before the first of the so-called " May laws " could be passed.

The essence of these laws consisted in the obligation which was imposed upon the bishops of reporting to the president of their province the names of the clergy whom they wished to nominate, an obligation which in a number of other states had long been recognised by the Curia. It was the refusal of this demand that made the struggle an acute one, because it led to the accusation and deposition of the bishops by the state, in the spiritual courts which in the meantime had been instituted.

Nothing, however, caused so much bitterness as the letter of the pope to the German emperor in which the latter was openly treated as the pope's subject by virtue of baptism (August 7, 1873).

The bishops, deprived of all independence by their acknowledgment of the infallibility, were forced to do service to the foreign enemy of their people. In frank repudiation of the oaths which they had taken at their institution into office, they carried the war into the parishes by intentionally leaving their religious needs unprovided for. The pope called the evils thus produced a Diocletian persecution of the Church. And the association of German Catholics, founded and directed in Mayence, carried on (simultaneously with the French " revenge processions " to Lourdes) an open revolutionary agitation.

The government then sought another temporary expedient in the new May laws of the year 1874 concerning the right of election of parishes and the dismissal of recalcitrant ecclesiastics. The first of these laws also sanctioned the inauguration of the so-called " state-Catholicism." The latter movement was in every way favoured by the state, while every effort was made to prevent the growth of the old-Catholic movement. A more effectual step was, however, taken when civil marriage was made obligatory. This was carried through in spite of severe conscientious scruples on the part of the pious emperor.

The so-called May laws are commonly held to have been the occasion of the conflict between Prussia and the Vatican, but the real origin of this trouble is to be traced farther back, to the *coup d'état* of the Vatican Council and the papal desire for intervention in Italy. Among the first answers to the May laws we recognise the attempt on Bismarck's life by Kullmann (July 13, 1874) and the papal encyclical *Quod nunquam* (of February 5, 1875). The first showed, according to the explanation given by the *Germania*, the " intensification of Catholic anger over the ecclesiastical policy of Bismarck "; the encyclical gave the most clear-cut expression to the irreconcilable opposition of the infallible ecclesiastical autocracy to the modern state. The Prussian laws were characterised as not being made for free citizens, as not appealing to a rational obedience, but as being imposed upon slaves and forcing obedience by the power of terror. Not enough with this theory: the pope expressly declared the laws of the state to be null and void, because in contradiction to the divine constitution of the Church. All those impious men who incurred the crime of accepting a spiritual office without episcopal nomination were visited with the major excommunication. There followed a series of other, in part childish, demonstrations and commendations of recalcitrant bishops.

The Christmas allocution of the same year raged

against the second Nero, other addresses stormed against the modern Attila. At the same time, the French desire for a war of revenge was in every way fostered, and in Germany a close alliance was entered into with all other tendencies working for the dissolution of the state; indeed, the various alliances between the Ultramontane and the Social-Democratic parties more than anything else stamp this religious war with a peculiar character.

The laws of 1875 followed, as the next step on the part of the state, after the papal declaration of invalidity against the state laws; they were the following: the so-called "Sperrgesetz" (law of inhibition) concerning the administration of episcopal incomes (April 22d),[1] the exclusion of all orders with the exception of those that devoted themselves to the care of the sick (May 31st), the formal cancelling of certain articles of the Prussian constitution (June 18th), and the changes in the administration of property (June 20th). The last received the approbation of the clerical party; against all the other laws protest and agitation was renewed at every conceivable opportunity.

As long as the reign of Pius IX. lasted, the mutual embitterment increased more and more. The party of the Centre and the clerical press understood so well how to discipline the dependent classes of society that every election brought them new victories. To be sure, this did not imply any positive success. The laws were universally executed. In spite of all agitation, the general result was such that it would only have required a few years of peace to make the new system of laws at home in the popular life. Towards the end of the reign of Pius IX., the condition of affairs forms a striking parallel to that period of the reign of Innocent III. which

---

[1] This law stopped payments from the state to the bishops and other clergy who would not pledge themselves in writing to obey the laws of the state.

immediately preceded the assassination of the emperor Philip of Suabia (1208).   Modern researches have established the fact of an undoubted yielding, in this period, on the part of the most powerful of the mediæval popes.   It was the assassination of Philip that gave the final victory to the Papacy.   The same significance for the parallel struggle of the nineteenth century attaches to the attempts upon the life of the emperor by Hödel and by Nobiling (1878).   Only Pius himself did not live to reap the fruits of these events in the furtherance of his own plans.

The other German states had been drawn into the struggle of the Papacy against Prussia in so far as many of the measures necessary for protection concerned the empire.   But aside from this, almost every one of the states had its own *Kulturkampf*.   The only exceptions were Saxony, whose dynasty retained the position taken since the conversion of Augustus the Strong, and Würtemberg, where Bishop Hefele, an opponent in the council, had by the favour of the court and the anger of the pope been changed into a peace-bishop.

In Bavaria, on the other hand, the " patriotic " party in every Landtag attempted repeated attacks upon the ministry.   The latter made concessions to the clericals and used every means at the disposal of the bureaucracy to render the old-Catholic movement ineffectual.   Nevertheless it was not sufficiently compliant to the so-called " extremists."   More and more concessions were secretly made to clericalism.   At the same time, the liberal party, which had shown its usual depreciation of the religious factor, suffered more and more losses in the representation and in the magistracy.

More violent was the war in Baden.   The archiepiscopal see, which had become vacant, remained unfilled, because the Curia would not accept the nominee of the cathedral chapter, Dean Orbin, who was acceptable to the government. The clerical revolutionary agitation, which was doubly dangerous in this border-state, prompted the ministry to pass the Church law of April 19, 1874, which defined more stringently the conditions for the appointments to parishes, and among other things made rules for the examinations of theological students in both churches. The Curia refused to accept this law, and parishes remained unfilled, but the liberal party in Baden lost a number of seats at every election by its own discord.

Even in Hesse-Darmstadt, the domain of Bishop von Ketteler, several new laws were adopted in the year 1875; these laws were in all essentials formed after the Prussian Church laws. Here, too, a number of parishes remained unoccupied, and after the death of the bishop the episcopal see shared the same fate.

The most curious proof of how unavoidable were the conflicts which the Vatican Council had forced upon all the states, lies in the extraordinary similarity between the *Kulturkampf* in the German empire and in republican Switzerland. An act of usurpation on the part of Pius IX., cancelling all former laws and agreements, called the Swiss confederation to the war: namely, the separation, carried through against all representations and protests, of Geneva from the diocese of Fribourg, and the nomination of an intriguer, Mermillod, to be the " apostolical vicar " of Geneva (1873). The undisguised contempt which he manifested for existing legal conditions forced even the peace-loving confederate council to expel Mermillod from Switzerland and to break off diplomatic relations with the Curia; the papal nuncio received his passes.

This conflict with the pope on the part of Switzerland was accompanied by a series of internal struggles in the majority of the separate cantons. There was a conflict in Geneva, where Mermillod from the neighbouring Ferney fostered the opposition to the authorities in every possible way, and where the state, following the example of other states, had to protect itself by adopting a new Church law.   This law left the choice of clergymen to the parishes, and as the papal faction would not consent to this, the most important parishes fell into the hands of the recently organised Christian Catholic Church. When the clerical agitation went so far as to attempt to deprive the commonwealth of its sources of income, the great council met this attack by the dissolution of all spiritual corporations and the prohibition of all religious processions and ceremonies in public places.   The clerical party then attempted to pass a law for the separation of Church and State.   So far their efforts have been futile. But there is no means of foretelling the future, where the government changes so often, and where these changes usually bring the opposite principles in ecclesiastical affairs into power.

Besides the disorders in Geneva there were disturbances in the diocese of Basle.   When the bishop of Basle, Lachat, under the influence of his chancellor, Duret, excommunicated and deposed pastors Egli and Gschwind, who had remained true to the old faith, official recognition of him was withdrawn by a majority of the cantons of the diocese.   Only Lucerne and Zug remained faithful to the bishop.   Berne became the centre of this conflict. The ministers who were attached to the deposed bishop refused obedience to the state laws.   They were declared to have forfeited their positions.   Against this judgment of the court they resorted to open force and produced such commotion in their parishes that the military had to be called in, and the agitators were driven from the country.   At the same time the new Church law which had been accepted by a large majority came into operation; the object of this law was to lay the foundation of a new Church by giving the choice of the minister to all Swiss citizens entitled to a vote.   The so-called " intrusion " of the new state pastors and the character of the agitation against them forms one of the most interesting chapters in the ecclesiastical history of Switzerland.

The then government of Berne showed a strict consistency of action, and if the conduct of the other cantons had been like that of Berne the result would have been wholly different.   But this canton, standing alone, found in the struggle with the papal world-power no help outside its own borders; on the contrary, it was rather disavowed by the federate council on account of the decree of banishment against the deposed ministers.   The final result was the amnesty declared at the change of government in 1878, and the effect of this amnesty was the complete destruction of the recently inaugurated state-Catholicism.   The Catholic theological faculty, which was founded during the course of these disorders, proved to be the only really promising result of the *Kulturkampf* in Switzerland.

Even Austria, which since the days of Consalvi had been held in high esteem at Rome on account of its proverbial good-nature, was not preserved from ecclesiastical quarrels after the Vatican Council.   Before the council there had already been marked premonitions of these quarrels.   Immeasurable concessions had been made by the concordat to the Curia.   But the constitutional state could not remain untouched by the general demand of the times for equality of the confessions, independence of the school, and civil marriage.   The protests of the bishops were futile, and the new laws received the imperial sanction on the 25th of May, 1868.   This brought out the papal manifesto declaring the " abominable " laws invalid.   The papal allocution declared: " We reject and condemn these laws on the strength of our apostolical authority, and by the same authority we decide that they have been and will be altogether void and without all authority." As a consequence, there followed further incendiary pastorals from the bishops. Warned by these proceedings, the Austrian government joined in the representations made in Rome against the proposed new dogma of infallibility. When these were disregarded, the concordat was, on the ground of the change in the situation consequent upon this dogma, declared abrogated (July 30, 1870).

In spite of this apparent energy, it was four years before the Austrian government brought before the Reichstag the new laws which were now rendered necessary. These fell into four groups: concerning the appointments to spiritual offices, concerning the support of the clergy and the improvement which it was thereby intended to effect in the condition of the lower clergy, concerning the recognition of new religious associations, and concerning monasteries. The House of Representatives accepted all four laws, while the House of Peers wished to have the law concerning monasteries modified. During the negotiations the pope issued an encyclical, in which he called upon the bishops for the most energetic resistance, and at the same time he appealed to the emperor in a letter demanding the veto of the laws. When the latter nevertheless confirmed the first three laws (May, 1874), the bishops issued a declaration to the effect that they would render obedience to the laws only in so far as they were in agreement with the concordat.

Hereby was declared the same opposition as in Prussia: the divine constitution of the Church against the temporal law-giving power of the state. But the papal policy had not forgotten the traditions of Gregory VII., who during the struggle with Henry IV. conceded to the king of France and the Norman dukes exactly the same things in behalf of which he waged a life-and-death struggle with the German king. The Curia, while at all times it recognised in the state of Frederic its mortal enemy, counted in Austria upon the slow but sure operation of influences favourable to itself.

As a matter of fact, the happy-go-lucky way which generally characterises the Austrian bureaucracy manifested itself again in ecclesiastical affairs. Although the separate articles of the new laws were partly even more severe than those of the Prussian code, yet, while in Prussia the courts were to decide in cases of collision, in Austria the decision was given to the administration, so that it depended upon the pleasure of that body whether they would apply or ignore the laws. When the long-pending law concerning monasteries had at last been adopted by the House of Peers, the nuncio succeeded by his influence in preventing the imperial confirmation. The law concerning marriages left the numerous abuses in force which had been called forth by the precedence of canonical over civil law. The incorporation into the university of the Evangelical theological faculty in Vienna was persistently refused. Officials high and low rivalled each other in abuse of the old-Catholics. The bishop of Linz, among other provocations of which he was guilty, vilified in the grossest manner the Evangelical deaconesses' institution, and the clericals of the Tyrol repeatedly excited popular fanaticism against the Evangelical foreign congregations of Meran and Innspruck. The emperor Francis Joseph showed repeatedly that personally he was very anxious for religious peace. But year after year a series of new events in all the provinces gave evidence of a continued forced retreat on the part of tolerant Josephinism before the advancing intolerance of the papal principle.

In this same period Spain as well as Austria was fated to feel the weight of the pretensions which followed as a

consequence upon the declaration of infallibility by the
Vatican Council.   Again, it was one of the revolutions in
this country, so devoted to the Papacy, which placed all
the boundlessness of these pretensions in the clearest
light.   The republican constitution of 1869 conceded,
with certain limitations, the long-suppressed religious
liberty, and the year 1870 saw a law for civil marriages
passed; but the restored monarchy (Alfonso XII., January, 1875) soon carried through a number of new limitations.   The decree of February 10, 1875, gave back to
the hierarchy the power to conclude marriages and the
administration of the marriage law, and civil marriage was
tolerated only for those " who profess another than the
true faith," and for " bad Catholics "; all marriages of
resigned priests, monks, and nuns were prohibited, and
such marriages already concluded were declared invalid.

The proposed new constitution tolerated dissenting
worship, but forbade all public manifestations thereof.
Pius IX. immediately protested against this article,
because it abrogated the concordat of Isabella in its
" noblest " part (namely, the suppression of dissenters),
and because it embodied a serious act of enmity against
the Catholic Church.   Nevertheless the Cortes of 1876
sanctioned the article in question.   But the Evangelical
congregations have since been exposed to numerous invidious and petty annoyances, whose origin is only too
apparent.   And the protest of the Papacy, renewed again
and again, against all toleration of other churches in
Spain has once more revealed unmistakably its never-
ceasing war against the civil rights of modern society.

The relations of the Papacy to Russia had become
embittered past remedy after the coarse insult which Pius
IX. had inflicted upon the Russian ambassador at the New
Year's reception of 1866, so that the Vatican Council could
hardly bring any intensification of the opposition in this
quarter.   But Pius has since then not only sought in

every way to intensify the internal crises of Russia, but has given his aid to Turkey in the war against the schismatic state. What the result has been, the participation of the pope in the oriental crisis and the internal condition of the Russian Church show.

As long as Germany was ablaze with the *Kulturkampf*, France, conquered in war, was the focus of a fanatical papal agitation. The third republic went beyond the *régime* of the Restoration, of the July monarchy, and of the empire in its subserviency to the papal principle, and the hope of an alliance with the black International in the war of vengeance against Germany by no means confined itself to demonstrative pilgrimages of hundreds of thousands to La Salette, Lourdes, and Paray le Monial, to the accompaniment of the pilgrims' song, *Sauvez Rome et la France*. The foundation of the so-called free Catholic universities owes its origin to the same situation.

It is so much the more remarkable that at exactly the same time that Germany sought an understanding with the Curia the *Kulturkampf* emigrated into France. One could hardly conceive of a clearer proof that it was a question of the same problems in all states, though through the adroitness of the curialistic policy these problems might present themselves in this and that place at different times. The conflict in France was not only quite equal to that in Germany, but the rigour of the opposition was rather increased by the alliance of the clerical tendency with the anti-republican parties. The passionate fury of the opposition to the educational laws of Ferry rivals the worst excesses of the German clerical press. The Curia itself interfered both directly and indirectly. It nevertheless succeeded in avoiding an official rupture in France, as it had done in Austria. The strategy of Leo XIII., different as it was from that of his predecessor, made itself felt in the French *Kulturkampf ;* and we shall therefore reserve the special consideration of this conflict until we speak of the general policy of this pope.

What is true of France is again true of Belgium. During the reign of Pius IX., it remained the centre of a clerical agitation whose influence extended to all neighbouring countries. And yet it was not spared its own *Kulturkampf,* and in the conflict with Belgium more than in any other country the diplomacy of Leo XIII. gave proof of its true moral character.

To what extent clerical encroachments have since the Vatican Council increased in England and Holland will appear later. Whether the acute or the lingering chronic *Kulturkampf* brings with it worse consequences for the ethical religious life of Catholic populations, is a question which we can decide only when we consider and compare the conditions of the countries under the former and the latter infliction. But the mere review of the acute struggles of the last period of Pius IX. would be incomplete, did we not turn our attention from European countries to America. The conflict of the Curia with the Brazilian government was for some time considered an instructive type by those European states which met the same fate. The Berlin official press, which a few years later liked to choose its foreign illustrations from among the concessions of other states to the Curia, at this time could not refer enough to the parallel with Brazil.

The origin of the struggle lay here no less than elsewhere in the impossibility of reconciling the protection which the state affords to liberty of conscience with the claim to exclusive right made by the papal principle. After long-continued religious oppression, especially of the immigrant Evangelical Germans, the Brazilian state finally declared its recognition of marriages performed according to Protestant rites, and the civil effects of excommunication were declared abolished. The same liberal government, which in these questions brought about the equal rights of all citizens, then endeavoured to protect itself against clerical agitation by sustaining the *placet* and by demanding that the bishops should give notice of newly appointed clergy. All these excesses of a " godless infidelity " were, as is customary in Catholic-Latin countries, attributed to freemasonry. The bishops, at their head Oliveira and Olinda, made the anathematising of Freemasons their favourite occupation. A papal brief (June, 1873) came to their aid.

As soon as the latter appeared, Oliveira published it without having obtained the *placet*, inflicted the greater excommunication upon a minister who belonged to the lodge, and placed all those fraternities under the interdict that refused to expel masonic members. Brought for this before the highest court, he was condemned to several years' imprisonment at the same time that similar processes began in Prussia against the rebellious bishops. The banishment of the Jesuits, who had distinguished themselves in the agitation against the Freemasons, made the parallel complete.

But even before Prussia inaugurated those measures which set a premium upon open violations of the law, Brazil had preceded it on this path. The amnesty for the transgressors of the law was soon followed by a complete clerical reaction. According to the accounts of the clerical press itself, the confinement of the crown princess, which was then imminent, was made use of in favour of this reaction. Such use Loyola himself had well understood to make of similar occurrences, and he had instructed the brothers of his order in the same policy.

In the Catholic Latin countries of South and Central America, we see the claims of the papal principle carried out more consistently than anywhere else. The concordat of Ecuador bears an especial significance in this respect. During the *Kulturkampf* in unbelieving Europe the clerical press repeatedly comforted itself with this model state. In the year 1873 the government of President Moreno, although it could not cover even the most necessary expenses in their own country, devoted a tenth of all the receipts of the state to alleviating the distress of the prisoner in the Vatican. In the meantime, the social condition of Ecuador was becoming from year to year worse. It was therefore not long before one of those revolutions so common in these half-barbarous countries broke out, and President Moreno lost his life (1875). The clerical press in Europe in innumerable articles extolled this *condottiere* as a saint and a martyr. But before the end of the reign of Pius IX. the concordat with Ecuador, which had so often been held up as a model to other states, was abolished (1877).

The greater the number of moral defeats which the policy of Pius IX. has suffered since the Vatican Council, the more has the papal press pleased itself by the comparison of his sufferings with those of Christ. The parallel was carried so far as to suggest a new incarnation of Christ in Pius. Even before the year of the council, we saw the Pius hymn used for the spread of the doctrine that a sinful generation found no sin in Pius. After the declaration of infallibility, men no longer shrank from the last consequences: the words of Christ, " Which of you convinceth me of sin ?" were applied directly to Pius.

He himself illustrated most drastically this sinlessness by an effusion of language which became every year more passionate. Probably no satirical author has ever added so much to the dictionary of abusive epithets. But abuse and invective were far outdone by his coarse caricature of biblical truths. The personalities which Curci has communicated concerning the self-deification of this pope during his last years are so disgusting that we cannot occupy ourselves with them ; yet the judgment of a

man who since the year 1842 had stood in personal relations to the pope deserves careful consideration.   Neither
may we forget the service which Gladstone rendered by
gathering from the official edition of Pius' *Discorsi* a
collection of his favourite expressions.   And we must read
the familiar addresses made to the faithful of all countries who were admitted to audience, if we would form a
correct appreciation of the agitations and conflicts of
which he was the author; for in these the nature of the
pope as such receives more unadulterated expression than
in the allocutions and encyclicals which are inspired and
corrected by others.

Secretary of State Antonelli took charge of the money
exactions.   The property which the latter left amounted
to more than a hundred millions; his natural daughter
(the Countess Lambertini) in vain demanded her part.
Before this celebrated suit revealed to his astonished contemporaries the private character of the cardinal, there
had already been drawn for the world of the " faithful "
a picture of Antonelli in the character of saint: this was
done by the German Monsignore Dewaal.   The canonisation of Pius IX. himself was agitated immediately after
his death.   His remains have long ago performed the
requisite number of miracles.

CHAPTER XIII

THE PEACE-POPE, LEO XIII.

AS Pius IX. advanced in age, the idea became prevalent among certain classes which had been violently excited by the clerical press, that this pope would not die until he had gained a victory over his enemies. The sufferings of Pius had already been compared with the passion of Christ, and the last prediction to the favourite disciple was applied to him: " This disciple shall not die." In the Vatican, however, they are accustomed to a more matter-of-fact calculation, and during the reign of the one pope thought is taken for that of his successor. Immediately upon the death of Pius (February 7, 1878), the conclave met, and after a session of only two days Cardinal Joachim Pecci was proclaimed pope. He took the name of Leo XIII., in honour of the predecessor, Leo XII., who had conducted him through the first steps along the path of priestly world-dominion. In fact, both the methods of his reign and its results bear a remarkable resemblance to those of his patron.

Leo XII. personally, though little loved by the Roman people, by his adroit management made himself sympathetic to the ministers of the foreign powers; Leo XIII. appears in contrast to his vain and loquacious predecessor as a diplomat of noble and dignified character. From the very first moment he understood the use of measured words and engaging speeches. He personally announced his accession to those states with which Pius IX. had come to an open rupture and gave expression to the desire for a resumption of friendly relations. This he did to the German and Russian emperors, and to the Swiss federate council. This mere act of courtesy would have sufficed for the politicians to give him the name of a peace-loving pope in distinction from Pius. But in official negotiations also Leo XIII. was never wanting in theoretical assurances of peace. The most celebrated of these is his brief of February 28, 1880, to the deposed Archbishop Melchers of Cologne, in which he expressed his willingness to permit the announcement to the state officials of newly chosen pastors. But the negotiations undertaken upon this *tolerari posse* (which afterwards became proverbial) showed clearly how little thought there was of any real concession.

Anyone familiar with the official utterances of Leo XIII. will find the talk of the papers about the " peace-pope " unintelligible. As bishop of Perugia he had in a pastoral letter characterised Protestantism as " a pest, the most pestilential heresy, a stupid, fickle system, originating in arrogance and godlessness." The knowledge of the Reformation which he here showed corresponded to the general standard of education of the Italian episcopate (admirably characterised by Rothe in the era of Leo XII).[1] But even after he had become infallible Joachim Pecci remained throughout true to the intellectual standard that had characterised him as bishop.

There has hardly been a single pope who considered the most contemptible falsification of history in regard to the Reformation as less beneath his dignity than Leo in his second encyclical. In this—making adroit use of the social-democratic and nihilistic assassinations—he praised to the terrified governments the Church as the sole guardian of society; and he took the same opportunity

[1] See page 80.

to stamp the Reformation, " the insane war which since
the sixteenth century had been waged by the innovators
against the Catholic Church," as the mother of the
" death-dealing pest " of socialism. Even more pronounced were his expressions about the Evangelical
schools in Rome, about " the impudence without parallel
with which in Rome even under the eyes of the pope
such schools were established, in which tender children
were fed with abominable errors, and from which proceeded influences the most harmful and the most injurious to manners."

As " supreme head of the Catholic Church " he took a
very positive stand. His very first encyclical appealed
expressly to the infallibility of the apostolical see and
asserted just as explicitly the condemnation of all errors
condemned by his predecessors. His references to Mary
as the immaculate queen of heaven, and to Joseph as the
heavenly patron of the Church, prove that he occupied
the same theological position as Pius IX. He also emphasised the necessity of the restoration of the temporal
sovereignty of the holy see, at the same time repudiat-
ing ambition and the lust of power, and declaring that
he was actuated solely by the desire for the public welfare and the salvation of humanity; and he renewed all
the protests of his predecessor against the secularisation
of the states of the Church.

The most significant, however, of all the utterances of
Leo for the appreciation of his personal attitude, and at
the same time the most pregnant of consequences by
virtue of its influence upon all the separate churches, is
his third encyclical (of August 4, 1879). This encyclical
made the philosophy of Thomas Aquinas the foundation
of all studies in schools and seminaries. Even this did
not disturb the belief of the liberal press in the peace-
pope, and it does in truth require somewhat more

knowledge of ecclesiastical history than newspaper writers and diplomats usually have at their disposal to appreciate the significance of the Thomistic system, not only for theology and the Church, but just as much for the state and for society. But anybody familiar with this system knows that even the most frantic outbursts of Pius IX. against the opponents of the papal principle are of inferior significance in comparison with the fact that the whole future generation, as far as the influence of the Papacy reached, were to be educated in views which with an unsurpassed consistency preach irreconcilable war against the modern world of ideas.

Knowing the educational methods of the Jesuits, one might have foreseen that their habit of setting up the Thomistic against the Kantian system would be made a model for other educational institutions. The Dutch and Belgian Jesuits, who to-day, as in the first century of the order, count among their number the real leaders of the society, had long ago adopted this contrast as the central point of their instruction. Thomas Aquinas had supplied the scholastic foundation of papal infallibility (upon the basis, namely, of the garbled editions of the Church-fathers which Pope Urban IV. had sent him); and therefore after the dogmatisation of the infallibility it was really only a question of time that the teacher of the middle ages should be declared *præceptor urbis et orbis* for the present generation.

Pius IX. was too much engrossed in the struggles of the moment and of too great ignorance — an ignorance strangely interwoven with his conceit of infallibility — to proceed as far as this. But his prudent successor did not wait long to take this last step. Indeed, his third encyclical was the necessary consequence of the second and of its vilification of the Reformation. In the latter the Reformation had been made the mother of socialism, and the tottering thrones had been referred to the rock of

Peter.   The next thing was to anoint with fresh oil the alliance, which dominated even the era of the Restoration, between spiritual and temporal absolutism.   What was better adapted to this purpose than the system of Thomas, which guaranteed to the princes their absolutism, if they only placed themselves at the feet of the higher authority of the Papacy ?

This political purpose was acknowledged without any ambiguity in the Thomas-encyclical of Leo: " Surely, families and civil society would be much more tranquil and secure if in the academies and the schools a healthier doctrine and one more consonant to ecclesiastical dogma were taught, such as is found in the works of St. Thomas." In all respects this system was to furnish that which the present time needed.   With regard to philosophy, Thomas has once for all set at rest the discord between reason and faith.   For,

while he has strictly sundered reason and faith and yet has kept both of them in friendly alliance, he has preserved the rights and exalted the dignity of both, in such manner that reason, borne by the wings of faith to the summit of human power, could hardly rise higher, and that faith could hardly expect from reason more frequent and stronger aid than it has obtained through Thomas.

Even greater is his merit in behalf of natural science. For,

one can hardly imagine what strength, what light, what aid this philosophy is able to give, especially in regard to the natural sciences.   It is a matter of importance to repudiate the wrong which has been done to this philosophy by accusing it of putting hindrances in the way of progress and of the growth of the natural sciences.   As the schoolmen have always taught in the science of anthropology that only from material things can the human mind raise itself to the knowledge of those things which are not bound to body and matter, so they have of themselves recognised that nothing is more useful to the philosopher than to search the secrets of nature and to occupy himself long and much with the study of physical things.

Nevertheless, all this eulogy of St. Thomas, as well as all the compliments paid to princes and statesmen, to philosophers and naturalists, in the last instance only serve the purposes of the papal monarchy in its suppression of every dissenting view.

The carefully selected teachers are to endeavour to infuse the teachings of Thomas into the minds of their pupils and to explain to them their eminent worth and excellence. But from those books, which are asserted to have been drawn from the fountain of St. Thomas, but which in reality have emanated from foreign and unwholesome sources, the minds of the young shall by your efforts be guarded.

This reference to the Index was calculated to prove how little the Thomas-encyclical of Leo was meant to be only a matter of theory. The new task which the pope thus imposed upon the Church was immediately undertaken. Father Beckx, the general of the Jesuits, testified in solemn audience the gratitude as well as the obedience of the society. The papal communication to Cardinal de Lucca (of October 15, 1879), ordered the formation of an academical association and of an official edition of Thomas' works. The command issued from Rome immediately became in every country the foundation of the entire clerical system of education. For Thomas Aquinas became the standard and the authority not only for the scholarship of the Church in general, but for the entire system of education. One of the most eminent authorities on the Thomistic system has pronounced judgment in the following words upon the dangers which this kind of training of the Catholic youth has created for Christian states: "Compared with the struggles which then become inevitable, the present *Kulturkampf* appears only as a childish, good-natured prelude."

For Protestant statesmen and the great mass of newspaper writers even this encyclical of Leo did not serve as a warning. They knew neither the thorough work of the Göttingen philosopher Baumann concerning Thomas' doctrine of the state, nor Holtzmann's striking exposition of its practical consequences. It was futile that an ecclesiastical historian of original research like Reinkens pointed out the historical contradictions in the papal document, and that a philosopher like Knoodt explained the significance of Thomas as an universal teacher in his influence upon the cause of Christian learning. The unwelcome proofs of old-Catholic scholars only increased the desire to render these disagreeable censors harmless. And the priest-rule which had invaded the Protestant ecclesiastical administrations once more did its best to help the pope.

We have considered it necessary to devote a somewhat detailed consideration to the Thomas-encyclical as fundamentally the most important measure of Leo. But his canonisations are of no less pathological interest. Joseph Labre, a man debased by indolence and filth, was set up as a type of papal piety. In the year 1786, the historian Schlözer wrote that this "wretched stinking lazy beggar would doubtless be put on the calendar as saint, did we not live in the eighteenth century." In the nineteenth century Labre has become a saint in good standing.

Clara of Montefalco, canonised at the same time, enjoyed the patronage of Leo XIII. much as the immaculate Virgin Mary enjoyed that of Pius IX. Leo declared in his address upon occasion of her canonisation, that he remembered with joy even now how as bishop of Imola he had twice visited her wonderful relics, and how he had read mass before the altar under which they rested, and added these emphatic words: " Now that we are placed at the head of the universal Church our veneration for this virgin is doubled, our trust in her is entire and perfect." This " veneration " and this " trust " of the pope were founded upon the more than wonderful fact that not only was the body of the saint well preserved since her death in 1308, but that more especially her heart (as the pope testified *ex cathedra*) showed traces of the instruments of the passion. Thus favoured by the highest authority, this virgin was of course accredited by a particularly large number of miracles. At the public celebration of December 8, 1881 (which on account of the continued " imprisonment of the pope " took place for the first time not in St. Peter's Church, but in the gallery connected with the Vatican), there were exhibited twelve pictures, of which six treated of the miracles performed by Clara, while only two fell to the share of each of the other saints (Labre, Giambattista de Rossi, and Lorence of Brindisi).

Such was the attitude of the pope towards modern culture, and analogous thereto was the position he assumed towards the modern state, founded as the latter was upon equal rights for all its members. The peace-pope occupies towards the state an attitude of almost greater hostility and intolerance than his immediate predecessor. We call attention in this respect to the fourth encyclical (February, 1880), which denies to the state every right of regulating the law of matrimony, because this belongs only to the Church. To this encyclical are traced all subsequent attempts to curtail the rights of other churches in mixed marriages.

Even more unambiguous in the expressions it gives to the papal hopes for the future, is the encyclical of September 17, 1882, recommending the Franciscan tertiaries.

These were the same tertiaries which in the war of
Gregory IX. against Frederic II. had rendered the most
valuable services to the Curia in stirring up the masses.
The changes of the laws which governed this order, made
under the authority of a special commission of cardinals
in June, 1883, testified to the special value which Leo
XIII. placed upon the organisation of clerical secret associations among the laity.   New indulgences were substituted for the old, " such as accord with the needs of
the nineteenth century."   The fourteenth year was determined as the time of reception into the order; married women were obliged to obtain the consent of their
husbands; from this condition, however, the father confessor could grant dispensation. The members are strictly
to avoid dangerous books and newspapers; a special
paragraph exhorts them to make their will in time.
Special visitors are appointed to watch over the observance of the rules and may punish and expel guilty
members.

In all the negotiations which Leo undertook with individual states, it was made manifest that wherever he
yielded in matters of secondary importance this was
always done with the reservation that the opponent accepted all other hierarchical pretensions of the Curia.   In
his ability in making the diplomats believe that the policy
of the Curia was inoffensive he surpassed even the great
master Consalvi.   The diplomats again lent their ear to
the papal insinuations; and not even in the era of the
Restoration after the Congress of Vienna, or in the period
of reaction after the revolution of 1848, did the papal
principle find more compliant adepts than it did now
among the diplomats.

Whence, we ask, was this general readiness in the face
of all the teachings of history, even in the face of the
very manifestoes of the pope, this readiness to accept

Leo XIII. as the peace-pope ?   The answer to this question is found in the all-important fact that now again, as in the days of Leo XII., when Bunsen, with his far-sightedness, showed how the Papacy was favoured by the tendency of the times, it was not so much the good or evil will of single individuals, but it was the general spirit of the times which set in motion the current towards the Church of Rome.

Let us consider somewhat more carefully, as typical of the change in the general sentiment, the condition of affairs in Germany.   Germany had been severely visited by ecclesiastical wars; and these ecclesiastical wars had become tedious to a generation accustomed to rapid living and devoted to material interests.   How could one ask men who had practical business to attend to that they should continue to " plague themselves with these ecclesiastical absurdities " ?   In the eyes even of educated liberals ecclesiastical matters were only the concern of stupid peasants.

On the other hand, whoever has traced the mutual relations of the clerical and the democratic press in Germany with any attention, must have been struck with the arguments which the *Frankfurter Zeitung*[1] brought forward to neutralise the measures of defence adopted by the state against the Church.   Even among the following of Eugene Richter,[2] for whom the religious problem for a time had a certain interest as a part of the *Kulturkampf*, antipathy against a compactly ordered state very soon gained the upper hand.   Just as happened in the year of revolution, this party found itself repeatedly side by side with the party of clericalism in its war upon the authority of the " police-state."

At the same time, " Gambettism " in France was cherishing thoughts of revenge, and the German government

---

[1] A radical sheet.
[2] The leader of the left wing of the radical party.

considered only the political necessity of hindering a clerical alliance with this foreign tendency, while it neglected the cares of its own household.

The pious soul of the emperor was disturbed by facts which came to his ears designed to prove that the war upon the Curia was becoming a war upon religion. It is true that clerical zeal played a large part in the collection and preparation of such facts. But it is no less true that the decade after the war with France was also the decade of Strauss' *Old and New Faith*, of Hartmann's *Self-Dissolution of Christianity*, and of Hellwald's pseudo-Darwinistic history of civilisation—to name only the most eminent representatives of modern naturalism. At all times has religious nihilism been the best ally of clericalism. And so it happened this time.

There followed the mania of crimes which fill the period of social-democratic and political-nihilistic revolution. The attempts on the emperor's life by Hödel and Nobiling (1878) followed in quick succession, and in their wake came that epidemic of murderous attacks from which hardly one of the crowned heads remained spared — the kings of Italy and of Spain no more than the queen of England. Not long after, the nihilistic era in Russia heaped horror upon horror. The greater the concessions of English statesmen, the more did agrarian murders in Ireland come into fashion. Even the President of the United States succumbed to the bullet of an assassin. And all these abominations were considered in large circles as triumphs of liberty, as meritorious acts in behalf of humanity in the war against tyranny.

It is one of the chief objects of the present work to make the reader understand that the Papacy owes all its triumphs, which largely make up the ecclesiastical history of the nineteenth century, to the ever recurring revolutions of this century. That which to-day seems a comical paradox to the enlightened Philistine, the future will make an all too serious reality. From the convulsions of the great French Revolution, through the great changes of 1830 and 1848, we have found the same course of events again and again repeated. Can we therefore wonder that the terrorism of the international revolution since the Paris Commune of 1871 has again led to the same rotation of events ?

In one of the great crises, between the two attempts upon the German emperor's life by Hödel and by Nobiling, there appears upon the scene a pope who is counted among the wisest of all wise calculators that have ever worn the tiara ;—a man who began his spiritual rule with the most friendly and the most harmless greetings to the state governments ;— who so feelingly recorded his wish for an abrogation of abuses and disorders ;—who presently offered himself as an ally against the death-dealing pest of the revolution. Such a " vicar of Christ " must have appeared to anxious souls a true messenger of peace. Of what significance were, compared with his promise of help, sundry theoretical differences in the use of language ? It was an accepted part of his office that the pope should anathematise the Reformation, as well as that he should be the eulogist of the good old times of the middle ages. But this style of the Curia was well known as an innocent thing; it had long become a matter of habit to overlook this sort of language on the part of the pope. Now as formerly the example of Niebuhr was considered as the proper one for imitation. Why should the antiquated theories which " it was so easy to forgive the good man " prevent one from grasping the hand, now proffered, of the long and ardently longed for peace-pope ?

We do not at all believe that in this hasty picture we have recounted all the factors that have come together in the legend of the peace-pope and have made it the favourite dogma of newspaper readers. But if one has a clear discernment of but one or the other of the motives which are so strangely intermingled, all the conquests in the various countries, which actually dropped into the lap of Leo, cease to be so puzzling as at the first glance they seem to be.

Let us begin our consideration of these conquests, just as we did that of the war during the last period of Pius IX., with the country of the Papacy itself, with Italy.

A careful consideration of the religious condition of Italy will afford us a view into one of the most severe crises of civilisation which a people that had fallen out with the augurs of its religion has ever had to pass through. The opposition between the spiritual life of the modern world and the influences of the hierarchy, begun at the restoration of Pius VII., confirmed through each of the following papal reigns, and intensified to its climax by Pius IX., was nowhere more acute than in Italy. Two different worlds, on the one side the satellites of the Papacy, on the other the representatives of the popular sentiment, were brought together on the same ground.

It has been said of France in the eighteenth century, that under the dominion of the Church it had lost religion, and the same may be said even more truly of the Italy of the nineteenth century. Scientific research which had taken a magnificent upward start, poetry which is cultivated by poet-heroes of giant stature, the newly flourishing schools of law which have chosen modern international law for their special field, indeed the whole national life as such occupies not only an indifferent, but mostly an hostile attitude towards the ecclesiastical régime. The accustomed Church form of piety has lost its magic influence over the younger generation; everywhere we meet a searching after something to take its place, and yet nothing has been found to satisfy the religious needs of this people, religiously so sceptical and artistically so productive. Neither the enthusiastic but obscure mysticism of the national hero Garibaldi, nor the several attempts of Gioberti, Passaglia, and so many others, to reconcile Church and people, nor the missionary labours of the Protestant churches, strangers as they are to the popular heart, have been able to fill the empty void. The tone-giving classes of society are hopelessly estranged from the Church, and alongside of these we find the immense mass of the illiterate, who with the majority of the women are now as before in the hands of the priests.

So long as Pius IX., by his violent language, stirred up the minds of the people, the hatred of the Papacy thus produced overshadowed all other party divisions. The wise counsels of Curci to give up the irrevocably lost temporal power in order to bring the people who stood in need of their old Church back into the fold, were spurned with contempt while Pius lived. But hardly had the reign of Leo begun,— although Curci himself was still officially disavowed and was even obliged to recant his own written defence—when the essence of his method was recognised and followed. Theoretical protests were continued as before, but the emphasis was laid upon practical ways and means of transforming universal suffrage slowly but surely into a tool in the hands of the clergy. The immaturity of the political parties and their constant war, which made a caricature of the parliamentary system, played into the hands of the clerical policy. A short-sighted liberalism poured a mass of unpractical measures over Italy, as it had done elsewhere. The dissolution of the theological faculties in the universities, greeted as a liberal measure of progress, took away the last means of exerting a reconciling influence upon the education of the clergy. On some occasions, as at the jubilee of the Sicilian Vespers or at the

erection of the Arnold monument at Brescia, popular indignation over centuries of suppression of the national
spirit by the hierarchy might find a pathetic expression.
But nowhere was there any strong organisation opposed
to the constant subterranean machinations of clerical
demagogism.

The elections, as well in the smaller as in the larger cities
(even in Florence), have already made the local magistrates
dependent upon the clergy.   It can be but a question of
time that the representation of the people and therewith
the government shall fall a prey to the same fate.   Not
until then will there be fully revealed the irreconcilable
opposition between culture and the Church.   But even
at this day it is beyond doubt that the reign of Leo XIII.
measures a long step on the road towards the new subjugation of the popular and state life by the Church.

What in Italy is a prospect of the future has in Germany become historical fact.   For here the fiction of a
peace-pope has sown the seeds of much more serious disorders than all the former reverses of the state.   The
situation which Leo found at his accession we have
already recognised as the most auspicious conceivable.
The correspondence which he opened with the German
emperor was interrupted by the attempt upon the latter's
life by Nobiling.   To the papal demand for a change of
the laws, the crown prince answered on June 10, 1878,
as regent in the name of the emperor, to this effect, that
no Prussian monarch could accede to such a demand for
changes in the constitution and the laws of the land according to the prescriptions of the Roman Church; but—
he added—although the differences of a thousand years
could not be reconciled, yet the manifestation of a spirit
of conciliation on both sides was not thereby excluded,
and ought surely to open for Prussia the way to peace
which had never been closed to other states.

But the results of all efforts were purely negative. The pope would not accede to the practical application of the duty of reporting nominations to Church offices, although he himself had said it was to be "tolerated" and although it was allowed without any difficulty in almost all other countries.

The events which followed show a reversal of the policy hitherto pursued by the government. In 1879 Bismarck made an alliance with the clerical party. Falk resigned from the ministry of public worship. Von Schlözer was sent on a special mission to Rome to open communication with the Vatican and the vacant bishoprics were filled. These measures mark the end of the *Kulturkampf*, and the Vatican remained master of the field.

The most remarkable parallel to the achievements of the first years of Leo XIII. in Germany is found in the Church's progress in Switzerland. The letter to the federate council, in which the pope expressed a wish for the restoration of the former relations, had at first no direct result. A political and religious reaction had, however, set in in Switzerland and elsewhere, especially in the canton of Berne, and Leo (here as everywhere carefully calculating) gave to the Roman Catholics of the Jura permission, which before had been denied on principle, to take part in Church elections. This enabled the leaders of the clerical party to take their stand apparently upon the ecclesiastical law of Berne and to dominate the liberal faction. The cantonal synod of Berne itself became in this manner the tool of the Ultramontanes, and the newly formed state-Church organisation in the Jura came to a premature end.

Italy, Germany, and Switzerland represent those states which, whether through the force of political influences

or on account of the mixture of confessions in their populations, lived in a state of continued illusion with regard
to the significance of the papal system, and as a consequence, the peace-pope everywhere reaped a series of the
most important triumphs.

Very few events in the history of the modern Papacy
have brought to it greater advantages than the restoration of the Prussian embassy at the holy see.[1] The
thoroughly unnatural character of this political representation at an ecclesiastical seat of authority for such a
state as Prussia has been demonstrated by the losses
which the state suffered in rapid succession; and the
Curia showed a masterly proficiency in putting to good
use in its negotiations with other powers the favours received from Prince Bismarck (which in the clerical press
were represented as a manifestation of good-will on the
part of the holy father towards the hostile state).

As in the era of Consalvi and his concordats one state
was played against the other, so now the acts of the great
German statesman were held up as a model before the
Russian, the English, the Swiss, and the American governments.   Here it was the Irish, there the Polish-
nihilistic troubles, against which the good services of the
Church were extolled as the universal remedy.   In
Switzerland, every new case of official dishonesty and
every form of social evil were attributed to the sins of
the *Kulturkampf*.   The vanity of young America was
flattered by the bestowal of cardinal's and chamberlain's
titles and by papal blessings upon clerical editors.   Above
all was it now possible to frighten the Italian state, which
was being undermined by the Irredentists, with the threat
of Bismarck's help towards the restoration of the papal
monarchy.   In the fall of 1882, a much discussed article
in the Berlin *Post* actually placed a policy of this nature
in view.

[1] See page 207.

The German chancellor was obliged to subordinate his relations to the Curia as well as every other question to the purpose of securing the external position of the young empire against the hidden and the open plans of revenge on the part of France. His accustomed mastery on his own ground again proved itself most brilliantly at the very time that the Curia counted upon his aid in its plans against Italy. As just before the French war of 1870 the secret compacts entered into after the war of 1866 with the South German states were made known to an astonished public, so there now loomed up unexpectedly above the horizon the great peace alliance between Germany, Austria, and Italy.

The disappointment which the Triple Alliance caused to the Curia in its hopes for the destruction of Italy was presently manifested by its coquetting with France, which was allured with the prospect of the aid of " the greatest international power," if it would desist from its *Kulturkampf*, and by the reproaches heaped upon Austria that it had so basely repudiated its sacred duty at all times to sacrifice itself for the holy father. The same double game that the Curia had played towards Napoleon between 1859 and 1870 it played again after the restoration of the Prussian embassy, by putting forward its political side in ecclesiastical questions and its ecclesiastical side in political questions. While the new conservative Prussian government recognised hardly any higher obligation than the satisfaction of the religious needs of the Catholic population, and to secure this object descended to the most humiliating and inconsistent conduct, the policy of the Curia, aspiring to universal dominion, had more important ends in view than such trivialities.

The sagacious use made by the pope of the Oriental crisis appears in so many special symptoms that it must be referred to a separate chapter. But our survey of the

14

policy of the peace-pope would be one-sided did we not
here again turn the reverse of the medal to the light.
For while the schismatic and heretical nationalities, as
well as those of mixed confessions, were more and more,
long before they suspected it, drawn within the sphere of
power of the Propaganda, the reverse took place in the
territories where the papal system had before held undisturbed sway and for that very reason had already become
known by its fruits.   The very countries which Pius IX.
in his struggle against Italy and Germany regarded as
his most sure support refused their services to the over-
wise policy of Leo XIII.

The manifest reverses in Belgium and France may be
kept ever so much hidden from the faithful,— the moral
loss cannot be denied.   In France the Polish nuncio
Czacki was able to avoid an open rupture, and since the
publication of the Triple Alliance the " Catholic interests of France" in foreign parts have been more than
ever emphasised.   On the other hand, Belgium has before all the world broken off its diplomatic relations with
the Curia.   Not long after, the same thing happened in
the most aspiring of all the South American states — in
Chili.   Even in the most devoted of the papal countries
—in Ireland,—where Leo had long overlooked the crimes
committed (which in effect was equal to a direct coun-
tenancing of them), as soon as he expressed a mild
condemnation, the threat was immediately made of
" boycotting " the pope.

To make up for this, Colombia has received a new
papal nuncio, since whose arrival the religious exercises
on the streets have increased to an extraordinary degree.
And whoever from the central point of the Vatican attempts to survey the universal field can hardly fail of the
conclusion that the reign of the peace-pope has not by
any means reached the zenith of its achievements.
[Written in 1889.]

CHAPTER XIV

THE PAPACY AND THE ORIENTAL CRISIS

THE unheard-of and unhoped-for triumphs which it achieved in the German *Kulturkampf* justly surpassed in the eyes of the Curia all other victories and were extolled in every key by the official papers. They took particular pleasure in comparing the result of the modern struggle in Germany with the end of Frederic Barbarossa. And it was made sufficiently manifest that they hoped the subsequent phases of the Hohenstaufen epoch might be repeated. Indeed, the hatred with which the popes of the middle ages persecuted the house of Hohenstaufen appeared insignificant compared with the language now used by the curialists against the Prussian state and its dynasty, where the press was free to express its opinion, as in Switzerland and Holland.

The triumph achieved in the young German empire has exerted an incalculable influence. But in the eyes of the Papacy the German empire forms after all only a fraction in its all-embracing calculation. Only the Curia knows by what powerful material means it is to-day supported in the great republic beyond the ocean, or what advantage it is destined to derive from the constant conspiracies in Ireland and the ever-renewed conversions among the upper ten-thousand in England. The ancient cradle of European liberty in the Netherlands stands on ground that is already undermined. And already the press of the Propaganda proclaims with rejoicing that Denmark and Norway and Sweden are beginning again to become " Catholic."

Nevertheless all that has been achieved in American and European countries, which once were counted the supports of Protestantism, is insignificant in comparison with what has been set on foot in the East, and with the concessions which since the Congress of Berlin the diplomats have made to the Curia.

Let us first make clear to ourselves the steps which, since its restoration, the Papacy has taken towards the solution of the Oriental question in its own sense. Consalvi himself was not content with distributing in the several European countries the inflammable material which was intended to undermine one state after another and make it pliant to the pretensions of papalism. The lecture which he gave to the successor of Pius VII.[1] proves to what extent even he had fixed his eye upon the remote East.

Neither Leo XII. nor Pius VIII. nor Gregory XVI., in spite of all that occupied them nearer home, left out of consideration the schismatic Oriental churches. Almost every year the Propaganda occupied new stations in the East. The rapid increase in the orders offered useful instruments in plenty. The Jesuits especially have been able to win positions all over Asia, by direct and indirect means, in ways similar to those by which the first generation of the old order drew India and China and Japan within their sphere. Just as the inquisition at Goa, in the sixteenth century, extirpated the Thomas-Christians of India (the Nestorians of those parts) who had dared to defend their independence, so the mountain tribes of the Nestorians have in our century been for the most part annihilated.

[1] See page 71.

From the same Mosul, where the plans against the Nestorians had been prepared, the Roman outposts have spread themselves over the most remote parts of inner Asia.   The large number of settlements of religious orders in Syria and the strong colonies of monks in Egypt, and on the other hand the wretched condition of the Oriental churches, heavily oppressed by the state-system, leave no room for any illusions.   Even in Palestine, where the Greek Church, supported by Russian means, had its securest position, and where even the Evangelical mission had the advantage of the Roman, the latter has more and more outstripped its rivals.

One of the first acts of Pius IX. was the installation of a Latin patriarch in Jerusalem in opposition to the Greek and the Evangelical bishops.   The same pope issued the bull *Reversurus* to cripple the independence of the United Armenians [1]; and the patriarch of Babylon learned at the Council of the Vatican how much the Jacobites had to submit to from the pope.

The wisely calculating and indefatigable tactics of Leo XIII. tended greatly to the exploitation of the Oriental crisis in the interests of the Papacy.   For the reign of Leo, even in its first years, has done more than all his predecessors in distributing the forces for the approaching world-conflict around Constantinople.   One cannot fail to see that in Rome the time was considered to have come for playing the cards that had hitherto been kept concealed.   From the invitation given to the Slavic churches to adopt the faith in the infallible pope, down to the so-called restoration of the patriarchate of Alexandria — again with disregard of the rightful holder of this dignity — a long series of papal measures affecting the East has come to our knowledge.

The papal bull concerning the adoration of the ancient

[1] The ancient Christian Church of Armenia.

apostles to the Slaves, Methodius and Cyrillus, openly expressed the hope that under their patronage the schismatical churches of the East might be brought under the obedience of the Papacy. It was for the purpose of playing the part of leader in this struggle that the Croatian bishop Strossmayer did penance for his opposition at the Vatican Council. His pastoral letters concerning the necessity of a union of the Slavic churches with Rome sought to make the liturgy serviceable to this end. Not yet is all opposition overcome. The national jealousy of the Croats among the Serbs prompted the archbishop of Agram in 1882 to order the giving up of the celebration which Strossmayer had appointed in Diakovar for the 5th of June (the day of the apostles to the Slaves). Not yet is all remembrance of the mission of Methodius and Cyrillus, which originally proceeded from the Greek Church and which only after long opposition yielded to Roman oppression, obliterated from the popular mind. But, aided by its silent allies in the Austrian bureaucracy, the papal Propaganda gains one parish after another. And nowhere is any compact organisation opposed to it.

Great as is the importance of Strossmayer's activity in Croatia, officially sanctioned by Leo XIII., Galicia is even more important for forming a judgment upon the operations of the Curia. Long has the Society of Jesus attempted to undermine the Russian Church from Galicia as a basis.[1] In this quarter, also, the time has come for an open advance. On the 15th of June, 1882, the monasteries and the property of the Ruthenian order of Basilians were delivered over to the Jesuits. This was done by means of a *coup d'état*, such as the Society of Jesus

[1] The Galicians are made up of Poles who are Roman Catholic, and Ruthenians, who belong to the United Greeks, a branch of the Greek Church which acknowledges the supremacy of the pope.

frequently resorts to in its dealings with other corporations. The same papal bull that sanctioned this shameful breach of law prescribed the erection of a central institution for the training of novices in the monastery of Dobromil, in which Catholics of the Latin rite are received and at the same time are given permission to accept the Greek rite; the pope thereby sanctioning the " dispensation from the public exercises of religion " for which the Swiss convert Haller and the murderer of William of Orange, Balthasar Gerard, received secret absolution.

All preparations had been secretly made to render the enemy quite defenceless against this sudden attack. As the only Greek Catholic order and of great influence upon the Ruthenian and the neighbouring Russian population, the Basilians had long been a thorn in the eyes of the Jesuits. A provincial of the Basilians, by the name of Farnicki, was employed as a tool for the suppression of the order and the spoliation of its goods. He asked for reforms from the pope. The kind of " reform " in which the Latin monasteries of Galicia were superior to the Greek was shown in the year 1869 by the legal action of Barbara Ubryk in Cracow. But without any more ado the apostolic letter of Leo ordered the surrender of the Basilian monasteries to the order of Loyola. They applied to the government for redress. But Vienna had forgotten the proverbially approved faith and loyalty of the Ruthenians. The Polish national hatred of the Ruthenians dictated the answer, that " the government found no occasion for intervention, because the ecclesiastical reform in question had been carried out by the supreme authority of the Church, in agreement with the supreme authority of the state."

The metropolitan Sembratowicz of Lemberg (in Galicia) continued to oppose the measure. He was soon after set aside and supplanted by a Roman-Polish coadjutor. Afterwards he was superseded by a successor of

the same name, and the first pastoral of the latter exhorted his people to obedience to the holy father, to
whom they owed so much gratitude, and to union with
the Polish " brothers."

So much we know from facts that have reached the
public.   A correspondent of one of the organs which
zealously seconds the contemporary Oriental policy of
Austria (the *Kölnische Zeitung*) has gone so far as to
assert that " the Greek Catholic Church is being offered
as a sacrifice to the alliance of the Hapsburgs with the
Latin Church."   In the eyes of the Curia the so-called
union of the United Greeks with Rome has never been
considered otherwise than as a transition to their complete subjection.   And the champions of this union
themselves are no longer able to deny that this object
is in view.   In January, 1883, Provost Naumowicz addressed his celebrated memorial to the pope, in which
the union of the Greek Catholic Church with Rome is
declared to be impracticable for the future.   In a letter,
written at this time, to the *Vienna Allgemeine Zeitung* he
complains of " the truly incredible intrigues of the Jesuits," which call to mind the methods of the Inquisition.

In Bosnia, the Roman Propaganda derived the greatest
possible advantage from the Austrian occupation.[1]   A
system of oppression of the Oriental Church in favour of
the Latin was immediately begun.   Ecclesiastical questions played a prominent part among the causes of the
insurrection of 1881.   Since the beginning of the year
1883 interesting stories have been told of a so-called
" auxiliary association for Bosnia and Herzegovina,"
which has gained many members among the clerically
disposed section of the aristocracy in Austria.   The Ultramontane newspaper *Vaterland*, in Vienna, has declared
the purpose of this apparently innocent association

[1] After the treaty of Berlin in 1878.

to be the "bringing back" of the adherents of the
Greek Catholic Church in the occupied provinces to
"Catholicism."

Roman agitation, under the wings of Austrian diplomacy, has extended as far as Servia, where it caused the
overthrow of the national ministry Ristic, after which
young king Milan deposed the Servian metropolitan.
Almost as much has in the last years been accomplished
by the Papacy in Roumania; while the advance of the
papal interests in Bulgaria cannot be even approximately
calculated since the Roman emissaries succeeded in bringing about the Bulgarian schism. The Curia appears so
sure of its success that it no longer considers it necessary,
as heretofore, to throw a veil over its proceedings. The
Osservatore Romano has made the following announcement
(November, 1882):

As the first practical result of the latest pastoral visit of Mgr.
Vanutelli, apostolical delegate and patriarchal vicar in Constantinople, we publish the joyful news that an entire Bulgarian
village, Allihodoilona, consisting of seventy families, has been
converted to Catholicism. We have every hope that this conversion will be followed by others, and that perhaps the time
is not distant when the whole Bulgarian nation shall return to
the Catholic faith. Such an event, to realise which without
doubt all the efforts of the holy see are bent, will undoubtedly
exert a wholesome influence upon the future of the Bulgarian
nation, upon its political fortunes, and upon its civilisation.

In Turkey itself the papal gains are even greater than
in the countries separated from Turkey. Not for nothing
had Pius taken the part of the crescent in the war of
Russia against Turkey: his reward was, among others,
the violent suppression of the party inimical to the
Papacy, the anti-Hassun faction of the Armenians. And
Leo XIII. has been no less active in this direction than
his predecessor. At the time that the "Armenian

question " was again brought before the public by England, a brief of Leo (February, 1883) ordered the erection of an Armenian college in Rome. The patriarch Hassun was nominated as the first patron of this college; the pupils were to be selected by the bishops out of their dioceses and sent to Rome.

At the same time clerical emissaries from Bosnia are labouring for the further extension of the Austrian-Roman occupation. Repeatedly have reports come from Scutari that the former members of the Albanian league and other prominent Albanians have addressed to the emperor a request to occupy Turkish Albania with Austro-Hungarian troops.

The Slavic-Roman Propaganda, which is everywhere planning further inroads into the domain of the Greek Church, is here as elsewhere favoured by the results of the last Oriental war to such an extent that it already considers the game won. Vienna is influenced by the political motive of holding the orthodox Montenegrins in check by means of the " Catholic " Albanians.

As long as the realisation of national unity in Italy and in Germany was prevented by force, a lasting peace in Central Europe was impossible. Does not this experience point the way to the only natural solution of the Oriental crisis ? But while the papal diplomacy, opposing itself to this natural solution, has kept its end steadfastly in view, German newspaper readers have been instructed in the wisdom of the policy of patching up the Turkish state, although it is evidently doomed to dissolution. In order to further the plans of the Papacy, German and Russian interests have been represented as irreconcilable —contrary to fact. Attempts were systematically made to foment a war between Germany and Russia. In alliance with the Polish emigration, Vambery and his Magyarised Jewish associates have repeatedly sought to incite the English against Russia. The more far-sighted measures which Gladstone had in view were covered with ridicule by the German papers. Döllinger's sober references to what was brewing in the far East were treated no better. They were considered the fixed ideas of a childish old man. The fact lay far beyond the comprehension of the wise men of the day that, unless a decided change took place, the Papacy must triumph in the East as it had triumphed in the West.

Throughout the unnatural evolution of European history, before the solution of the German and Italian questions, we have everywhere been led back to one and the same point of departure: the Congress of Vienna, devoting its energies to the policy of papal restoration. To-day we ask ourselves this question: Will not the coming generation pronounce a similar judgment upon the consequences which have followed upon the Congress of Berlin? If we examine without bias such results of this congress as are already manifest, we shall again see the chief advantage fall to the Curia.

The official organs of the Austro-Hungarian press assert more and more openly that the great future task of this state is, marching under the banner of the Roman Papacy, to conquer the ground from under the Oriental schism, supported as it is by Russia. In proportion as the German element in Austria is sacrificed to the Czechs and Poles, to the Slovenes and Magyars, the more clearly appears the idea of the future which dominates the Roman Catholic Slave and Magyar state. At the settlement of the concordat with the Curia it was asserted that the many-tongued state stood in need of an ecclesiastical cement, and now the good-will of the pope is expected to secure to Austria the dominion of the East.

The consequences of the concordat were made manifest in the years 1859 and 1866. Austria, as long as it followed the leading ideas of Joseph II., fought its way through all the struggles of the Revolution to a glorious victory over the emperor of the Revolution. The Austria of the concordat, on the other hand, reaped at Solferino and Königgrätz the harvest of its priestly rule. And to-day, Austria's confidence in the help of the Curia is doomed to disappointment; for whoever in the Balkan peninsula marches under the banner of the Papacy will never win the heart of Servian or Roumanian, of Bulgarian or Greek.

What for Austria has been a distant fear to far-seeing patriots, has become for Russia a melancholy fact. After a bloody war with Turkey, in which the most terrible sacrifices were made, came a peace which gave Cyprus to the one rival for the dominion of Constantinople, Bosnia to the other. It is surely not surprising that the embitterment produced by such a result played into the hands of the revolutionary party. For here too we must look to the violent suppression of natural forces for the cause of the volcanic eruption. As in the aspiration for unity in Italy and in Germany, so in the rising national instinct of the Russian people there had been a natural force, which was not understood by the politicians who over commercial interests and exchange speculations forget that nations no more than individuals live from bread alone. No more did they understand that the restoration of an Oriental Catholicism, cherished by a whole people, was a higher ideal than that represented by the hierarchical artifices of the Papacy. And so the Papacy won its victory, and as a consequence we have witnessed in Russia the fall from the height of an enthusiastic popular faith into the abyss of nihilism.

In the survey of the Oriental crisis the horrors committed by the nihilists come under our consideration only so far as their authors have sapped the health and strength of their own country. The crises of the unhappy country are still on the increase. Almost every new chemical discovery has put new weapons into the hands of the heroes of dynamite. Those unfortunates who sacrificed themselves for their crimes were utterly unable to understand that no popular welfare can grow out of revolutionary deeds of terror. In the meantime, the moral force of the state has been more and more weakened. And who profited by this but the ever-watchful Papacy ? The same year, 1882, in which the Basilian monasteries of Galicia were sequestered by an arbitrary papal act, saw the " compact of peace " between Russia and the Vatican. The six articles of the compact comprehended nothing but concessions made by the state to the Curia, to whose tender mercies even the United Greek Church was given over.

Russia demoralised in its vital parts, Austria aspiring to oppose the papal banner to the Greek cross, France following the traditional policy of supporting its " Catholic mission " in the East, Italy internally and externally crippled by Roman priests, Greece an untimely birth to begin with,—who can be surprised that the papal policy is emboldened in its attempt to solve the Oriental question in its own sense ?

But how few of those politicians who can accurately weigh all external factors have an eye for the religious-ecclesiastical forces which in this Oriental question play a more important part than anywhere else ? Who remembers to-day that it was the provocation of the French Jesuits among the Maronites which led to the Syrian butchery of 1860 ? Other questions have caused it to be forgotten that the cause of the Crimean war grew out of the question of the holy places.

As often as the French government pleases to emphasise the " Catholic interests " of France in the East, the other great powers simply stand aside. This was seen in the destruction of the national faction of the United

Armenians; it was again seen ten years later in connection with the vice-royalty of Syria.   Under the moderate and energetic Rustem Pasha the long and sorely visited province enjoyed some years of peace.   France demanded his recall.   The demand was conceded.   Rustem was obliged to yield his place to the " Catholic " Wassa Pasha.   There is a deep significance in this: for Syria and Palestine are the most important battle-fields in the ever-recurring struggle between the Greek mother-Church and papal usurpation.   Neither Wittenberg nor Geneva, neither Dordrecht nor Westminster, possess over against the name of Rome any such moral power as there is in the name of Jerusalem.

Human foresight cannot foretell what will be the future phases of the Oriental crisis.   The craftily woven nets may suddenly break.   The history of the Jesuit order is made up of a remarkable combination of high-flying plans and sudden defeats.   For the present only one thing is certain: that the curialistic policy is operating in the East with the same far-seeing calculation with which it had long before the event spun its threads for the Vatican Council, and that, as with the council, so now it thinks it can count upon opponents who are unprepared and in disagreement among themselves.   Perhaps Gladstone's Egyptian expedition will give a new shape to the complicated situation on its ecclesiastical side as well as the political.   [Written in 1889.]

CHAPTER XV

THE INFALLIBLE PAPACY IN ITS RELATIONS TO SOCIETY, TO LEARNING, AND TO RELIGION

OUR survey of the history of the Papacy since the Restoration has shown us a continuous growth of power. While it is true that hitherto no princes have been deposed as in the middle ages, that heretical nations have not been extirpated by crusades, and that the Inquisition has not been set to work as in the time of the counter-reformation of the sixteenth century, yet this difference, due to modern progress, is only formal. All former pretensions of the Papacy have remained the same. It is considered a damnable error to suppose that by deposition, crusade, and Inquisition the Papacy has ever exceeded its prerogatives. The popes of our own century have declared laws of the state which demand equal rights for all subjects to be null and void; and recalcitrant peoples have been coerced by a new kind of interdict. The same papal principle which created the Inquisition has sworn irreconcilable war upon the modern ideas of freedom of faith and of conscience, and has claimed as a divine right the supremacy over all baptised people.

The tone assumed in papal allocutions and encyclicals is at present more one of lamentation over the hindrances that now restrict the exercise of this divine right than of joy over what it has achieved. But a calm review of

the triumphs won by the Papacy forces upon us the conclusion that they are simply preliminary successes, that far
greater triumphs are bound to follow.　As to the remoter
consequences of the infallibility-dogma, we get very
clear ideas of what will inevitably happen from the written opinions of the minority bishops during the council.
And the decade that has since elapsed has only confirmed
their forebodings.　The seeds sown from land to land
are even now ripening.

The historian of the future, unlike the historian of the
present, will have to deal not with a Papacy which aspires
to infallibility, but with a Papacy which has attained
infallibility.　What is its relation to Society, to Learning,
and to Religion ?　By what means has it been enabled
to lay a ban upon one and the other, to a degree not
thought of even by Gregory VII. and Innocent III. ?
Let us consider, first, the relation of an infallible Papacy
to Society.

Whoever compares the means at the disposal of the
Papacy with those of its opponents, temporal as well as
ecclesiastical, will at once recognise the former as far
superior.　For while the leaders of the state dispose only
of political ways and means, and religious conviction is
the only sphere of influence open to the churches free
from Rome, the essence of the papal principle is the
exploitation of religious ideas for worldly ends.　The
external body of the Church is put in the place of the in-
dwelling Spirit.　The faith of the pious in an invisible
world with its spiritual gifts and heavenly treasures is
used in the interest of a visible world of external power
and worldly pomp.　The religious needs of the human
soul are made available to further the interests of a hierarchy which is devoid of religious character.　The religion
of Jesus itself is placed in the service of the same cæsarism
which centralised the ancient world-dominion of Rome.

This ancient world-dominion brought with it the end of Roman liberty: in order that the empire might be preserved, the central and commanding place was given to the emperor, and he was raised to a position among the gods. A corresponding necessity has brought about the proclamation of papal infallibility; and it is probable that in the future course of history the modern papal-cæsarism will experience the same consequences of self-deification that the ancient cæsarism did. But whatever may be in the future, there is one fact of present and undoubted reality: no single temporal prince, however absolute, has ever claimed and exercised such super-human sovereignty as the successor of Pius IX. What is the secret of that power?

The answer to this question will be found in several reflections. First of all: this limitless papal absolutism is proclaimed as the true principle of liberty. The rule of the pope must — so it is said — guarantee the freedom of the Church; freedom, namely, from the police-guardianship of the secular governments. This thesis, in itself, carries immense moral weight; all the greater from the opposition in which it is placed to the Byzantinism in the other churches. There is good reason why in every struggle between Byzantinism and papalism the former has succumbed.

But beyond this: in the very idea of the papal system, as it is developed by the Jesuit order, there lies a magic power. For there is no slight inspiration in the thought, when a man knows himself to be a link in the chain which embraces the whole world. What statesman is able to place prospects so grand before his followers? Vulgar ambition aspiring to external titles cannot compare with the inspiring feeling of being a silent partner in this world-dominion.

The most important factor, however, in the great power of the Papacy is found in the exploitation, already

15

mentioned, of the religious needs and aspirations of the great masses of people to further the political ambitions of the Papacy. Innumerable simple pious souls find in the sovereignty of the pope over the world-powers the image of divine Providence. In the use made of this and of all other latent forces which belong to the Catholic-ecclesiastical religious type, we find the ultimate cause of the rehabilitation of the papal power after every defeat. Not only did a Luther surpass in moral influence a Charles V.; a Francis of Assisi also wields a power compared with which the best-drilled army corps is insignificant. The religious orders, which have so greatly increased in numbers and in importance during this century, give us a measure of the powers which are in the service of the Papacy. As long as these forces remain enslaved we cannot hope for a permanent triumph over the Curia. And our own generation has, more than any former, placed them at the disposal of the pope. The entire political development of the nineteenth century in all its crises has been steadily serviceable to the Papacy.

We have traced the first beginnings of the papal rehabilitation back to the storms of the Revolution. We have learned that the papal principle owed its subsequent triumphs to the general tendencies of the Restoration era. The type of statesmanship which under the ægis of Metternich had obtained the ascendency in the various countries sought to overcome revolutionary ideas by the so-called solidarity of conservative interests. The international police system of the great powers, inaugurated at the various congresses following the Congress of Vienna (at Aix-la-Chapelle, Troppau, Laibach, and Verona),[1] and at the still more fatal Carlsbad conferences,[2] made no objection to the worst measures of the so-called legiti-

[1] 1818, 1821, and 1822.   [2] 1819.

mate governments; the national ambitions of the people, on the other hand, were treated as capital crimes. Popular aspirations, thus suppressed, took refuge in secret associations, formed on the models of the Jesuits and the Sanfedists. Therefore, these associations, the Carbonari, Freemasons, and others, were now looked upon as the incarnation of the satanic spirit of the times. To cast out this spirit seemed possible only by shutting out the modern world of thought from the spiritual life of the nations and by bringing back the pre-Revolutionary or rather the pre-Reformation circle of ideas. Who was better able to do this than the Papacy, which had opposed itself with its ban to the entire development of things since the Reformation ? The rigid unchangeableness of its principles, which, even in the stormy years when the foundations of all the states had been shaken, had been at least apparently preserved, was imposing to unbelievers even more than to the faithful, and Protestant diplomats saw in the anathemas pronounced upon toleration, in the pretension to dominion even over Protestant souls, only one reason more for their admiration of the Papacy, while the reversal of history practised by the romanticists extolled the time when the Papacy held sway not only over the souls but also over the bodies of men, through the state acting as its bailiff.

Not only was the general atmosphere of the Restoration favourable to the Papacy, so was also the trend of public policy in the several countries. The restoration in France of the *ancien régime* with the shadows clinging to it of the massacre of St. Bartholomew and of the dragonades, the tearing asunder of Italian nationality into quivering shreds, the annihilation of the constitutional aspirations in Spain, the suppression of the Greek struggle for liberty : — all these measures were in accord with the papal policy and favourable to it.

Especially was this the case in Germany, the country

of the Reformation.   While Arndt was suspended[1] and
Schleiermacher disciplined,[2] the papal emissaries were
able to cast their nets in the centre of Protestantism, and
secret converts were intrusted with supreme authority
over the Evangelical churches.   It is more than half a
century since Schleiermacher wrote his last prediction:

Living piety and free-minded courage will more and more
disappear from the clerical profession; the rule of the dead
letter from above, anxious, spiritless sectarianism from below,
will approach each other more and more closely, and from
their conjunction will arise a whirlwind which will drive many
helpless souls into the ready nets of Jesuitism.

Since then innumerable multitudes have taken the way
to Rome.

The Restoration policy — thoroughly unnatural as it
was — brought in its train new revolutionary outbreaks.
So we have the July revolution in 1830, and after it the
revolution of February, 1848, which shook all Europe to
its foundations.   Since then, one revolutionary movement has followed another.   Each new movement undermined the established order of the state, and thereby
brought to the Curia new acquisitions which surpassed
in importance even those made during the era of the
Restoration.

We have already seen, in tracing the history of one
pope after another, how the Papacy profited by the repeated revolutions.   The same popes who were looked
upon as bulwarks against the revolution have again and
again added fuel to the spirit of revolution.   At the very
time that legitimacy saw in the pope its best support for
the suppression of unwelcome aspirations for liberty,
Lamennais had given out the watchword that the Papacy
had ever been the guardian of liberty, that Gregory VII.

---

[1] From the chair of history in the university of Bonn, in 1819, because he
insisted on the constitutional reforms which the king had promised.

[2] Charged by the Prussian government with "demagogic agitation."

had been the patron of all those who fought for popular liberty against tyrants. The immense success of the ideas of Lamennais is proved not only by the history of French Catholicism, but also by the Church history of Belgium, Ireland, Poland, and Germany. The author himself succumbed to the disagreement between his ideal and his idol, yet the school which he founded has become more and more influential and therewith more and more demagogical.

Thus has the Papacy of the nineteenth century found ready allies in the most opposite quarters. We can hardly conceive of any form of constitution where it did not know how to apply its lever. In the absolute monarchy, there meet us in the nineteenth as well as in the seventeenth century the affiliated members of the Jesuit order in the guise of chamberlains and ladies of the court, who know all the side doors and back stairs. In the constitutional monarchy, the leaders of every policy, liberal as well as conservative, are made to feel the power of a party to which every political question is but a means for the strengthening of clericalism. In parliamentary states, where all continuity of government perishes in the quickly recurring intrigues for position, the Church militant has found it so much the easier to gain possession of one attribute of the state after another. In most republics, the constantly changing majorities offer the surest guarantee that in a few years the opposite principles will have the ascendency. Only one thing remains the same in this continual change, and that is the masterly skill of the Curia in making instantaneous use of every favourable moment in every suitable place.

The truest interpreter of its tactics is the German party of the Centre, as in the one year it allies itself with the social democrats, in the other with the high conservatives, in the third with the followers of Eugene Richter.[1]

[1] See page 201, note 2.

The party of the centre has used in the interests of the Papacy all those factions which from whatever motive opposed themselves to the modern state. The only factions which enjoyed its perpetual hostility were the hated middle parties of the national liberals and the free conservatives, precisely those which through all changes of policy have laboured for the strengthening of a state system founded upon equal rights for all its citizens.

In this relation of the papal system to political parties there is nothing less than chance. The papal Church can attain its purpose of assuming to itself the functions of the state only in weak states. And its purpose is very far-reaching. For not only school and educational systems, not only state and municipal authorities, not only the property of congregations, but also industry and art must be subject to this Church, in a state which acknowledges the Jesuit liberty of the Church. The state is allowed to retain the collection of taxes. In return for this it is obliged to yield willing obedience to the divine right of the infallible hierarchy. Its first duty consists in preparing the way for true toleration and a genuine religious peace by preventing other religious communions, which may claim the same rights as the papal Church, from defending themselves against its attacks. In mixed marriages the state is bound to guarantee the freedom of the Church to claim the children for itself alone and to declare marriages performed by other clergymen to be concubinage; and it is the duty of the state to prevent every unwelcome criticism of the divine attributes of the infallible pope as well as those of the fathers of the council who proclaimed this infallibility.

Alsace and the Dutch provinces afford at this time the most striking object-lessons. In these countries municipal and state authorities are being brought into subjection to the Roman clergy, and there is not a social position whose occupant has not been taught by experience that his material existence is in the hands of this same clergy. In the countries of the Reformation the conditions are hardly better than in France, of which the historian Nielsen testifies: " In proportion as Ultramontanism is victorious in France, Catholicism loses in France the character of a Church and sinks to the position of a party." The evidences of the influence which this party has exerted upon popular morality in the various countries meet us again and again, from the war of Don Miguel in Portugal and the repeated Carlist wars in Spain, the revolution in Belgium, and the Swiss war of the Sonderbund, down to the bands of pious assassins in Poland and Ireland.

If the history of the past and present affords any indication of what is to be expected in the future, we cannot doubt that the triumphs so far achieved by the papal policy over secular politicians will be very much increased. The majority of statesmen treat the Church only as a means to an end; ecclesiastical offices are, in their hands, only a means of compensation in matters of the excise and the custom-house. To-day they assume one position toward ecclesiastical questions, to-morrow exactly the opposite. This is really quite in the nature of things, inasmuch as their public functions accustom them to deal with entirely different matters. And it is quite natural, too, that the representatives of each state think only of their own state; whereas all these separate states are comprehended by the Curia in one general survey of the whole world. Its nets are laid everywhere. At all times and in all places it acts according to the same unalterable maxims, which, however, allow the greatest flexibility of method in regard to the existing position of affairs.

The instruments and agencies which are at the disposal of the Papacy for the realisation of its plans are many and various. We find in the first place that the most influen-

tial social strata have rendered the most willing service.
The number of converts alone from princely families and
from those of counts and barons is not smaller than the
representatives in the pay of the pope of the so-called
youngest of the great powers—the press.   More indefatigable still, as affiliated members of the restored order
of Jesuits, is that class of noble ladies, whose type is the
Empress Eugenie.   Loyola himself had taught the order
to make use of the influence of ladies of high position for
ecclesiastical purposes, and their female penitents have in
our century rendered very considerable service to the
cause.   From the autobiography of the Prince-Bishop
Sedlniczki, we know how important a part the converted
duchess of Köthen and a mistress of Prince Hardenberg
played in the intrigues which led to the resignation of
this long-suffering prince of the Church.   The Arch-
duchess Sophie of Austria through her various sisters
frequently exerted a decisive influence upon the other
German courts.   Moreover, among the most obedient
female servants of the Curia are those who to outward
appearance are of another faith.

Together with these female influences, which were too
often decisive, we find the great majority of male diplomats and leaders of the state closely allied with the papal
interests.   There is no temporal state which can so richly
reward its servants as the so-called vicar of Him whose
kingdom was said not to be of this world.   Orders and
promotions and titles of all kinds are given to those to
whom the hope of what is beyond possesses little reality.

The rank and file of the Catholic clergy have been
made to feel the masterly skill of the Roman policy,
which makes use of the mutual jealousy of the various
orders of monks in order to dominate them all.   Especially in the war upon the national-Church tendency
within the several ecclesiastical bodies have such indirect
methods played an important part.   When we add to

this that the opponents of the Curia within the ranks of the clergy were usually quite defenceless, not even protected by the representatives of their own states, but again and again betrayed by the latter into the hands of the common enemy, we have an adequate explanation of the complete change that has taken place in by far the largest part of the Catholic clergy. On the one side were alluring prospects, on the other the danger of moral or material annihilation. When no other handle was found against Bishop Wessenberg, his honourable name was assailed. When Sembratowicz protested against the spoliation of the Basilian monasteries,[1] he was denounced to the government as a traitor. The farther removed from the scene of action, the more unhesitating the use of the accustomed Jesuit means. The methods which the clerical press employed in dealing with the lives of the reformers is now applied to contemporaries. If anyone dreams of any possible rights as belonging to the state or to another Church or to science, the attempt is first made to intimidate, and if that is impossible, to bring moral ruin upon him. The enormous means at the disposal of the Church militant make it an easy matter to spread the clerical literature to the remotest parts, and to silence dissenters. How many an opponent has finally become discouraged and has given up the battle which he has waged single-handed against the world-ruling organisation!

And yet, all these factors would not have sufficed to secure to the Papacy the yearly increasing influence over all social conditions, had not again and again the help of the Protestant Jesuits come to the rescue. The tendency which aims to bring back Protestantism to the standard of traditional orthodoxy is of the greatest service to the Papacy. The self-rending in which the Protestant leaders have been pleased to indulge has now, as before, played

[1] See page 215.

into the hands of that Roman arrogance which considers the destruction of the schismatic churches as merely a matter of time.   In order to suppress a displeasing theological tendency, the Protestant hierarchs have exposed themselves to the ridicule of the Ultramontanes, who assert that Protestantism owes the preservation of whatever faith is left in their decaying churches to their alliance with the papal party.

Such are the forces at the disposal of the Papacy, and no one familiar with the position of affairs can doubt that any of the pope's present following will refuse their services in the future.   And now consider all these forces marshalled by the rigid dictatorship which the new dogma has introduced.   For the society of the future no longer faces the old ideal conception of Catholicism, which in its essence coincides with the idea of the invisible Church of the Reformation, and whose claims of exclusive power of salvation really only amount to this, that it promises salvation to all who do not maliciously harden themselves. This Catholic conception of the Church has been destroyed and the papal system put in its place.

It was not for a theoretical fancy, for an altered theological formula, that the Jesuits spent more than ten years in making their preparations and in conquering every opposition.   Papal infallibility has very real practical ends.   Hitherto the scholastic and Roman element has been second to the religious and Christian; the Roman Catholic could be devoted to his country and could have a heart for science; the hope of the future for a reunion of the separated churches was based upon the presumption of a mutual approach.   All this has been changed since the Council of the Vatican.   In distinction from the mild and pious type of Catholicism which in spite of all oppression preponderated in the hearts of the people, a fanatical Jesuitism has been declared the only authorised religion.   Jesuitism and papal rule are now inseparable conceptions. Clothed with divine authority, the dictator in Rome demands the blind obedience of all Catholics. By divine right there is claimed the subjection of all baptised heretics under the ever-renewed incarnation of Christ in the pope. By divine authority the temporal rule of the state is restricted, and the independent exercise of the divine prerogative of the state is called in question.

The ideal Church hitherto existing has been completely materialised and sacrificed to the world-dominion of the pope. The minority bishops at the Council of the Vatican entreated the pope not to sanction the theory of the bull, *Unam Sanctam*. But in spite of their entreaty the constitution, *Pastor æternus*, was issued, July 18, 1870, and precisely what they wished to avoid has happened. The same bishops immediately gave the most unambiguous proof of the change that had taken place by proceeding with all the means at their disposal to persecute those who before had shared their own views. As vicars of the pope they have no more sacred duty than to persecute dissenters and to teach the faithful that the worldly magistracy exercises authority over them only by the grace of the pope. For the prophecy of the one shepherd and the one flock means in the future that every creature must be subject to the pope.

Analogous to this position of an infallible Papacy towards society and the state is its relation to science and learning. Along with the denial of rights to dissenters and the refusal to acknowledge the laws of the state when they conflict with the infallible oracles of the Papacy, goes the papal proscription of the liberty of scientific investigation; and no possible means is neglected of destroying all independent research and of putting obedience to the revelations of the pope in its place. In the first period of this century Catholicism, especially in Germany, could boast of numerous schools full of the spirit of independent research. One after another, they have been suppressed by the Curia. At this day the Roman Index has become the highest authority over science wherever the power of the Papacy extends.[1]

At present its decrees preserve only the believers in the Papacy from dangerous literature. The question of the future will be of establishing its authority over unbelievers. Measures looking to this end have already been taken. The Prussian laws, *e. g.*, threaten with three years' imprisonment whoever exposes to hatred and contempt any institution of the Roman Catholic Church, and only one more step is required, namely, to define these institutions as synonymous with those of the Papacy. The state has allowed Vaticanism to be put in the place of Catholicism. Thereby both the congregations of the Index and of the Inquisition have in fact been placed under the protection of the law.

The protection of these institutions by the power of the state is now one of the prerequisites of the peace between Church and State, and it will not be long before the courts are called upon to protect the religious peace, as it is guaranteed by the Index and the Inquisition. The Protestant pastor of Geldern was compelled against his will to decorate his house on Corpus-Christi day. He afterwards gave an exposition of the reformed conception of the mass. For this he has been condemned by the court. In the same week the *Germania* newspaper, which had declared the legal marriage of a Prussian school inspector to be concubinage, was acquitted (November, 1882).

The law of the state is obliged to protect the Roman "dogma." In accordance with this dogma the religious peace is violated if anyone dares to give the actual his-

[1] Compare the admirable monograph of Reuss, *The Index of Prohibited Books.*

tory of the Papacy, or if anyone has the hardihood to speak of the blessings of the Reformation or to look upon the characters of the Reformation in any other light than that which is permitted by the infallible pronouncements of the Papacy.

The same infallibility which controls the action of the government prescribes rules to the historian. " The tradition am I," said Pius IX. " Dogma has conquered History," boasted Manning after the Vatican Council. When Hefele's [1] history of the councils, revised after the decrees of the Vatican, appeared, it was found that the bishop had overcome the scholar. How could it be otherwise ? The condemnation of an heretical pope by an ecumenical council cannot be allowed to have taken place. The Council of the Vatican has declared it impossible. What, compared with this, do the sources of history signify ?

With good reason did " Janus " [2] on the eve of the council point out the one essential condition for the general triumph of the dogma, namely, that all libraries should be burned and that the civilised nations should become strangers to all knowledge of their past, somewhat like the Maoris of New Zealand. The disciples of the pope are well advanced on their way to this goal. The achievements of the Reformation era in the destruction of unwelcome books and historical documents have been well-nigh surpassed in the nineteenth century. The disappearance of the most important documents in the archives of Würzburg, testified to by J. B. Schwab, has numerous parallels. Augustine Theiner has witnessed to the same thing in regard to the original records of the reign of Clement XIV.; the minister of public

[1] Bishop of Rottenburg in Würtemberg, one of the most learned scholars of the Roman Catholic Church, author of a standard history of the Church councils, which he was subsequently obliged to revise in accordance with the decrees of the Vatican Council. See page 158.

[2] Döllinger.

worship, Falk, in regard to irreplaceable documents of the Prussian ministry.

The leaders of the papal party make no concealment of this noble principle. The valuable collection of the *Gallia Christiana* contained the history of the pre-Revolutionary Church of France, and in that history were many awkward facts for the papal system. Abbé Guéranger of Solesmes issued a new edition. His principles of historical research made no secret of the fact that the interests of the Papacy must be the highest criterion to the historian. The extent to which the new edition of the *Gallia Christiana* followed these principles was shown by the words in its praise spoken by Veuillot (in the *Univers* of August 28, 1874), to the effect that in redressing the expressions of the old authors no pains had been spared to " create a monument worthy of the devotion to the vicar of God."

The Fribourg Church-lexicon has been transformed on the same principle. In the second edition important sentences in many articles of the first edition have simply been placed on their heads, and that without the slightest indication of the total transformation of the former account. In a short period the first edition will have disappeared, and no one will be able to compare the two. Then it will be possible to teach coming generations that the infallibility of the pope has been taught always, everywhere, and by all. Numerous drastic examples of the same method have been given from French catechisms and manuals and from German books of devotion.[1] We already have Müller's translation of the *Imitatio Christi*, approved by Melchers, the archbishop of Cologne, in which at a certain place we read for licentiousness " in the monasteries," licentiousness " in the higher classes."

[1] The latter by Bishop Reinkens, the former by Michaud, professor in the old Catholic seminary at Berne : *De la falsification des catéchismes français et des manuels de théologie par le parti romaniste, de 1670 a 1868.*

Until now nobody had known that *in cœnobiis* meant " in the higher classes."

It would be unjust to charge this systematised falsification of historical documents to the dogma of the infallibility. For the authority of the Papacy rests from the beginning upon the same system. An unbroken chain extends all the way down, beginning with the fairy tale of St. Peter's Roman bishopric. From the falsification of the Nicene canons and the invention of the synod of Sinuessa,[1] which never took place, we are led to the pseudo-Isidorean decretals; and again from the falsifications of the Gregorian era to the deceit practised upon Thomas Aquinas through the pseudo-Cyril sent him from Rome.[2]

There is system and method in this never-ceasing imposition. It is the same method as that which maintains the belief in witches and demons (identified with the Christian faith since the infallible pronouncement of Innocent VIII.), as that which is used in the miracles of La Salette and Lourdes and Marpingen, as in the revelations of Marie Alacoque and Catharine Emmerich, as with false relics confirmed as genuine by papal seal and documents. The works of eminent scholars have exposed these facts.[3] But these works are placed upon the Index. The faithful may not read them. To secure unbelievers from temptation, such unpleasant books, as soon as the moment appears favourable and no new edition is to be feared, are bought up and rendered harmless. For years it has been impossible to obtain a copy of the writings of Gratry and Maret against the infallibility and of many similar works. " Janus " also is disappearing.

[1] Said to have taken place in the year 303.

[2] Compare page 195.

[3] Compare on this subject the writings of " Janus " (Döllinger); also " Paulinus ": *Märtyrer der Katakomben und die römische Praxis ;* Reusch : *Die deutschen Bischöffe und der Aberglaube ;* and Friedrich : *Mechanismus der vatikanischen Religion.*

The conception of history that Papalism has put in the place of " infidel " research is sufficiently illustrated by the Roman breviary, the daily reading of all the Roman clergy.   Besides this—to choose but one out of the hundreds of papal periodicals—we mention the *Monthly Roses*, disseminated in all languages for the adoration of the Sacred Heart.   The so-called " historical " works on the " miracles " in the nineteenth century, approved by the Church, are almost innumerable, and are spread abroad in countless editions.   To cite only a few examples: we call attention to the work of the Abbé Curicque, *Voix prophetiques ou signes, apparitions et predictions modernes* (specially approved by Bishop Räss of . Strassburg), to the work of Sausseret, translated into German and scattered abroad in several editions, *Apparitions and Revelations of the Most Blessed Virgin Mary*, to François Joseph's *Miracles de Salette*, and Marie Antoine's *Manuel du pélérin de Lourdes*.   But—how many Protestant scholars are familiar even with these easily accessible works?   And yet it has long been evident that these are the sources from which clerical parliamentarians have derived their knowledge of history and their judgments. And already the bold attempt has been made to set up this idea of history, as it is disseminated in clerical pamphlets, against the results of modern science.

During the sessions of the Vatican Council there appeared a pamphlet by Scheeben: *The Pope and his Latest Calumniators*, directed against the warning voices of " Janus " (Döllinger) and others.   The judgment here pronounced upon Döllinger (1869) is characteristic:

The manner in which Janus fulfils the conditions of scientific investigation and the mendaciousness with which he conceals his true views and purposes warrants us in concluding that we have before us no competent historical scholar — that there are in theology and history, as well as in conduct and life, bunglers and swindlers.

And wherein consists this lack of the "conditions of scientific investigation"? The answer is contained in one word on the last page: Döllinger gives a "heretical representation of the ancient constitution of the Church." Whoever applies the light of history to the pretensions and impositions of the Papacy gives a "heretical" representation. For it is the business of dogma to prescribe to history what it may tell and what not.

Even more explicit is the announcement made in the "historical-political papers," where the "dogmatic-historical method" is upheld as the only valid one. This is the definition of Dr. Pohle:

In the Church of Christ breathes and rules the Holy Ghost, and by virtue of this breathing and ruling dogma and history form a wonderful harmony. There are reasons in the very nature of the case why there can be no fact of Church history which should stand in any real contradiction with dogma, or even with the spirit of dogma. Ecclesiastical history possesses in dogma an unerring guide through the manifold historical transformations of the centuries—and the interpretation of historical facts must lean closely and submissively upon dogma.

This "leaning" upon dogma is to be understood to apply first and foremost to the account of the Reformation. "Infallible" judgment on this event is given in the bulls of Leo X. The historian has simply to follow these bulls. "A Catholic author must consider it his strict duty to make the alone valid and therefore objective ecclesiastical view of the religious schism a distinctly emphasised principle of his own historical conception."[1]

Formerly these beautiful theories were found only in orthodox seminary books, pamphlets, and periodicals, and in the clerical press, whose method of refutation

---

[1] See vol. iii. of the *Historical Manual of the Görres-Society.*

16

was not by reasons but by vilification of dissenters. But since the triumph of the infallibility dogma they appear in the open light of day with the claim to infallibility and exclusive right. At the convention of Catholics in Frankfurt (September, 1882), the same convention which in the name of Germany welcomed the cult of St. Teresa a Jesu, Herr Windhorst declared explicitly that the whole of German history had been falsified; that history falsified was taught in popular schools, in gymnasia, and in the universities. It was important that a correct account should be given; here was the arsenal which Catholics required to furnish them with weapons for the struggles that were forced upon them every day.

The watchword given out by the leader of the Centre has been promptly taken up by the clerical press in Germany. The *Schlesische Volkszeitung* expressed against those who were going to celebrate the four hundredth anniversary of the birth of Luther the threat, that if this was attempted an answer would be given in the shape of a picture of the real Luther, at which every decent man would have to be ashamed. The promise was literally fulfilled in a biography prepared for the Luther-jubilee.

There is nothing new in this whole method. Only the boldness is new with which it is publicly applied, now that the defeat of the German empire in the *Kulturkampf* has been followed by its inevitable consequences. For with a defiance which can hardly be exceeded the Protestant heresy is treated as in reality a thing of the past. Like mushrooms the books spring up which enlarge upon the text furnished in the statements made by Leo XIII. on the Reformation as the origin of all the evil of our time.

One repeats what the other has said on the papal construction of history, until the number of echoes really appears as a sort of public opinion. The modern fabrication

of books does not demand any effort of the mind.   Ham-
merstein's *Recollections of an Old Lutheran* takes its data
concerning the Reformation and the reformers from Evers'
Catholic or Protestant ; Evers has collected his tirades from
Janssen's *History of the German People*.   From the latter
work the entire clerical press dates with touching unanimity a new era in the writing of history.   And in fact
no work is so well fitted to stand as a type of the position of an infallible papalism towards historical science. [1]

The conception underlying Janssen's book does not in
the least differ from that of the whole papal literature on
the Reformation.   This literature had in the eighteenth
century retired from the public gaze into obscurity, but
since the beginning of the nineteenth century it has
everywhere again come to the front.   None of the tricks
by which history is perverted are new, as anybody knows
who is at all familiar with the school of the old as well as
of the new Jesuits.   The supercilious appearance of

[1] Janssen's *History of the German People from the End of the Middle
Ages* appeared in 1876 and the following years.   It claimed to be purely
"objective."   It is in effect a reconstruction of German history from the
Ultramontane point of view.   It was one of the literary sensations of the
times.

The following commentary on the method of Janssen and his school will
be found instructive.   It is taken from a review, published in *The Nation*
of May 17, 1900, of Dr. Gasquet's recent book, *The Eve of the Reformation*.   The appearance of this volume proves that the style of historical
literature against which Nippold protests is spreading from Germany to
England.   After stating the title of the book, the review begins :

"Under the above title Dr. Gasquet, known to scholars chiefly by his
book on *Henry VIII. and the English Monasteries*, has grouped a series
of 'studies' upon various aspects of the English Reformation.   'Studies'
is an attractive but misleading word.   One studies in order to learn something ; but that has not been the purpose of Dr. Gasquet's investigations.
He knew beforehand all that was necessary for him to know, and he has
studied only to find illustrations of a thesis with which he starts.   He is
avowedly a disciple of Janssen, whom he quotes at length and whom he
describes as 'the historian of Germany' for his period.   His method, which
is the same as that of his master, was bound to be applied sooner or later
to this phase of the Reformation, as it has been already with so much effect

superiority which Janssen assumed in his answer to " my critics " was possible only because of the almost entire ignorance until then prevailing among Protestants, as well of the inner life of Catholicism as of the papal representation of history. On one side was the incessant, indefatigable claim for the reversal of all history according to the infallible oracle in Rome, on the other side was the customary ignorance of Catholic literature.

What Protestant critics remained ignorant of was clearly appreciated among Catholic scholars. The real intellectual leaders of Catholic theology have long ago freed us from the trouble of exposing the means used by Janssen and his followers. Döllinger's address on sectarian and non-sectarian teaching of history, *i. e.*, on the *contradictio in adjecto* contained in the former, gives us his judgment on the work of Janssen. Bishop Reinkens has characterised Janssen's transformation of history and his methods in the following language: " Apparently he allows the documents to speak; but by suppression, by a slight colouring, by unnoticed transposition of cause and effect, he says the opposite." Various well-informed authors, such as Hoffmann, for many years his literary associate, and Baumstark, have given a faithful characterisation of Janssen and of the diametrical opposition between his

in other directions. It consists in laying down certain propositions and then supporting them by contemporary evidence, carefully selecting such as bear in the desired direction, and ignoring all that might seem to weaken the case. An essential feature is also the apparently frank admission of certain errors and weaknesses on one's own side, and of a certain proportion of good intention on the side of the opponent. Such a method aims to disarm criticism at the outset. It would produce its effects by an appeal to the sense of fairness and of logical sequence."

The last sentence of the review will be interesting to readers of this volume as expressing—almost in identical language—one of its main theses : the irreconcilableness of the Papacy and the modern world : " We welcome this book and all its kind, for the service they do in showing the irreconcilableness of the issue between the Roman principle and everything the modern world has come to value and respect."

" objectivity " and the honest writing of history. All
this only proves how necessary it is to heed the warning
of the gospel against those who come to us in sheep's
clothing, but who inwardly are ravening wolves.

More celebrated than Janssen as an exponent of the
same construction of history is Conrad von Bolanden,
who has " corrected " almost every period of German
history. In his *Enemies of the Empire*, the chancellor,
Marcus Trebonius, the author of the first Diocletian persecution, bears the features of Prince Bismarck; his four
volumes of historical novels on Frederick the Great have
drawn the picture of the founder of the Prussian state
after the method usually applied to Luther; and his other
books caricature the German character and vilify the
Reformation and the modern world of ideas. Yet no
German author has so widespread an influence.

At the same time the fabrication of novels, which has
been begun in the papal interest, has undertaken to
satisfy the demand for such reading, and no other literary
products of this class but those that have passed the
censorship of the confessor can find an entrance into
Catholic families. Whoever studies the catalogues or
even the shop-windows of the great clerical book concerns in the centre of Catholic Germany, will find every
year new works in numerous editions of which the ordinary history of literature takes hardly any notice.

More influential than the thick volumes of history with
their learned notes, more influential even than the so-
called Catholic novels, are the numerous collections of
pamphlets, to which we have already frequently referred,
from which the speakers of the Centre have for some time
derived their historical knowledge. The same methods
are here used to bring awkward historical data and the
problems of natural science and philosophy into harmony
with dogma *ad majorem dei gloriam*. Whether the representations agree with the truth is a matter of **very**

little moment.   There had been, even before the council, a good deal of activity in this direction.   Nevertheless we observe after the council a world-wide difference
from before.   For from the proclamation of the infallibility dates, strictly speaking, the rise of the clerical
press, which disseminates the papal construction of history
among the masses.   From year to year the organs of
clericalism have increased in number.   And now the
same language, which before they had only dared to use
against the Hohenstaufen emperors or the reformers, is
applied to the great leaders of the classical period of
literature.   The Jesuit father, Baumgarten, has already
achieved the moral assassination of Goethe.

Not yet has the effort been successful, as it was in the
seventeenth century, to separate the German people into
two hostile camps.   But Holland is to-day a striking
illustration of the far-reaching results of Jesuit training
systematically carried out.   The periodicals and newspapers of the Jesuits have there trained up a generation
which has lost every feeling for the glorious struggles for
liberty in the Netherlands.

The effect of the clerical universities upon the popular
life is shown by the condition of Belgium.   The French
imitation, under the third republic, of these so-called
" free " universities is of too recent date to show the same
effects as in Belgium.   Germany has followed suit, and
an attempt has been made to establish " free " German
universities.[1]   This has not yet been successful.   But in

---

[1] The following notice found in the New York *Nation* of July 14, 1898,
will be of interest in this connection in explaining the true nature of the
Roman Catholic " free " universities :

" A curious episode in modern university annals was the migration, about
half a year ago, of eight professors of the so-called ' free ' Roman Catholic
University in Freiburg in Switzerland.   This institution was established
some six or seven years ago for the special purpose of demonstrating that
freedom of scientific research was perfectly compatible with the spirit and
trend of the Church.   It was called ' free,' in contrast to the universities of

all the state universities sectarian associations of students have been formed, who now possess their own song-books with thoroughly " corrected " songs, and in which the young generation is systematically taught to look for the ideals of the future, not to Frederic II. and Joseph II., but to Ferdinand II.; not to William of Orange, but to Philip II.; not to Gustavus Vasa and Gustavus Adolfus, but to Sigismund of Poland; not to Elizabeth, but to James II.

Not only history, but every other scientific discipline has been similarly affected by the malign influence of papal infallibility. The science of law has been obliged with much labour to clear a path through the immeasurable network of frauds upon which has been built the pseudo-Isidorean papal law. Natural science has not only had to lament the persecution of Giordano Bruno and Galilei, but is to-day challenged by every new canonisation and every new pretended miracle. We claim, however, for historical research the position of an advance guard. Building upon the foundation of empirical investigation as laid by natural science, and yet, as the history of man, fixing its attention intelligently upon

Germany, Austria, and Switzerland, which were regarded as controlled unduly by the state. Experience has now shown that in this ' free' university, the ' Lehrfreiheit,' the ideal so dear to continental scholars, has not been able to establish its throne. The professors who have severed their connection with the Freiburg University, namely, Drs. Effmann, Gottlob, Hardy, Jostes, Lörkens, von Savigny, Streitberg, and Sturm (all, we believe, Roman Catholic laymen and Germans), have united in the publication of a Memorial (*Denkschrift*), in which they give the why and wherefore of their exodus. From this document it is apparent that the French Dominican monks are in absolute control of the University, and any teachings not in conformity with the interests of this order have in recent years brought down upon the heads of the offenders the opposition and even persecution of the fathers, which finally ended in withholding the salaries of several teachers who would not withdraw views not acceptable to those in authority. The *Denkschrift* is an interesting and instructive document, and again shows how inevitably ecclesiastical authority and freedom of scientific research merely for truth's sake come in collision."

the deepest impulse that humanity knows — religious enthusiasm, beyond all other branches of science it has to bear the most embittered hatred of Vaticanism. For that very reason, under the leadership of Döllinger, it bears the banner in the never-ceasing struggle between a truth-loving science and the conceit of infallibility.

The undermining of the state and the destruction of the scientific sense of truth do not exhaust the fatal heritage which the principle of infallibility leaves to the future. For the state and science, however fundamental as factors in the development of civilisation, are but subordinate to that factor which, after all, makes men men — religion. Only the knowledge of what religion has become under the influence of papalism enables us rightly to judge its real nature.

In order to obtain a complete survey of the effect upon religion of the infallible dominion of the Papacy, we should be obliged to give our first consideration to those countries in which heretical influences are as good as excluded. But with the success of the policy which seeks to build impassable barriers between the Roman Catholic population and their fellow-citizens, the conditions in countries of mixed population approach those of Spain and South America. In Germany it has proceeded so far that Baedecker's guide-books, because they bear the stamp of no sect, are forbidden by the clerical press, and others are substituted, which along with the sacred places recommend Catholic hotels and Catholic shops. In Germany again, where there are state and communal savings-banks, we find also institutions of credit founded for Catholic apprentices and Catholic masters, who through them reap larger dividends, but also greater dependence. There are even musical associations and concerts with the sectarian stamp; the interdict is placed upon mixed societies as well as upon mixed schools.

No one who has not from infancy lived in a Catholic atmosphere can form any judgment of the systematic transformation of a population by nature tolerant, as it has been gradually brought about through sectarian schools forced upon them by unwise statesmen, and as it has been intensified to a degree of overbearing arrogance in consequence of the surrender in the *Kulturkampf*. It is no longer questioned that Christianity consists in the subjection of the nations to the pope, or that the faith of the individual rests upon the sacrifice of the reason. The realisation of this faith in life consists in the hatred and persecution of dissenters. Whoever resists the motherly love of the Church must sooner or later fall a prey to God's vengeance. Every means is allowable for the making of proselytes. A man like Cardinal Diepenbrock could declare to a Catholic priest that it did not matter even if the man whom you wished to convert did not believe in anything himself, if only by his submission his children could be won.

The prevalent disgraceful language of the clerical press is an indication of an increasing deterioration of all ethical conceptions among the people. What Father Curci reports of Italy, that the gospels of the New Testament are the book least known to the people, represents an ideal which, among the other nations subjected to the Papacy, is more and more approaching reality. Can it be otherwise, when all that Christ censures and opposes is made the criterion of Christianity, when demonstrative processions and public reading of the breviary take the place of the prayer in the closet, when the worship of God in spirit and in truth is materialised, when the infallible man in Rome is put in the place of Christ ?

The entire literature of devotion is carefully purified from the evil works of the last century, which know a true life of Christian piety only as an ethical life. What happened in France in the eighteenth century after the prohibition of Quesnel's work on the New Testament is the case in Germany to-day. In the place of a devotion which fostered the ethical life in the pursuit of life's vocation, the modern Jesuit religiosity has placed Madonna-visions, the cult of the Sacred Heart, exorcisms, and stigmatisations. The fact that Catharine Emmerich was judicially proved to be an impostor was no bar to the ecclesiastical celebration of her jubilee and the glorification of her miracles in special pamphlets. A drastic revelation of the influence of the modern Jesuit cults upon the popular life is given by the legal action connected with the miracles of Marpingen.[1] The latter were a favourite argument for the infallibility in the German *Kulturkampf*, and in the historical manual of Cardinal Hergenröther they are treated as undoubted facts.

"God will allow a stronger and a worse Papacy to come up, because we have too readily submitted to the papistical maxims." The nineteenth century has taken every pains to fulfil this prediction of the pious Spener and to leave to the twentieth century an inheritance similar to that which the seventeenth had prepared for the following century, before the second reformation to which God called Spener. Will the twentieth century return once more to the likeness of the " Frederician era " ?

[1] The Virgin and Satan were said to have been seen by children and miracles were wrought, in 1876. See *The Marpingen Miracles before the Royal Police-Court, Saarbrücken. According to the stenographic report* (in German), Saarlouis, 1879.

PART II

CATHOLICISM AND PAPALISM IN ENGLAND AND AMERICA

CHAPTER XVI

THE SO-CALLED CATHOLIC EMANCIPATION IN GREAT BRITAIN [1]

FRANCE, the land of the great Revolution, is the centre of the papal reaction in the nineteenth century. From France the movement has extended in all directions, just as the French fashions did in the reign of Louis XIV. and in the era of the encyclopedists. The leaven spread from France first to its northern neighbour, the Netherlands; but it affected in no less degree Catholic Switzerland and Western Germany.

In all these countries of the European continent the teachings of the new Papacy found the soil already prepared. For not only had a large part of the Catholic population remained devoted to the papal interests through the era of Illumination in the last century, but the same population had suffered almost more than the French from the horrors and the havoc of the Revolution, and had naturally become so much more susceptible to the influence of the Restoration-spirit. These conditions,

[1] It has been the custom among Roman Catholics in Germany to represent the repressive and precautionary measures which the English government since the Reformation has from time to time adopted against English Roman Catholics as the extreme of religious intolerance and persecution. This must be borne in mind by the reader as the point of view from which the present chapter is written. Our author's protests against the perversion of English history and the false ideas of religious liberty have in view the misrepresentations current among the papists of Germany.

however, which told powerfully in favour of papalism, were entirely absent in England, among the people of the twofold reformation, the victorious opponents of the Revolution.

And yet, even during the storms of the Revolution the triumphs of the Papacy in England were most pronounced—a fact whose explanation is to be found not so much in local as in those general causes which lie in the very nature of our modern spiritual life. The victories of Roman Catholicism in England are but the counterpart to the progress of Protestantism in all those countries which had before been hermetically closed against it. There is a remarkable balancing of gain and loss between the opposing churches, as is seen by a comparison of general statistics. And this peculiar phenomenon is the result not only of the physical changes that have taken place, of mixed intercourse, of more frequent travelling, and of the mingling of the most diverse nationalities; but is largely due to the modern principle of liberty of conscience.

For, ever since this ancient Christian principle has won the battle over ecclesiastical ambition and greed, the oppressed of every country enjoy the advantages of free motion and general toleration. And, in England as elsewhere, the oppressed minority has profited by the modern spirit. Catholic emancipation, long resisted and finally carried out by its former opponents, is directly traceable to the universal spiritual process, which has made itself everywhere felt since the American war of revolution and the so-called ideas of 1789.

More difficult to understand than Catholic emancipation is the immense stream of conversions, by which the English, so proud of their liberty, were brought in droves to submit to the authority of the pope. Nevertheless, with emancipation to prepare the way, we shall learn to understand these conversions as in no way the result of mere chance. But not only do the general causes and the several stages of this movement deserve a closer examination than has hitherto been given them; we must turn our attention also to the reaction and to the ultimate effect of these conversions upon the English Church itself.

Catholic emancipation and the multitude of conversions raised the hopes of the Curia for the ultimate submission of England to the Papacy, and Pius IX. knew what he was about when, in the year 1850, to show his gratitude for the Emancipation Act, he established the papal hierarchy alongside of the national. He showed a like prudent calculation a few years later (1853) when the same step was taken in Holland. In both cases the result was the same. After a period of high but short-lived popular excitement both England and Holland submitted to the papal encroachment. England has been taught by her experience in Ireland the consequences of the complaisance she has shown to the Papacy. The history of Ireland in the last years affords the most instructive illustration of the blessings of infallible Vaticanism in its influence upon faith and morals, upon domestic and national welfare; and the almost uninterrupted series of open assassinations and secret conspiracies, by which every act of leniency and of toleration on the part of the English was answered, may well be considered a prognostic of the ultimate influence which the British conversions will exert upon the following generation.

We take up now the first of those memorable phenomena, about which the entire Catholic Church history of Great Britain in the nineteenth century groups itself, the so-called Catholic emancipation — that is, the repeal of those laws which limited the political rights of Roman Catholics. So many erroneous opinions are still held in regard to these laws, that their origin and execution demands some explanation.

It is not to be denied that English history contains abundant evidence of intolerance towards Roman Catholics, and we have no desire to palliate the far-reaching consequences of religious hatred such as prevailed in former generations in Great Britain.   But we must also remember this lesson, which English history teaches us, that English legislation against the Church of Rome was not simply the expression of religious persecution.

It is not just to compare the duty of self-defence against an open enemy, whose challenge is to a life-and-death struggle, to whom all means for the destruction of his opponent are equally just, with that spirit of persecution which is of the very essence of the papal principle. The inalienable duty of the national leaders to find means of protection against the political dangers with which the papal policy for centuries threatened England, brought great hardships upon the British Catholics.   But we have no right to blame the result and to ignore the cause.

The history of England since the Reformation shows frequent attempts to repeal the oppressive laws.   Such were the transactions of the year 1648.   It was proposed at that time to extend toleration to all those who should repudiate the following three propositions : that the pope had the power to release a subject from obedience to his government, that he could grant dispensation from an oath given to a heretic, and that it was lawful upon his command to kill those whom he had condemned as heretics.   Fifty-nine English Catholic noblemen, besides a number of priests, had declared themselves against these propositions.   But Innocent X. immediately pronounced that whoever had subscribed to this declaration made himself liable to the penalties imposed upon the denial of the papal power.   '' For this reason the penal laws against the Catholics remained in force for more than a century longer." [1]

Let us, in the interest of unbiassed history, stigmatise every religious persecution, but let it be done with even-handed justice, wherever we find it, in this church or in that. It is not just to speak of the martyrdom of papists under Henry VIII. and to ignore the fact that he condemned to death a far larger number of those of the reformed faith. It is equally unjust to parade the oppression of Catholics under Elizabeth and to conceal the number of Protestants Bloody Mary had sent to the stake. It is unhistorical to paint romantic pictures of the beautiful Mary Stuart and to draw a veil over the attempts upon the life of Elizabeth by her adherents, attempts whose plans are traced very near to Mary herself.

Up to the present time only timid efforts have been ventured towards attributing the expedition of the great Armada to Philip II.'s interest in religious liberty. But this is what we are coming to, among those who talk of the suppression of religious liberty in England, who would lead you to think there had never been such things as the papal deposition of Elizabeth, the powder plot under James I., the Irish massacre under Charles I., and the intrigues against popular liberty of the convert James II.

It was precisely these events which obliged England to have recourse to measures of defence. Nor was it otherwise in the last great duel between Louis XIV. and William III. of Orange. The reign of William taught mutual toleration to warring Episcopalians and Presbyterians, and even relieved the hated revolutionary sects of Baptists and Quakers of the persecutions they had suffered. But is it reasonable to expect, at the time when Louis XIV. gave to French Protestantism its death-blow, that William III. should rise to the standard

[1] Quirinus, *Roman Letters from the Council.*

17

of the nineteenth century and risk his own and his country's very existence ? It is true that, after the battle of the Boyne, the Orange lodges of Irish Protestants imitated the example of the Jesuits; it is also true that the London festival of Guy Fawkes' day in so far copied the *autodafès* as to burn an effigy in revenge for the death agonies of hundreds of thousands of living victims. But we may not forget that only with the dawn of the eighteenth century, when the creation of Louis XIV. had crumbled into ruins, did the idea of general religious liberty become first a philosophical doctrine and then was made the common possession of all those whom the Papacy declares to be unbelievers.

Nevertheless, however necessary the laws against Roman Catholics may have been for the defence of England, this does not alter the fact that these laws were opposed to the recognition, now rapidly spreading, of the modern principle of universal liberty of conscience. If from the time of the papal deposition of Elizabeth to the days when William III.'s life was attempted and the time of the repeated invasions of the Stuart pretenders (1715 and 1745) it was high treason, not only in name but in fact, to obey the commands of the pope against the government of the country, the consequent liability of every Roman priest to the penalties of felony could not but be pregnant with evil for the future. Still more invidious was another measure, by which the property of a Catholic went to the nearest Protestant heir, if the former had been educated in foreign parts, and every Protestant son of a Catholic father was permitted to claim his inheritance during the life of the latter.

As a matter of fact, the very measures which were designed to secure the outward influence of the state Church could not but very seriously undermine her moral power. The exclusion by the Test Acts from public office and from Parliament alienated Roman Catholics from the rest of the population. The adherents of all other forms of worship were obliged to pay tithes to the Episcopal Church, and had at the same time to provide for their own churches and schools, while the state Church was suffering from a system of sinecures in the hands of a mercenary clergy. And naturally, this condition of things won increased respect among their flocks for the poor Roman clergy.

But it takes, as a rule, a long time before such experiences impress themselves upon the popular imagination. When in 1780 Lord Saville proposed some slight mitigation of the " Act for preventing the further growth of popery " of William III., the dangerous Gordon riots (described in Dickens' *Barnaby Rudge*) proved how deep-seated in the popular consciousness was the feeling against the Papacy. Nevertheless, before the end of the last century a change had taken place in the position of English Catholicism. For not only was Lord Saville's law soon afterwards passed in spite of the Gordon riots, even the establishment, by Thomas Weld, of the Jesuit college of Stonyhurst, near Liverpool, was sanctioned, and many French priests, who had refused the oath and fled to England, found a welcome there and were able to exert a certain influence in the times of the first conversions to Rome.

Immediately after the period of the Revolution, the liberal party embodied in its platform the repeal of the Test Acts which had closed the public offices to Roman Catholics. The spirit of the times was in favour of the abolition of the old restrictions. As early as 1817 a motion for the repeal was made in Parliament. For a considerable time the attempt was frustrated by the resistance of the Upper House. As late as the year 1824 the Peers rejected the so-called Emancipation. But resistance only increased the efforts of those who were determined to extend the principle of liberty of conscience even to its opponents. Consalvi, acting for the pope, brought his expert influence to bear upon English statesmen. The Chevalier Bunsen, as Prussian ambassador in Rome, used his English connections to the same purpose.

The chief objection which was made by those who stood up for the old laws lay in the papal encroachments and pretensions. This objection was overcome by the official declaration again made by the Roman Catholic bishops of Ireland (following upon former declarations made in 1661, 1757, 1788, 1793, and 1810), to the effect that the Catholic Church does not teach the infallibility of the pope. This " declaration," made in the year 1826 by the Catholic bishops, the apostolic vicars, and their coadjutors, not only stands as an unequivocal testimony to the doctrine of the Church as it was then held, but is invested with a peculiarly solemn character, because it was upon the ground of this declaration (sanctioned by the Curia) that emancipation was demanded. And during the sessions of the Vatican Council in 1870 a number of the older English bishops expressed themselves emphatically to the effect that English Catholics had obtained their political and legal position in consequence of the repeated declaration and upon the express condition, that they do not teach the doctrine of papal infallibility. Gladstone's pamphlet on the Vatican decrees has recorded the arts of deception which have been resorted to in order to gloss over this inconvenient fact.

The declaration of the bishops seemed to prove that the repeal of the Test Acts threatened no danger to the state, and under the last ministry of the Duke of Wellington and after a celebrated speech by Sir Robert Peel, the Tories carried through the programme of the Whigs. On the 13th of April, 1829, the royal sanction was given to the act of both Houses, which opened Parliament and the public offices to Roman Catholics on condition of taking an oath of allegiance which was worded in general terms.

The stone once set rolling, almost every year brought new gains to the Papacy. The Irish Ecclesiastical Endowment Act, which abolished a half of the bishoprics of the Irish state Church and thereby called forth the first opposition of the Puseyite party, was a new concession to the papal Church. The same motive induced the Peel ministry to enact the inheritance bill, by which testaments in favour of the Church of Rome and her institutions, orders excepted, were permitted. Not long afterwards followed the state endowment of the Jesuit seminary of Maynooth. In 1847 four more royal colleges were established at the expense of the state, at which religious instruction was left in the hands of the Church. But when Pius IX. proclaimed the so-called restitution of the hierarchy in England, the hopes of the Curia had been raised to such a degree that attendance at these state colleges was forbidden.

CHAPTER XVII

THE ENGLISH CONVERSIONS AND THEIR CONSEQUENCES FOR THE ENGLISH CHURCH—THE OXFORD MOVEMENT [1]

WE have traced the so-called Catholic Emancipation chiefly to the spirit of the times; but this explanation will not suffice for the second phenomenon to which we now turn our attention: the stream of conversions to the Church of Rome.   There must be other deeper lying causes for the fact that large numbers of this people, so proud of its ancient liberties, bowed their necks under the Caudine yoke of recantation, and more especially, that it became the fashion among the upper ten thousand to kiss the pope's foot.   A correct appreciation of these causes is of far greater importance to the historian than the statistics of the converts with their titles and incomes, which is the favourite theme of the Vatican press.

Among the motives which led to the conversions were some which were specifically ecclesiastical, but we shall also have to consider a series of more general factors in the process, partly preparatory, partly co-operant.   And, in a reactionary tendency such as we have before us, we must not fail to look for those underlying ideals, without which we shall be entirely unable to understand the significance of this or indeed of any other movement.

[1] The German point of view from which this chapter is written must again be borne in mind.   The Romeward movement in England was the cause of exultation to German papists, and they made a great show with the names of English converts.

262

Among the preparatory causes we place the social influence of the immigrant foreign priests, and the romantic literature and poetry, in which the influence of Scott,[1] Byron, and Moore was supreme. But it lay in the nature of things that the seed already sown could bear fruit only after emancipation had prepared the soil. How great were the expectations which emancipation raised in Rome is proved by the well-known statement of the Count de Maistre, who declared the acquisition of the Church of St. Peter in Geneva and of St. Sophia in Constantinople to be the necessary consequences of English Catholic emancipation. And we read elsewhere this prediction, that " with the 25th of April, 1829, there begins a new era; the entrance of O'Connell into Parliament and his refusal to take the oath of supremacy have given the signal for the religious regeneration which sooner or later, but inevitably, must lead to the most complete victory of the new faith." In fact, we see that the concessions obtained through emancipation were used as a stepping-stone to new favours for the papal Church.

Among the factors which from the beginning co-operated towards the same end, we have also to consider the political events since the July revolution of 1830. The friendly relations to the young Belgian state, and especially the high estimation in which King Leopold was held among the leading classes of England, influenced English statesmen more and more in favour of the

---

[1] " The following of Walter Scott's novels are especially used in the interests of the Papacy : *Waverley*, with the character of Flora ; *Rob Roy* (where the heroine and her father represent the Roman faith) ; *Montrose* and *Woodstock*, with the struggles in behalf of Charles I. and II. ; more particularly, *Old Mortality* and *Heart of Midlothian*, with their repulsive caricatures of puritanical fanaticism ; and *Peveril of the Peak*, where the papistical conspirators appear as patient lambs and the defenders of Protestantism as persecutors. The novels of the crusades, also, as well as *Ivanhoe* and *Quentin Durward*, throwing a romantic nimbus about the middle ages ; and the twin volumes, *Monastery* and *Abbot*, especially in the last part, are used with great skill."—Note in the literary-critical supplement.

example which Belgium had set in the treatment of religious questions.

Other causes, of entirely different nature, contributed to bring about the same result.   The distrust, which had prevailed in Great Britain since the time of Frederick the Great, towards German neology was greatly increased by the appearance of Strauss' *Life of Jesus* and Feuerbach's *Nature of Christianity*.   At the same time, the Prussian ecclesiastical policy with its police interference appeared to the English as one of rude violence.   And the increasing alienation from their former allies, from the home of the Reformation and of modern philosophy, carried with it an alienation from the lasting impulse of Reformation ideas.   Furthermore, with the growing inroads of the dissenters among the adherents of the state Church grew the opposition of the latter towards the so-called sects; and the Church itself was driven more and more in the opposite direction.   The greater, in fact, the progress of political and religious radicalism, so much the more reactionary grew the conservative tendency in politics as well as in religion.

The prevailing tendencies of thought outside the Anglican Church help us to understand why within the Church itself anti-Protestant inclinations so frequently triumphed over its Protestant character.   But we must take into consideration also the reaction from the evangelical school, in order fully to understand the new high-Church tendency.   This school had been very influential towards the end of the eighteenth century, and from its union with dissenters proceeded the great Bible and missionary societies, and with them the aspiration towards an ideal Catholicism.   But, as had been the case with Lutherans and Calvinists on the Continent, so here Anglican sectarianism took up arms against these creations of an era of tolerance and enlightenment.

At the same time, the repeal of the Test Acts drove

the high-Church party into opposition to the policy of
the government. And not without reason. For, the
ecclesiastical convocations having fallen into disuse and
Parliament having assumed ultimate authority over
Church affairs, the constitution of the state Church was
dangerously affected by the repeal. Dissenters and
Roman Catholics now sat in the House of Commons.
And the House of Commons did not hesitate to pass the
Irish Ecclesiastical Properties Act, by which ten Irish
bishoprics were dissolved, without any consideration for
the apostolical succession of their occupants. Cambridge
being the centre of the low-Church tendencies, the bitter
feeling over these measures made itself particularly felt
at Oxford. Here Thomas Arnold, Whately, and Hampden had not long before taught in the spirit of the later
broad-Church school. But from the year 1833 (the year
of the Irish Ecclesiastical Properties Act) Oxford became
the centre of Puseyism.

The movement which is associated with the name of
Pusey was really far from new. It had a number of precursors. From the very beginning the English Church
had intended to occupy the middle ground between
Catholicism and Protestantism, and the old high-Church
school had emphasised their relationship with the Church
of Rome and their repudiation of Protestant sects.

Without doubt this middle position of the Church of
England is an important factor, not only in the national
development, but in the universal progress of humanity.
And the hope that the amalgamation of the Catholic and
the Protestant principles, first realised in England, is
destined to play a highly important part in the future, is
justified by the victorious opposition of a national Catholicism in the United States of America to the invasion of
Roman ecclesiasticism.

Nevertheless we may not ignore those elements in the

Catholicism of the Church of England which might easily cause a gravitation towards the Church of Rome.   The Church of England has never realised the Catholic ideal in its purity: for it has lacked the necessary attributes of freedom and independence.   Henry VIII. and Elizabeth, and, to a greater degree, the Stuarts and the first Hanoverians, exercised an arbitrary ecclesiastical tyranny, and the system of James I., under the principle " No bishop, no king," made of the Church a means to a political end.   The supremacy of the crown thus appeared to be inconsistent with the independence of the Church, and it was quite natural that the only alternative should seem to be the primacy of the Roman bishop, whose authority the king had usurped.

The very defects of the national Church thus led to an idealisation of the papal system.   But it is also to be noted that the Anglo-Catholic conception of the Church itself carried with it an element which would necessarily favour a tendency in the same direction, and as a result of this tendency we find in the Tractarian movement a decided approach to Roman doctrine.   Not the invisible kingdom of God, but the visible Church, represented by the hierarchy, was held to be the sole exponent of revelation.   The bishops have received from the apostles the gift of the Holy Ghost.   Without this apostolical succession there is no true Church.   The fellowship with Christ is conditioned upon the fellowship with the bishops as the successors of the apostles.

With the teaching of the apostolical succession is connected that of ecclesiastical tradition.   The more dissenters appealed to the Scriptures against the high Church, so much more were the defenders of the latter thrown upon tradition—" a turn of the dispute," so an acute observer said, " which led the party farther in the Catholic direction than they had wished or intended."   And, as a logical consequence, the Bible was accepted as the rule of faith only as interpreted by tradition, and the right of authoritative exposition of Scripture was allowed solely to the Church as the keeper of tradition.

The same tendency affected the doctrine of the sacraments. Baptism, not faith, justifies. The Holy Communion stands or falls with the real presence of Christ. And finally, the rest of the Catholic sacraments, celibacy and the monastic life, the adoration of saints and relics, were justified; it is only necessary to guard against the abuse to which for a time they were liable. This reactionary tendency was only partially carried through in the so-called Puseyite movement; it was left to Ritualism to supplement what was wanting.

We find these fundamental ideas of the " Catholic movement " emphasised by Pusey's American biographer, John Henry Hopkins, in the *American Church Review* (January, 1883), who himself claims to be an enthusiastic adherent of this movement. He, too, asserts that the conception of the Church lies at the foundation of the Catholic movement, the Church as founded by Christ and the apostles, and therefore independent of Parliament or of Congress. He finds the apostolical succession as well as the doctrine of the sacraments, especially the real presence, justified by the belief in the divine life of Christ in the Church and its worship. His contentions give not only to the Tractarians but also to the Ritualists a more reasonable basis. The revival of ancient ecclesiastical architecture, music, and hymnology, the restoration of old forms of dress and rites, not only have for their object the honour and glory of ecclesiastical mysteries, but also serve the pedagogical purpose of increasing the attraction of the Church for the uneducated masses. Either, says Hopkins, the workingman must be won for the Church by these and similar means or he falls a prey to Moody and Sankey and the Salvation Army on the one hand, to the Roman Propaganda on the other.

The *Tracts for the Times*, whose publication began in
1833, which is generally supposed to mark the beginning
of the Roman movement in the Church of England, have
a long introductory history, and before we enter upon the
consideration of the Tractarian movement, in its various
stages, and of its after-effects, it will be in place to take
a survey of the earlier more isolated cases of apostasy to
the Church of Rome — sporadic conversions which we
must distinguish from the Puseyite movement proper and
its later excrescences.

As early as the end of the eighteenth century occurs
the name of one who preceded Manning and his associates in their new ecclesiastical career, the subsequent
London apostolical vicar and bishop *in partibus*, Bramston
(died 1836), and we read a similar story in the life of
Baggs (died 1845), who was influenced by his Irish
mother, and was afterwards particularly favoured by
Gregory XVI. In the first decade of this century we
meet only with a few officers and noblemen, converted
in France, important for nothing but their names, like
Lord Stuart and Lord Holland, and with a number of
ladies, who either married into French families (Polignac,
Choiseul, Delange), or were influenced from France; who
in their turn influenced a larger number of others, of the
nobility and of the middle classes.

It is interesting to note that in the long list of annual
conversions the female element is predominant and has
precedence in point of time. Modern proselytism in
England began with the women, in order by their influence gradually to win over the families, at least in the
second generation. In this process there was little scruple
as to the morality of the means, as is proved by the
account of Miss Loveday's conversion, which has been
published in German as " a memorable contribution
to the history of religious toleration in the nineteenth
century " (1822). The deluded father is here pictured

as the representative of intolerance. The truth of the matter was that his daughter had not only been secretly converted, but was hidden from him for a considerable time in various French convents, so that the French Parliament engaged in lively debates upon the subject of this outrageous abduction.

Still more characteristic is the story of Miss Pittar's conversion, translated into French by Mermillod (1861), the title of the translation representing her as " a Protestant woman converted by her Bible and the Prayerbook." She was influenced to conversion behind her husband's back; and after his death she took away her children from the care of their guardians. As a reward for her pains, both of her sons became Jesuits.

Among the female converts before the time of Newman and his friends we find a Miss Gladstone. Her illustrious brother had himself been strongly influenced by the Tractarian movement, in the time when he wrote his first work upon Church and State. It may have been chiefly his close relations with Bunsen which counteracted Newman's overpowering influence, to which many of Gladstone's nearest relatives and friends succumbed. It is necessary to recall these earlier years of Gladstone's development in order to realise in its full significance his later attitude against " Vaticanism." With this anti-Roman position of his maturer age the subsequent attitude of his sister presents a remarkable parallel. In spite of her conversion to the Roman Church we find in her the same distinction of papalism and Catholicism, which afterwards placed even Newman for a time in opposition to the new dogma and brought him into discredit with Pius IX. Miss Gladstone died some years after the Vatican Council under the spiritual ministrations of the old-Catholic pastor Tangermann in Cologne.

More important, however, than the list of converts is the polemic literature of the time which appeared under their names. Miss Agnew's *Geraldine, a Tale of Con-science* (1837), became the type of an extensive literature of fiction representing the course of conversion. *Geraldine* passed through numerous English editions and three successive translations into German were undertaken. Among other books of the same kind we may mention Sir Leopold Wright's *Return to the Catholic Church*, in the form of a letter, which appeared not only in English but also in German and French. Not long after we note the writings of Richard Waldo Sibthorp, who in two letters answered the question, "Why did you become a Catholic?" and of Francis Wackerbath, who before his conversion had written a similar letter to Sir Robert Peel. Lisle Phillips wrote about *The Future Union of Christendom* (1857). Henry Digby was, among the older converts, an exceedingly industrious polemical writer. Before his conversion he wrote *The Rock of Honour*. Later he published a large number of works, each of many volumes, which, however, never became popular, because they were too "learned" for the younger fanatics. We mention the *Mores Catholici* of ten volumes, the *Compitum*, or *The Meeting Ways of the Catholic Church*, of eight volumes, and *The Chapel of St. John, or a Life of Faith in the Nineteenth Century*, not to speak of several collections of poetry and devotional writings.

Much has been made of converts who had made names for themselves in other spheres. Especially characteristic are the biographies of the painters Stanfield and Herbert and of the architect Pugin. One would gather from such works that modern England possessed hardly any other artists of note. The same is true of the antiquarian Turnbull.

But the most significant in the older literature of apostasy are the detailed biographies of George Spencer, subsequently the "Father Ignatius of St. Paul," and a most zealous proselytiser, and the fiery Frederick Lucas, founder of the *Tablet*. These biographies afford the best opportunities for the study of the psychology of conversion before the era of Tractarianism. The cause of Spencer's conversion (which happened in the year 1830) was the confusion of faith and dogma. His argumentation is as follows: There can be but one faith, therefore the English Church, divided into so many parties, cannot be the true Church; such can only be the Church which preserves the unity of the faith.

The conversion of Lucas took place in the year 1839, when the Tractarian movement had attracted general attention. Lucas had been interested from the beginning. But he, Quaker by birth, never shared the pious attachment to the English Church which was so strong in Pusey and his friends; to him, therefore, the scruples which for a long time held Newman back were as unreasonable as the more pacific disposition of born Catholics. Nevertheless, his *Reasons for Becoming a Catholic* (1839), an attempt to make Roman doctrines acceptable to Protestants, appears in a certain sense as a model of what shortly afterwards *Tract Ninety* attempted to do for the Thirty-nine Articles.

After this survey of the older forerunners, we enter upon the Tractarian movement itself. It is necessary to distinguish its several stages. Even before the publication of the *Tracts for the Times*, which gave to the movement its name, the Tractarian tendency had given signs of its existence. Perceval's *Christian Peace-Offering*, for instance, had manifested the sympathy for the Roman Church which characterised the *Tracts* from the beginning. This writing, published at the time of Catholic emancipation, intended to prepare the way for the intercommunion of Anglican and Roman " Catholics." All errors and defects of the papal Church were represented as mere excrescences on a true branch of the true Church, which did not touch the vital parts. And while the author expressed the hope of complete reunion in this direction, hardly any abuse was strong enough for Independents, Baptists, Calvinists, and Lutherans.

With Perceval we reckon Froude as one of the earlier forerunners of the young Oxford school. It was he especially who reverted to the ecclesiastical ideals of Laud; he characterised the Reformation as a badly knit fracture, and saw in the " rationalistic " spirit which proceeded from the Reformation the antichrist of the Apocalypse. Keble's programme, in the *Churchman's Manual*, for united action and for changes in the Catechism, also dates from before the *Tracts for the Times*. We find, furthermore, before the movement proper, large numbers of sermons and treatises in reviews and newspapers, and an extensive literature of stories, poems, and romances; the type, as it were, of an industry which was afterwards carried on openly in the interests of the Papacy.

Far more influential than all the above-mentioned names, even at that time, was the man who gave to the whole movement its name, Edward Bouverie Pusey. The number of Puseyites who went over to the Roman Church runs high into the thousands, if we include the laity. Pusey himself remained to the end of his life true to the declaration which he made at the most difficult period, that he would live and die in the bosom of the English Church, and that this should be his only answer to all attacks upon him. And however men's judgments formerly differed as to his work, at his death in 1882 he carried with him into the grave the universal respect of his fellow-men. The organs of all Church parties in England recognised him as one of the most eminent men of the whole country. His American biographer goes so

far as to call him the greatest theologian the English
Church has ever had. And it is certainly highly significant as regards the position and influence of an English
theologian, that he was neither archbishop, nor bishop,
nor even dean, but simple professor, and yet he guided
the entire development of his Church into new channels.

Pusey's studies in Germany had exerted no less influence upon him than the same studies had in his time
upon Cranmer. Only this influence was in the opposite
direction. He had learned to know German biblical
criticism, but at the same time to hate it with his whole
soul as undermining the authority of the inspired Scriptures. If even at this day his otherwise clear-sighted
admirer Hopkins condemns German critics as enemies of
the holy Scriptures, we may form an idea of the frame of
mind in which the youthful contemporary of Hengsten-
berg returned to England. But we cannot deny to him
an accurate knowledge of the hated criticism. He also
occupied himself extensively with natural science and
was unusually familiar with rabbinical literature. His
preface to a work upon the Jewish expositors of the 53d
chapter of Isaiah has become almost proverbial for its
rabbinical learning. The list of learned works and
treatises by his pen is imposing; large literary undertak-
ings were started by him, such as a comprehensive commentary to all the books of the Bible and a new edition
of the Church-fathers. He personally contributed to the
former a commentary on Daniel and the Minor Prophets,
to the latter the Ante-Nicene Christian Library. At the
same time we find him in the forefront of all ecclesiastical
movements, everywhere contending for the authority of
Church doctrine, but even more for the practical tasks of
the Church in the popular life; and the Tractarian movement brings him before us as the first leader of a party
to which a great future was assured.

These much-talked-of tracts are themselves by no

18 .

means the work of one man, but represent the outcome of discussions concerning the defects of the Church and the means of remedying them, in which Pusey, Newman, Palmer, Keble, and Hook participated.   We find in them from the very beginning all the fundamental ideas which we have already designated as the heritage of the Laudian tendencies in the high Church: above all, the importance assigned to the apostolical succession as the sole means by which the Holy Ghost is transmitted, and to ancient ecclesiastical tradition as the source of doctrine alongside of the Scriptures and as the standard of interpretation.   From these premises are drawn the natural conclusions as regards the doctrines of justification and of the Holy Communion, the prerogatives of the clergy, and liturgical rites.   The Catholic character of the English Church was emphatically maintained and all fellowship disclaimed with so-called Protestantism.

There is, however, as yet no purpose discoverable in any of the tracts of a separation from the English Church. It was rather the express object of the authors to maintain the Church's doctrinal basis in the Thirty-nine Articles.   This was done even by the famous *Tract Ninety*, although it openly proclaimed the break with all the principles of the Reformation.   For it aimed particularly to show that it was possible upon the basis of these very articles to defend the specifically Roman doctrines.   Purgatory and absolution, adoration of images and transubstantiation, the worship of Mary and the invocation of the saints, celibacy and the papal authority: all these are, according to the author, not absolutely, but only in corrupted form, contrary to the Thirty-nine Articles.   It is possible to be a loyal Anglican and yet to accept the decrees of the Council of Trent.   The Roman Church itself is the older sister Church; Protestantism is the religion of the corrupt human heart and the Protestant Churches are anti-Christian sects.

The author of *Tract Ninety* will now claim our attention more than any other, even than Pusey. For the latter gave place in the course of the following years to Newman. And the several periods of Newman's life form, as it were, the pivots about which moves English ecclesiastical history during the next score or more of years.

Pusey's American biographer, as well as his English friends, ascribe to Newman a power of personal attraction quite indescribable; at the same time he is spoken of as a man who felt strongly the need of authority. Newman's theology has in fact something of the *genus varium et mutabile semper* which Virgil ascribes to women. From the evangelical school he turned to the high Church, from this to Rome. But after he had refused to follow Manning's agitation for the infallibility dogma and had characterised the Society of Jesus as an insolent, aggressive faction, he stood in the last years of Pius IX. as good as under the ban. And, in spite of the wise policy of Leo XIII., who sought to cover up these differences, there is no doubt, as Hopkins rightly remarks, that Newman was much more honoured and loved in the English Church than in the Roman; while the romanising tendency of his influence ceased with his secession, the personal devotion remained. But before we consider Newman's personal influence upon others, we shall have to examine the effects of *Tract Ninety* and of Tractarianism in general.

Hardly one of the tracts gives any evidence of a scientifically honest investigation in the German meaning of the word (that is, where the result was not certain before the investigation). It is true that there was no lack, among the authors, of patristic learning and of dialectical skill. And their courage grew not only with their successes but also with opposition. Among their successes we count the favour they found with the majority of the bishops, who saw the considerably weakened authority of their office strengthened by the Oxford men. Foremost in opposition was the *Christian Observer* (representing the evangelical party), which as early as the year 1834 pointed out the dangers of the new tendency for the Church. At that time Newman had propounded his *Via Media*, in which he vindicated for the English Church the middle position which in fact represents her peculiar character.

The struggle grew from year to year more intense, and more and more unmistakably the new school claimed not only toleration but sole right in the Church. This was shown in 1836 in the Hampden dispute, when the Oxford men attacked Hampden's nomination as professor. Thomas Arnold at the time vigorously defended his friend against the charge of infidelity. The following year, 1837, witnessed a new conflict, occasioned by Williams' tract on official reserve in the communication of religious truths. The publication of Froude's Remains in the years 1838–39 increased the intensity of the antagonism by revealing the real nature of the ends Froude had been pursuing. " It was now made perfectly plain that the younger generation had been taught to see in the Reformation a deplorable calamity, to treat the other Evangelical Churches with contempt, and the Roman Church as the older sister of the English, or in fact as her mother."

But it was *Tract Ninety* which finally knocked the bottom out of the barrel. Its sophistical character was only too evident. Newman did not so much investigate the doctrinal intentions of the Thirty-nine Articles; his endeavour was rather to ascertain how far they could be twisted and interpreted, in order to reconcile the doctrines rejected by the authors with the letter of the articles. It was a real Jesuitical *reservatio mentalis*, by means of which the young generation was taught to give a different meaning to the obligation of ecclesiastical formularies. Wiseman, from the Roman side, could point out with little trouble that such a position must necessarily lead farther.

The subsequent events in which were manifested the consequences of the premises enunciated in the *Tracts for the Times* are to be sharply distinguished from the attitude of the authors at the time. They were as yet very far from thinking of leaving the English Church; on the contrary, they hoped so to increase their influence as to bring about ultimately the reunion of the separated Churches, that is, to bring over their whole Church to the Papacy. It is therefore necessary to leave their later writings out of consideration, in order at this point to fix our attention upon the situation as it had been created by *Tract Ninety*. The challenge which it contained was of course too peremptory for the bishops who had hitherto favoured the movement to look on in silence. In March, 1841, the vice-chancellor of Oxford broke with the Tractarian party. Bishop Bagot of Oxford, personally much inclined towards the party, notified Newman that *Tract Ninety* was offensive and calculated to disturb the peace and the quiet of the Church. The archbishop of Canterbury forbade the publication of further polemical tracts. Newman submitted by his letter of March 29, 1841, to the bishop's order, and stopped the publication of the tracts.

Pusey, who until now had covered the whole party with his name, attempted to defend Newman's position. He himself was suspended for three years from the university pulpit, on account of a sermon which had been too controversial. But he did not follow Newman in the latter's subsequent career; he contented himself with "deprotestantising" the English Church. Pius IX. afterwards said of him, he had rung the bell for the entrance of England into the Catholic (*i. e.*, Roman) Church, but himself stopped at the door.

This period of transition, before the conversions in
large numbers had begun and Newman himself took the
last step, illustrates the attitude which his party originally
endeavoured to assume and to occupy.   A few months
after he had outwardly submitted to his bishop Newman
took it upon himself to suggest to the Protestants of the
Continent to submit themselves to the Roman bishops of
their dioceses.   The claim, put forward at a later time
by Bishop Martin of Paderborn, that his jurisdiction extended to the Protestants living in his diocese (to " all
baptised persons "), was sanctioned in principle by Newman in the declaration which he made to the Evangelical
pastor Spörlein of Antwerp: to the effect that he, as a
cleric of Antwerp, was subject to the spiritual power of
the bishop of that city.   The circle of young men sur-
rounding Newman expressed their agreement with this
view.

Even after the crisis occasioned by *Tract Ninety*,
Newman remained for more than four years on the divid-
ing line between the two Churches.   One after another
of his disciples and friends preceded him into the Church
of Rome.   Among them are many of slight importance,
but also no small number of those who before their conversion occupied prominent positions and who by their
ascetic piety as well as by their learning and their power
of logic exercised an influence upon large circles.   The
numerous writings by these men, partly before, partly
after their conversion, represent at this day an important
chapter of modern English ecclesiastical literature.

They are not always agreeable reading; nevertheless
in the period now beginning we have before us one of the
most powerful spiritual movements of our century, one
which for those who were caught in its influence was all
but irresistible.   In his pamphlet on the Vatican decrees,
Mr. Gladstone has expressed himself as follows: " The
ecclesiastical historian of the future will perhaps conclude

that Newman's withdrawal was a more important event
than the partial alienation of John Wesley, whose loss to
the English Church is the only one which, in magnitude
can be compared with the loss of Newman.'' He emphatically designates him as the leader, at the time, of
religious life in England; no one but Newman himself
was able to deprive him of this office and this power.
Newman was, according to Gladstone,

in the extraordinary, perhaps unparalleled, position in a critical
period to give to the religious thought of his time and his
country the most powerful impulse it had long received from
any man; then to be the principal, though without doubt in-
voluntary, cause of an equally remarkable dissension and dis-
sipation of the representatives of this mode of thought into a
number of divided and mutually antagonistic groups.

The testimony which Gladstone bears to the existence
of dissensions will be confirmed by those who, in the
literature of the years 1841 to 1845, trace the remonstrances and the warnings on the one side and on the
other follow the writings published in increasing numbers
by converts. It is manifestly a period of separation of
heterogeneous elements, which came about in the natural
order of things and then just as naturally assumed ever
larger dimensions. Many of those who were formerly in
favour of the Tractarians began to hesitate: among them
the same Perceval who had been one of the first pro-
moters of the movement, and an increasing number of
bishops. Measures are now taken to dam the stream,
more, to be sure, in the spirit of the seventeenth than of
the nineteenth century: such as greater stringency in the
requirement of subscription to the Thirty-nine Articles
at matriculation in the universities. On the other hand,
the advance guard of the army, which is looking towards
Rome, more and more engages our attention.

As yet it is mostly younger men, with unknown names,

most of them personal pupils of Newman, who shared his hermitage at Littlemore and then left it in order openly to transfer their allegiance to the Church of Rome. Somewhat better known are William Lockhart, who went over in August, 1843, and Charles Seager, who in October of the same year took the same step in Rome. Charles Scott Murray, who followed them, was the eighteenth immediate pupil of Newman who since 1841 had taken this step.

A much greater sensation was made by the course which William George Ward pursued. He had been the editor of the *British Critic*, in which Newman, after the cessation of the *Tracts*, had defended his position. Ward published, in 1844, his *Ideal of a Christian Church*, in which he went far beyond the principles of *Tract Ninety*. This writing is characterised, on the papal side, as the boldest which the Puseyites had till then published. Ward in fact endeavoured to represent the promulgation of the most pronounced Roman maxims as entirely compatible with his official position in the Church of England. The universal opposition which this called forth, and the legal action instituted against him, which ended with his deposition, obliged him to relinquish his office. After his conversion Ward undertook the publication of the *Dublin Review*. He also published a number of writings upon special topics, of which we mention one which was written in the true Jesuitical spirit of quibbling, concerning *The Authority of Doctrinal Decisions which Are not Definitions of Faith* (1867).

But even Ward's far-reaching audacity was soon surpassed by that of Frederick Oakeley. He too had begun his literary activity by a defence of *Tract Ninety*, in which, like Ward, he went beyond it and recommended auricular confession, celibacy, and a form of worship which served as a model for subsequent ritualism. Now he entered the lists in defence of Ward and claimed even more decidedly than the latter the right of retaining spiritual office in the Church, in order that he and others might fulfil their mission for the conversion of their parishes. He tried the patience of his colleagues in the Church until it became necessary to take legal steps against him, which ended in his deposition.

There is thus evident, even while they are both on the way to Rome, a certain divergence in the two lines of procedure, that of Ward and Oakeley on the one hand, of Newman on the other. Oakeley's polemical zeal afterwards carried him farther and farther and greatly intensified the confusion existing in the company of the converts. He finally had the audacity to glorify as " the Church of the Bible " (1865) the same papal Church which in every way had sought to counteract the dissemination of the Bible and, where it could not altogether prevent it, had sanctioned the grossest falsifications.

And yet even Oakeley's infatuation was surpassed by that of his friend, Frederick William Faber. Besides Faber's own writings, the *Sights and Thoughts in Foreign Churches*, written before his conversion, the customary letter to a friend concerning the motives of his secession, and a large number of ascetic and proselytising works dating from the latter part of his life, we are in possession of a laudatory biography of him by Father Bowden. If anyone desires a superabundance of malicious expressions of defamation poured out upon everything connected with the Reformation and with Protestantism, he could hardly find a better source to draw from. Even the heroes of English literature, a Milton, a Shelley, a Byron, are treated by Faber in the most contemptuous tone. His associate and peer in this berserker madness was his bosom friend, William Anthony Hutchinson. The latter had the hardihood to write a special pamphlet (soon translated into German), in which he represented the Loretto fable as true history, and we are not surprised that this orthodox papal " historian " treats a scholar of Dean Stanley's eminence as if he were an ignorant schoolboy.

We have selected these names from among a large number of theological converts, because they exercised a decisive influence upon the man who had hitherto been the head of the school. It is evident that the " leader, at the time, of the religious spirit in England," in the more than four and a half years from the suppression of the *Tracts for the Times* to his secession, never gave up the hope of being able to avoid the last step, and that he sought to avoid it because he thought it possible to carry his whole Church over with him to Rome. With this purpose in view he attempted several large literary works, such as the *Lives of English Saints*, which dates from the period of his hesitation. Most of these works came to a standstill, and even his *Essay on the Development of Christian Doctrine* remained a fragment. The book gives clear evidence of how the author was drawn hither and thither and could not rise above an attitude of vacillation. More and more did the man, who so long had influenced others, become the object of others' influence. Even such young men as Dalgairns, who had reported to the Paris *Univers* the situation as it was created by *Tract Ninety*, are seen to exert an increasing influence upon his decisions.

It was Dalgairns who brought Father Dominicus, the priest who occupied himself with receiving " recantations," to Newman. The journey of the father on a rainy day has been neatly dressed up in true novel style. Dalgairns had gone over on the 29th of September, 1845, Ambrosius St. John followed him on the 2d of October. On the 8th of October, late in the evening, Father Dominicus came to Newman, took his confession, and received him into the true Church. During the next days there followed a large number of friends, who had only waited for Newman to set the example: Bowles and Stanton on the 9th of October, Woodmason on the 10th, and soon afterwards Coffin, Newman's companion on his journey to Rome.

Newman's literary activity is too comprehensive to be exhaustively treated in this connection. Immediately after his secession he published the open " retraction " of his errors (antedated the 6th of October). He expressed himself somewhat more fully in *Loss and Gain, or the Story of a Convert* (1848). But his activity consisted from this time mainly in the introduction into England of the congregation of the Oratorians, of which he himself had become a member. From 1852 to 1858 he presided as rector over the university of Dublin. Quite naturally, a large number of the younger converts made their confession by preference to him.

With Newman's apostasy begins the first period of a regular pilgrimage to Rome. The mere names of the theologians who went over in the years following fill a number of pages. We select only those who have recorded the reasons for their apostasy in any noticeable writings. Among these are Thomas William Marshall, Edward Browne, Albany Christie, William Wingfield, Leicester Buckingham. The first belongs to the older group who with Newman sought to avoid isolated action. Witness his *Notes on the Catholic Episcopate*. But after he had recognised the inevitableness of recantation, he drew up a list of twenty-two motives by which he endeavoured to persuade others to follow him. Later he wrote a larger work on missions, in the style of Wiseman's *Millions and Martyrs* (the former represented as the means of Protestant, the latter as the power of Roman Catholic missions). Browne's conversion pamphlet bears the form of a letter to the editor of the *Church and State Gazette*. Christie wrote for the glorification of the Papacy (identified

with Catholicism) as the only real counterweight to political tyranny.   Wingfield began as Anglican with a defence
of prayers for the dead; at a later time he wrote books of
travel in the interests of the Papacy.   Buckingham finally
added another to the many Jesuitical fabrications whose
aim was to prove the innocence of Mary Stuart.

More interesting, however, than any of these is a pair
of friends whose mutual relations remind us of those of
Faber and Hutchinson.   They are James Spencer Northcote and Healy Thompson.   Northcote wrote his first
work upon the fourfold dilemma of Anglicanism (1846);
later he wrote on the Roman catacombs and the Virgin
Mary (proving the papal dogmas concerning Mary out of
the gospels).   Both together founded the *Clifton Tracts*,
in which, by the boldness of their method of reconstruct-
ing history, the authors have out-distanced even the
" historians " of the German tract associations, who certainly are not to be accused of too great modesty in this
respect.   The first seventeen issues of the *Tracts*, or the
first division, treated the Reformation in the light of the
papal bull against Luther.   The second division has
" made the refutation of historical falsehoods, such as
are current in England, its object "; the third consists
of dogmatic, the fourth of devotional or entertaining
treatises.

Among the theological controversialists of the year
1846 we name a few who are particularly eminent: Henry
Formby, author of a popular illustrated Church history
and of a pamphlet against rationalism in education; David
Lewis, author of an exceedingly violent work on the nature
and the extent of the royal supremacy; the two Morrises,
one Pusey's assistant in the Hebrew professorship, the
other afterwards the secretary and biographer of Wiseman; Richard Simpson, author of a number of works on
the persecution of Catholics in England and of a life of
the Jesuit Campion.   With these theologians go a few

forerunners of the subsequent droves of converts from the aristocracy: the Scottish Lord Monteith, who with his large fortune rendered material services to the Propaganda; and Lady Georgiana Fullerton, who followed in the steps of the authoress of *Geraldine*, and wrote numerous proselytising novels, which have been all translated into German.

Among the converts of the year 1847 John Gordon leads the way. His work, *Some Account of the Reasons of my Conversion to the Catholic Church*, passed through seven editions in ten years. From out of the circle of the Oxford school there followed him in the same year his brother William Thomas Gordon, Richard Gell Macmullen, Thomas Wilkinson, Edward Caswall (known among Romanists as a poet), Robert Ornsby (author of a life of Francis de Sales and companion of the young duke of Norfolk), and a number more. Early in the year 1848 these were joined by Robert Knox Scouce, whose work, *A Few Plain Reasons for Submitting to the Catholic Church*, was widely circulated.

Most of these Anglican theologians became after their conversion Roman priests or monks and as such devoted themselves with energy to the making of new converts. The movement which proceeded from the clergy extended more and more into other strata of society, as we see from the lists of the same year, which contain the names of General Tyler, Lord Macaffrey, the lawyer Wetherfield, the painter John Pollen, and the publisher James Burns.

The stream of converts steadily increased, even before the Gorham case, when the attitude assumed by Manning in consequence of the decision gave it a new impulse and a new character. Even during the storms of the year of revolution, 1848, the movement did not stand still. Among the converts of this time is James Burton Robertson, a poet of some talent, whom the papal press places

on a level with Milton and above Young.   We find also
the name of the baronet William Drummond Stewart,
whose wealth enabled him " to form the nucleus of a
Catholic congregation in a region wholly Protestant ";
also that of Colonel Jerrett, the rich landed proprietor
and justice of the peace, and Thomas Yonge, " nephew
of Lord Senton and member of one of the most prominent
families in Hampshire," and various judges and lawyers.

The great majority of writings by converts dating from
that time breathes the fanaticism of infallibility.   In
justice to the authors we are bound to acknowledge that
they were men of conviction, who unflinchingly followed
duty wherever it led them.   There can be no doubt that
in them the English Church lost a number of highly
gifted and influential members.

And yet—if we candidly compare the time before and
after 1845, we can hardly resist the conclusion that the
crisis brought about by Newman's secession acted like a
storm which clears the atmosphere.   However great was
outwardly the loss to the English Church, the gain to its
inner life was much greater.   These men in fact no longer
belonged to a Church which after all was rooted in the
Reformation.   The English Church occupied an untenable
position so long as the Tractarians held their places in her.
Hence the sultry, oppressive atmosphere caused by the
feeling of an imminent, inevitable catastrophe.   When
the dreaded event had happened, when the inevitable
separation had taken place, the Church seemed again to
breathe freely, like the newly sown field after the thunder
and lightning of the storm.   All respect for Newman's
learning and — we accept Gladstone's testimony for it —
his subjective honesty.   Objectively there is scarcely
conceivable a greater piece of dishonesty than *Tract
Ninety*.   No candid man can blame Newman because
his conviction led him into the papal Church.   But we
may justly blame him for delaying so long.

To be sure, if we consider Newman's later life, we shall understand why the step was so difficult to take. Again we say, all respect for the weight of his personality, and that not only in view of his earlier, but even more in view of his later activity. But was the latter not a labour of Sisyphus? We read the answer in his own writings. There is hardly anything more pathetic than his auto-biography (published after long delay in the year 1864) and the controversy with Pusey to which it gave rise. How touching are the repeatedly expressed regrets for the happy years from 1833 to 1841; and how significant, when we compare the broken life of the following years! And why broken? It was not the attacks of his former associates in the faith that clouded his after-life, but those of his eager disciples to whom the master was not sufficiently zealous. He was obliged to relinquish his position in Dublin after many painful experiences. And when at last he was about to realise his dearest wish, the establishment of an oratory at Oxford, he was most humiliatingly disavowed by Pius IX. (1867).

The manner in which the orthodox papal press at that time spoke of him is paralleled only by the treatment accorded to Döllinger after his celebrated lectures in which he advocated the abandonment by the pope of the temporal power. He was accused, with Döllinger, of an attempt to " germanise " the Church, which must be protected from this fate by the Papacy. Newman did not conceal his opposition to the dogma of the infallibility. But when the crisis came, he lacked Döllinger's strength of conviction. Such unreserved opposition as that which was shown by born Catholics would have meant for the convert a disavowal of his whole former life. It is the fate of numerous converts that they are not able publicly to retract their recantation without stultifying themselves. Newman is a prominent illustration of this. After maintaining for some time his refusal, he had to resign himself to accepting the cardinal's title from the peace-pope Leo XIII., and suffer himself to be represented as bought over.

Although a large number had followed Newman in his apostasy, still the years we have been considering do not by any means bring us to the real climax of the era of apostasy. This was brought about by the Gorham case (1849), that new crisis in the Anglican Church, in consequence of which the antagonistic elements diverged more than ever, following a sort of centrifugal movement. In all previous party divisions within the Anglican fold, the question had practically been between the two parties of the high and the low Church. But the appearance of Puseyism within the first party, together with the opposition of evangelicalism, with its more practical tendency, had called forth a more strictly scientific movement. We trace its beginnings in the opposition of the older Oxford men, the school of Thomas Arnold, Whately, and Hampden, to their younger successors.

As the "romanising" tendencies of the Puseyites became more evident, the "germanising" movement asserted itself more decidedly in opposition. The united action with Germany in the establishment of the Jerusalem bishopric called forth from Newman a decided protest; on the other hand it drew closer, among a large number, the connection with Germany. The growing strength of the so-called broad-Church school, which maintained intimate relations with German theology, forms one of the most interesting phases of Protestant Church history in England; but in the chapter of that history which brings before us the progress of Anglo-Catholicism we meet only with an intensified antagonism on the part of those who would have nothing to do with the German Reformation, with German theology, and with what they were pleased to call German unbelief.

The Gorham case first brought these new antagonisms into prominence. Gorham really opposed the magic conception of baptism as identical with conversion. But as the Thirty-nine Articles maintained this conception even more decidedly than the Lutheran symbols, he departed from the confession of faith as much as *Tract Ninety* had done in the opposite direction. It is the peculiarity of the crisis that attaches to his name that the party which hitherto had been the occasion of the increasingly numerous conversions to Rome now set itself up as the guardian of the faith and would tolerate no other interpretation than its own. Gorham's Tractarian bishop refused to confirm him in the living to which he had been presented, and the bishop's proceedings were approved by the higher ecclesiastical court; but the royal privy council acquitted Gorham of the charge and instituted him in his parish. This action, in the eyes of the Puseyites, showed more than ever the supremacy of the crown in the light of a tyranny and the Church as hopelessly subjected to the state. Hence a growing excitement and more and more angry protests, in which Pusey himself took part. But again he separated himself finally from his associates.

It was the subscribers to the so-called Gorham protests whose submission to Rome marks the real climax of the whole stream of conversions. And both Newman and his friends and the old-Catholics of England were more and more pushed to the rear and deprived of their influence by those who from this time on went over to the Church of Rome.

Again, we find a number of *dii minorum gentium* leading the way. Almost all of them entered the service of the Roman Church and henceforth devoted their lives principally to the conversion of others. The fact that at the one Church of the Redeemer at Leeds almost simultaneously five of the clergy took the same step proves to what extent the action of one man determined

19

that of another.　Soon the forerunners of minor importance were followed by the real leaders, such men as
Wilberforce, Manning, and Palmer.　And to these men,
who since then have been the heads of the new Roman
hierarchy, were now added regular processions of the
aristocracy to the rock of St. Peter.

With the theological leaders of the new movement as
well as with the Tractarians, we must unreservedly
recognise the ecclesiastical ideals which determined their
action.　We find these expressed in the words of the
men themselves.　For we meet now, even more than
before, with a voluminous controversial literature.　Prominent among the writings in which the new converts
justified their action is the " farewell letter " to his
former parishioners of Henry William Wilberforce.　A
few years later he was followed by his brother, Robert
Isaac Wilberforce, who at his conversion published a
pamphlet against the royal supremacy.　The third
brother, Bishop Samuel Wilberforce, became, with Pusey
and Keble, the leader of the subsequent reaction.

If we compare the literature as a whole which belongs
to the new era with that which dates from the earlier
days of Newman's secession, we observe a considerable
disparity.　In place of the earnest, conscientious struggles
which characterised the former period, we now find a
tendency to rhetorical pathos; in place of the ancient
Church-ideals we find a growing emphasis placed upon
the Church as a world-power.　Vulgar materialisation of
religious ideas is mingled with a still more vulgar ambition.　The reason of this change is not far to seek.　The
older forerunners made sacrifices for their convictions;
the younger generation followed the favourite fashion.
Newman and Manning have been much compared; but,
aside from the fact that both entered the Church of
Rome, the parallel is justified only in so far as both became cardinals.　But even touching this external fact the

difference is striking: Manning won the coveted title by his agitation for the new papal dogma, while Newman was reluctantly prevailed upon to accept it. As the religious-ethical attitude of the two men was one of contrast, so was their outward position: the successor of Wiseman in formal capability and hierarchical dexterity far excelled Newman, whose coveted ideal was the hermit's life. Manning therefore exerted upon the latest development of the papal Church, under an infallible pope, an influence which extended far beyond England.

Manning's course, before his conversion even, shows very vividly the contrast between the two periods of conversion, the one led by him, the other by Newman. Manning, even in his earliest controversial writing, in connection with the Tractarian movement (1842), took his stand upon the mere external mechanical conception of Church unity. It was in consequence of the Gorham decision that he identified this conception with the exclusive claim of his own party to represent the Church. He stood personally at the head of the protesting movement. He himself described at a later time the scene at the subscribing of the protest: " At the moment of subscribing, one of the authors of the protest, turning to the others, exclaimed: ' If the Church of England does not repudiate this judgment, I suppose we are all ready to leave her ? ' ' For my part,' answered one of us, ' I shall never leave her, cost what it may.' " The one that put the question was Manning, the other was Pusey.

The protest was repudiated by the bishops, and the subscribers were considerably embarrassed. They had recourse to an appeal, against the bishops' judgment, to the rest of the clergy. This meant, from their point of view, to whom the apostolical succession of the bishops was the corner-stone of the Church, open revolution. But the appeal had no great success.

In order to understand Manning's plans in connection
with the general ecclesiastical situation, we must not forget that the year of the judgment in the Gorham case,
1849, was the year of the establishment of the papal
hierarchy in England.   This wisely calculated *coup d'état*,
carried through regardless of consequences — the expression of the pope's gratitude for Catholic emancipation, which made clear to those who had laboured to
bring about emancipation that the Papacy did not recognise its opponents' rights, — will be fully considered in
another connection.   But in reviewing Manning's earlier
and later position, the fact is of no slight importance that
he delayed his open conversion until the furious storm
occasioned by the " anti-papal aggression " had calmed
down.   It was not until October, 1851, that he considered
the time propitious for the contemplated step.

The first three years after his conversion were spent in
Rome, and from there he returned as *Doctor Romanus*.
As such he was affiliated with the Jesuits.   His wife had
died, and there was therefore nothing to prevent his entrance into the Roman hierarchy.   He had in Rome
been admitted to the order of Oblates of St. Charles Bor-
romeo, and after his return he founded a monastery of
this order in Bayswater, a suburb of London.   Bayswater
is said to have become, in consequence, a half-Roman
suburb.   Somewhat later Manning also transplanted the
Sœurs du S. Sion and the Geneva school brothers to
England.   During the last years of Wiseman he almost
forced the latter into the background.

More significant still are the events at his nomination
to succeed Wiseman.   This was a new act of violence on
the part of the Papacy, in no way inferior to that which
had been inflicted upon the English Church by the imposition of the Roman hierarchy.   Both the chapter and
the provincial bishops had proposed three other can-
didates.   Pius IX. simply forced his favourite Manning

upon them. The latter entered upon his new dignity with the public expression of the hope that the English schism, like the Arian and the Donatist, would fall to pieces and in the course of a few centuries would remain only as an historical curiosity.

The position of primate of the Roman opposition Church in England gave to Manning the outer form, and it depended upon him to give to this form a substantial meaning. In this he was successful. To render an account of what he did for the Roman world-power by means of his many sensational demonstrations would require a special work. One of his first acts was " the erection of a cathedral commensurate with the size of the Catholic population and the dignity of the archdiocese." One of the many rich converts, Sir John Sutton, furnished the means for the purchase of the ground.

Such outward manifestations are proper to the nature of the papal Church, which devotes itself by preference to spectacular exhibitions. Far more important were the attacks made by the new archbishop upon the Church of the land, whenever the latter passed through a new crisis. These later crises, which ensued as by a law of nature in consequence of the forced union of three heterogeneous tendencies in the Church of England, are not to be overlooked, if we would fully grasp the reasons for the continual progress of the Roman Propaganda in England. Every time broad-Church criticism or low-Church friendliness toward dissenters made itself prominent, the high-Church party renewed its opposition. So it was with the agitation called forth by the *Essays and Reviews*, with the opposition to Bishop Colenso, with the growing animosity against the modern methods of nature study; so it was, again, when the efforts of Moody and Sankey, of Pearsall Smith, or the comedies of the Salvation Army were patronised by the " Evangelicals."

With a dexterity in which he was equalled only by

Bishops Dupanloup and Ketteler, Manning understood how to use these crises in such a way as to force the conviction upon the Anglo-Catholic party that their ecclesiastical ideal was capable of realisation only in union with Rome.   We mention, by way of illustration, his letter to Pusey at the acquittal of the authors of the *Essays and Reviews*.   The very title, *The Crown in Council*, was admirably calculated to stir up the Puseyite antipathy to the supremacy of the crown.   The first letter (which Pusey did not answer) was soon followed by a second, on *The Work of the Holy Ghost in the Church of England*. This work of the Holy Ghost consisted, of course, principally in conversions to Rome.   It is a question whether Pusey would have made any reply to the renewed challenge, had not Newman's *History of my Religious Opinions* demanded an answer.   At any rate, we may say of Pusey's *Eirenicon*, in which, over against Newman's and Manning's defection to Rome, he gave the reasons for his remaining in the Church of England, that it had a considerable effect in staying the stream of theological conversions.

All of Manning's attacks upon his mother Church witness to the same talent and also to the same fanaticism. His zeal turned every means to account.   There is in the contemporary history of England, political as well as ecclesiastical, hardly an important event with which the Roman primate in one form or another has not connected his name.   It is true, as has been said, that he " obtained a position in English society such as no Catholic (*i. e.*, Roman) bishop has had since Reginald Pole."   The personal peculiarities by which Manning gained this position have been described as " his many connections and his fine manners."   The etiquette of the salon offered to the representative of Rome the best field of operations for his intended conquests among the society of the nobility.   The courtesy of the cultured

Englishman smoothed the path, step by step, for his further plans. Scarcely an appeal can be found in behalf of a philanthropic work which is not subscribed to by the delegate of the pope in England.

But the same man, whose advances were met in the most friendly spirit by the representatives of the religious circles of England, more and more unreservedly set papalism in the place of Catholicism. In full opposition to Döllinger and Newman he dared, as early as 1865, to defend the temporal power of the pope with arguments which nowhere sounded more sophistical than in Great Britain. The new dogma of Pius IX. found hardly any more passionate defender. Although Manning liked to have his name appear in connection with movements outside the Church, yet when in 1866 the establishment of an association of prayer for the reunion of the churches was agitated, he forebade the participation of the faithful in it. The reason was given that " it was of questionable expediency, even dangerous, for a Catholic to take part in such associations, because in spite of the strongest faith he might easily be induced to make the most serious concessions."

What the state as such had to expect from a realisation of Manning's ideas is made clear by one of his latest writings on *The Catholic Church and Modern Society*. In the final conclusions which he draws in the fourth section we read this sentence:

The Catholic Church can only to a limited degree maintain political relations with those European states that have separated themselves from the unity of the faith. In them we find either regalism introduced, as in England, Denmark, and Sweden, or cæsarism, as in Prussia. Inasmuch as these states have departed from the canon law of Catholic Christendom, they have rendered cordial co-operation impossible.

What the " canon law of Catholic Christendom," in other

words, the papal system as founded upon the pseudo-Isidorian decretals, demands, has been made sufficiently evident since the Vatican decrees. The departure of these states from this " canon law " consists in the fact that they acknowledge, not only the " rights " of the Propaganda, but also the rights of other beliefs. As long as they are unwilling to renounce this fundamental error and to place the temporal power at the disposal of the " unity of the faith " for the extirpation of heretics, they have " rendered cordial co-operation with the Catholic Church impossible."

But it is time to turn from Manning himself to those who followed his example. For with all the difference between the personalities of Newman and Manning, the conversion of both had the same result, in so far as it became the signal for a number of those who were of the same mind. In the one year 1851, in which Manning's defection took place, we count besides those already named twenty-two high ecclesiastics who took the same step. Nor did the movement come to a standstill in the following years, although it gradually somewhat abated. But we find in the number of later theological converts no eminent qualities or performances, excepting titles, connections, and property.

Only one name, and that the name of a man who was a leader in the beginning of the Tractarian movement, demands special mention in connection with Manning. It is William Palmer, the same who, as early as 1839, in his treatise upon *The Church of Christ from the Anglo-Catholic Point of View*, had shown evident tendencies towards Rome, and who in 1842 in his *Letter to a Protestant Catholic* hurled loud anathemas against Protestantism.

Nevertheless, Palmer did not immediately follow either Newman or Manning. On the contrary, we see him in

1853 entering into negotiations with the Russian synod concerning an alliance with the Church of England — negotiations which, like all others, failed on account of the *Filioque*. After his return, Palmer called down upon himself episcopal censure, because he had acted without the authority of the episcopate. His action, from the standpoint of the Episcopal Church, was as revolutionary as Manning's appeal to the clergy had been. Nevertheless, he made a similar attempt with the Scottish bishops, anticipating, in view of the Tory origin of their Church, a more favourable reception of his plans than he had found in England. Not till after this step had proved futile did he journey to Rome, in 1855. The exercises of St. Ignatius finally overcame his scruples against open conversion. He remained in Rome and wrote a pamphlet in which he turned history into romance by telling us what is not found in the catacombs, but what in the interests of the Papacy ought to be found there.

With Manning and Palmer there passed into the Roman Church the last leaders of the old Tractarian movement who left the Church of England. For not only did the closer circle around Pusey not follow them; Keble also, who in the beginning of the movement played a conspicuous part, afterwards turned back. In the subsequent development of the Church of England, Puseyism was succeeded by so-called Ritualism, whose object was to romanise the worship of the Church. The several usages which the ritualists gradually introduced into the service, vestments and candles, elevation of the host and incense, and many others, appear to be so trivial and childish that it is difficult to understand how serious men could busy themselves with such things. Nevertheless, even to a man like Hopkins, Ritualism stands for a genuine ecclesiastical ideal, and the tendency concealed at its first appearance a far greater danger than that of the old Tractarians. The dogmatic niceties of

Puseyism had little interest for the religious laity. Ritualism, on the other hand, was bound to exert a strong influence in accustoming the laity to Roman usages.

This enables us to understand the attention which the new movement attracted, and the many controversies occasioned by the youthful zealots who were its noisiest agitators. For it is a fact that British Church-history of the last twenty-five years is largely made up of renewed aggressions on the part of the ritualists and legal actions instituted against them (Bennett, Cheyne, Mackonochie, etc.). It was a natural consequence that of the accused and condemned ritualists a considerable number in the end found their way to Rome. We have, however—with the exception of the literary stragglers already mentioned — not been able to find any persons of eminence among the converted ritualists.

The English daily papers every year print the names of new converts, and the display made with these lists rather increases than diminishes. And yet there is the greatest conceivable contrast between this display and the reality. How different is the picture which Newman draws in his *History of my Religious Opinions*, a book which is considered by Roman Catholic authorities to mark the height of his fame and public influence and to represent the most considerable literary triumph which Catholicism has obtained in England, but which, on the other hand, called down upon the most eminent of all converts the irreconcilable hatred of Pius IX., and from whose publication (together with Pusey's *Eirenicon*) we date the first ebbing of the tide in the stream of converts. Why does Newman speak so emphatically of the " little band " ? Why does he make the remarkable declaration: " So long as we Catholics in England are so weak, the Church of England represents us " ? The effect of the secessions to the Church of Rome was not what was expected. In fact, ever since the Vatican Council the

Anglo-Catholic party has, more than all others, become conscious of the utter antagonism of Catholicism and papalism: a fact which forebodes for the future a continually increasing reaction.

Great parade has been made by the representatives of the Papacy with the names of converts of high position. But, although we do not deny the learning and the logic of the converted theologians, we have no such respect for those bearers of illustrious names who have figured so prominently in the lists of converts. Who, that has followed with interest the course of public affairs in the ten years after 1870, does not remember how in the most childish demonstrations against Bismarck's policy the names of Earl Denbigh, Earl Gainsborough, Sir George Bowyer, and many more were paraded before the public ? These gentlemen were made out to be the born representatives of the English Catholics. Most of them were in reality the mere irresponsible tools of adroit proselytisers.

And what shall we say of the ladies who belong to the same category, — the many duchesses, marchionesses, countesses, and baronesses ? Revelations, like those made by Earl Nelson concerning the unworthy means by which his son, still under age, was converted behind his father's back, are repeated with almost all these young converts. Indeed, the reading of the " conversions " too often creates the impression that these people were simple idiots. The authors of the lists of converts seem to have understood the principle that in matters of religion men are not to be counted but weighed, in the sense that not their persons but their money-bags were to be weighed. The great sums which the converts in different lands have placed in the hands of the papal party, rival the treasures of the greatest magnates of the exchange. But for this very reason the great majority of the cases which come under the head of conversions among the nobility afford neither a religious nor a theological, but only an exchange interest.

Lord Fielding, afterwards Earl Denbigh, was won over by Bishop Gillis. In the same year Sir George Bowyer seceded to Rome. His chief claim to fame lies in the introduction of the order of the Knights of St. John into England. Since then this order, together with that of the Holy Sepulchre, the papal order of the Golden Spur, and the Roman title of count, has played a similar part in the lists of noble converts as the dignities of papal house-prelates, prothonotaries, cardinals, and the like have played with converted clerics.

The number of gentlemen and ladies who followed at this time is legion. Among them are: Sir John Simeon, member of Parliament for the Isle of Wight; Sir James Hope Scott, by his first wife (a granddaughter of Walter Scott) owner of Abbotsford; Robert Biddulph Philipps, who spent large sums in restoring a ruined church on his estate and gave his library to a monastery; and the poet, Aubrey de Vere. In the one year, 1851, that of Manning's secession, sixteen other illustrious families are counted. It is a fact which hardly requires an explanation that after the " return " to Rome had become the fashion the number of those who took part in the movement steadily increased, and also that the religious motives which operated here and there in the beginning were more and more lost sight of. And as was the case with the large majority of the converts from the German aristocracy, so with their English associates we meet often with the most pronounced political reactionary tendencies.

Among the nobility, the conversions of the marquis of Bute and of the marquis of Ripon made the greatest sensation. The latter became afterwards, under Gladstone, viceroy of India. Of the female sex we find a still larger number, among whom are the duchesses of

Hamilton, Leeds, and Buccleugh, and Lady Herbert of Lea, who defended her secession in an open letter to her brother, and who wrote *Impressions of Spain*, which it is interesting to compare with the reality as it was revealed two years later at the expulsion of Queen Isabella. With the converts of this period we must also mention Miss Adelaide Procter, the poetess; and whoever cares to do so, may refer to the lists for a host of other names.

None of the conquests of the Papacy can, in outward splendour, be compared with the English conversions. We will therefore briefly sum up the statistics. In the year 1852 there had seceded 92 members of the university of Oxford, 43 members of the university of Cambridge; among the former 63, among the latter 19, divines. Ten years later, there were put down 867 proselytes of note, among them 243 former Anglican clergymen. In the year 1879, the *Whitehall Review* published a list of 41 pages, in which were 350 clergymen. From this list we extract this further information, that the number contained 1 field marshal, 7 generals, 4 admirals, 23 colonels and majors, not to mention the captains and lieutenants. The nobility is represented by 6 duchesses, 2 marquises, and many earls and barons. After these we find members of Parliament, lawyers, artists, etc. The list proves — what indeed we already knew—that the conversions were a fashion which had become prevalent in the upper world. As Cardinal Wiseman said, the whole movement " found most difficult entrance and the most sterile soil in the middle and industrial classes."

But quite aside from the large dimensions of the movement, whoever studies the literature of conversion will observe certain other peculiarities. One is particularly struck by the differences which existed among the converts themselves and between them and born Catholics.

The difference in the treatment given to a man like Newman by Pius IX. and Leo XIII. affords an instructive
insight into the mutually hostile tendencies in the same
Church of Rome, which was so proud of its unity.   The
main argument of the English converts had been that
ecclesiastical unity was to be had only in Rome.   Now
they found oppositions more acute than before.   Even
before the appearance of Newman's autobiography and
the dogma of papal infallibility, the greatest differences
had come to the surface among the converts themselves.
Before the Tractarian movement, in the time preceding
the real era of secession, we have this drastic description
by Oakeley:

In many important questions we found ourselves split into
different parties.   When the various persons, who as the ex-
ponents of Oxford opinions were generally treated almost as
one person, met one another in society, they were so little sure
of unanimity of opinion that the fear of quarrelling was anything but favourable to their mutual intercourse, and prompted
many of their sincerest friends to join societies which confined
enthusiasm within narrower limits, and thereby obviated the
danger of dissension.

Far more significant, however, is Newman's account
of the " old school," to which he belonged, and the
" new school," " which entered into the original movement obliquely from one side, crossed its line of thought,
bent it around and carried it in a parallel line backward."
He complains bitterly that the old friends had forsaken
him: " You throw me, whether I will or not, into the
arms of others "; and that he " could never devote himself to the persons and to the lines of thought, which had
come together in the new school, in the same way as to
the old circle "; although " I felt myself mightily attracted to their main purpose and moved in the same
direction with them."   But that he did this with a divided heart is proved by this frank confession:

So it happened that, when the new school had come to maturity and had begun to quarrel with the old, I did not have the heart and much less the power to refuse them; I placed myself on their side; at a time when I craved peace and rest I felt obliged to raise my voice, and so I incurred the reproach of weakness from some, while the great mass accused me of concealment of purpose, of false play and of equivocation.

Even those historians on the Roman side, whose object it was to make the new converts appear as a compact body, are not able to deny the manifest differences among them, and the German historian Rosenthal says of Ward: " He represents in English theology most purely, but with his own originality, the views of the Roman school and of the later scholasticism, while he has a certain antipathy towards that school of older theologians to which Newman is drawn." And another German, Alzog, makes this significant remark: " Cardinal Wiseman was very glad when the *Home and Foreign Review*, edited by Lord Acton, was started in opposition to the *Dublin Review*, whose tendency, under the editorship of the convert Ward, was altogether too extreme." This is the same Lord Acton who at the time of the Vatican Council went hand in hand with Döllinger; and his action proves unmistakably the existence of irreconcilable differences in the Church of Rome in England.

Wiseman, being a born Catholic, was able to hold the warring factions together. But when Pius IX., in the face of the opposition of chapter and bishops, appointed to the primacy the most zealous and the most hierarchical of all the converts, there was an end of peace. Manning belonged to the inner circle of the initiated in the management of the Vatican Council. At this same Vatican Council Bishop Clifford, recalling the sworn declaration of the Irish bishops at the time of Emancipation,[1] made the following statement:

[1] See page 76.

No one will convince the Protestants that the Catholics have not acted contrary to honour and good faith, when, for the securing of certain rights they publicly professed that the doctrine of papal infallibility was not a part of the Catholic faith, and then, when they had obtained the fulfilment of their desire, immediately receded from this public profession and affirmed the contrary.

Lord Acton and Bishop Clifford were no converts, but representatives of old Catholic family traditions. It was in the nature of things that, if the differences among the converts were so acute, the contrast between them and born Catholics should appear far more decided. And the biographies of the converts themselves repeatedly point out the many differences between the tendencies of born Catholics and those of the neophytes. In one of the earliest French works upon *The Religious Movement in England*, by Gondon (1847), the former are contrasted with the latter and reproached with " reserve and timidity." The same charge is made by the German author already quoted, who says that

the older Catholics avoided everything that could infringe upon the customs of their Protestant fellow-citizens, they observed Sunday with the same pedantry as the Protestants, their clergy wore no costume different from that of other classes, the rosary was rarely to be found in private houses and families, etc.

It is interesting to note the attitude assumed, even among the first converts, in the reviews and periodicals which they set on foot, towards the older Catholic generation. We take as an illustration the *Tablet*, founded by Frederick Lucas, in 1840. This is what Lucas' biographer says of the opposition which this organ called forth among the Roman Catholics:

With only one object in view, the furtherance of the in-

terests of his Church, including the most complete conservation
of the civil rights of its members, he spoke the language of a
man who was pursuing a purpose with entire and perfect sin-
cerity, and he had no patience for what seemed to him weak
and hesitating politics.   But years of oppression and persecution had not been without effect upon English Catholics, and
had left behind no little timidity and caution, nor were there
wanting other motives to moderate the fervor of their zeal.
Many of them, who had fought manfully for political equality,
considered themselves, after the passage of the emancipation
bill, bound by honour and gratitude not to be unreasonable
in urging further concessions on the part of their Protestant
friends and helpers.   Others, although sincerely devoted to
their religion, did not consider it necessary or advantageous
to make it prominent upon ordinary occasions or to connect
it with every object of public interest.   Others again were
under the influence of strictly aristocratic feelings, and shrank
from everything that looked like popular agitation, even in
favour of their own religious opinions.   To all of these Lucas
now addressed himself in a tone of indignant censure as to
those who had culpably neglected the talent committed to
them, and it is not surprising that they resented his language.
It must have been particularly offensive to those hereditary
leaders of the party, whose Catholicism had descended to them
with the estates and the honours of their ancestors, who in
dark and stormy times had held fast to their faith, who could
point to the names of confessors and martyrs in their family
histories, and whose old castles still contained the hiding-
places which had concealed the persecuted priesthood, as well
as the secret chapels in which in dangerous times mass had
been said.   For such it was really hard to be called to account
and to be accused of lukewarmness, not by a dignitary of the
Church or other spiritual authority, but by an obscure layman,
a convert of yesterday.

With the nomination of Manning to the primacy of
the Roman English Church, the leadership went entirely
into the hands of converts of his school, and the older

20

Catholic element has been pushed to the rear. Roman Catholic journals and periodicals have been almost without exception founded or at least edited by converts. This is true, among others, of the *Dublin Review* (Ward's organ), of *Atlantis* (Newman's creation), of the *Rambler* (edited in succession by the converts Capes, Northcote, Simpson, Newman, and Wetherell), of the *Home and Foreign Review* (conducted also by Wetherell), of the *Tablet* (founded by Lucas, afterwards in the hands of Ryley), of the *Weekly Register* (owned by the converted members of the Wilberforce family), and of the *Month* (edited by Coleridge).   The *Clifton Tracts*, the model of a German pamphlet-series, were founded by Northcote and Thompson.

In the field of general literature also, especially wherever there was a possibility of controversy, born Catholics are far behind the converts.   But we meet their influence especially in the daily press : not only are there numerous avowedly clerical sheets, but both in liberal and in conservative organs a large number of converts is employed.[1] Cardinal Manning is said to have founded a sort of seminary for the training of young men for this kind of press activity.

The numerous monasteries and congregations, founded and managed by converts, are anything but asylums for those who are weary of this world.   They are rather centres of the most energetic agitation.   To the congregations of Oratorians, founded by Newman and Faber, have been added the Oblates of St. Charles at Bayswater and an increasing number of institutions of Jesuits, Redemptorists, and Brothers of Charity, which are mostly filled with converts ; to say nothing of female orders and congregations.

[1] In one of our American daily papers the feeling in England against Germany was recently ascribed to the influence of Roman Catholic reporters for the English daily press.

The consequence of all this is that the born Catholics of Great Britain are now almost a neglected quantity. Quite different, however, is the final result of the whole movement as it affects the Church of England. For with the secession of those who corrupted the Catholic ideal, always strenuously insisted upon by the Church of England, and gave it a papal meaning, this ideal became purified from such excrescences. And as the Church of England became increasingly conscious of its historical position as the representative of the truly Catholic ideal, it became better able to assert this position outside of its own limits. From this point of view we learn to appreciate the renewed influence which the Church of England and the German Church of the Reformation have mutually exerted upon each other. The latter gave to the former its high intellectual aspiration, which seeks truth for truth's sake; and Germany learned from England to understand the necessity of the ecclesiastical factor for the popular welfare, which had been too much ignored by the philosophy of the closet.

From this point of view we also learn to comprehend the significance for the future of the old-Catholic sacrifice for conscience' sake. At a time when politicians and scholars in Germany had nothing but ridicule for a religious movement that did not materialise in numbers, the English Church did not refuse the brotherly hand. And their participation in the union conferences at Bonn, under Döllinger in 1875, proved most strikingly that the victory over an attack which shook its very foundations has taught this Church to grasp with far greater earnestness its world-historical mission for the future.

As in its attitude towards other countries, so in England itself the Church of England has become again the guardian of true Catholicism. Of its activity in the life of the people, of its culture of all intellectual interests, ecclesiastical annals may tell little.   It is with a church, which quietly and peaceably does its duty in the service of the kingdom of God, as it is in a happy marriage : not much is said of it.   As, on the other hand, the disputes of priests and doctors of the law have at all times been in evidence, so it has been with the papal party in England.   But genuine Anglo-Catholicism, fructified by the philanthropy of the low Church and by the scientific research of the broad Church, goes in security its earnest, quiet way, in closest alliance with the national culture. If we compare the state Church and the free churches of Great Britain, we shall find in the former a much wider and freer horizon.   The Scotch Free Church would not tolerate Robertson Smith; the English state Church has learned to appreciate more and more highly its Robertson and Kingsley, its Hare and Arnold, and no church of the present time has had a nobler representative of all the ideals of true church life than Dean Stanley of Westminster.

But while thus the association with the national culture has been preserved, the sundering of the bonds which the external connection with the state has imposed upon the established Church, which not without reason had challenged the opposition of the Tractarians, is now only a question of time.   The re-established convocations have already largely taken the place of Parliament. The disestablishment of the Church of Ireland has been accomplished.   The same is imminent even now with the Scotch Church, and the entire inner development of the Church of England propels it in the same direction.   A number of its ancient privileges have already been forfeited.   Both the Ecclesiastical Titles Bill and the University Tests Bill were repealed in the year 1871.   By the repeal of the latter, admittance for adherents of every form of belief was opened to all degrees in the universities of Oxford and Cambridge.   But in proportion as the special privileges, which were inconsistent with the spirit of the times, were abandoned, the moral power of the old Church of England has increased.

The process of purification, effected by the secessions, has thus brought a blessing to the Church of England. Since the Vatican Council the movement towards the Church of Rome has not only come to a standstill, but a reaction has set in. No theologian of the Protestant world is more highly esteemed in England than Döllinger. The " Catholic movement " has largely leaned upon him for support. He sees to-day (1889) in the English Church one of the firmest bulwarks of Christendom, for the same reason which made him recognise in the dogma of infallibility the seed of an incurable disease for the newly established German empire. And if we would appreciate the moral position which Döllinger has occupied since 1870 we must go, not to Germany, but to England and America.

Nor has the opposition between Catholicism and Vaticanism ever been more strikingly pictured than has been done by Gladstone; no less than one hundred and fifty thousand copies of his pamphlet on *The Vatican Decrees in their Bearing on Civil Allegiance* were in a few weeks spread over England alone. Littledale's writing also, *Plain Reasons against Joining the Church of Rome*, passed in a few years through more than thirty editions. And is it not for the future of Germany and of Switzerland a sign of the times, that the Catholic historian Dr. Lossen was the translator of Gladstone, and the Catholic Church historian, Dr. Woker, the German editor of Littledale, while the Catholic bishop Herzog furnished an introduction ?

Let us return once more to the judgment expressed by Pusey's American biographer Hopkins upon the results of the Catholic movement. One of the first effects in his judgment is the restoration of the ecclesiastical convocations, which had slept for a century and a half, as the true representatives of the Church in place of the temporal Parliament.   In close connection herewith is the strengthening of the Anglo-Catholic conception of the Church in its contrast to that of the papal system. The Anglo-Catholic Church itself in both hemispheres has grown so rapidly that, instead of the sixty-seven bishops at the beginning of the Tractarian movement, it to-day counts two hundred and fifteen.   Far greater, however, is the growth of the Church's influence upon the life of the people.   The restoration of voluntary confession is the result of the recognition of the pedagogical functions belonging to the cure of souls.   The so-called new orders, especially the sisters' homes, are asylums intended to meet and ameliorate social needs.   The Catholic name simply stands for what in Germany is comprehended under the name of " home missions ": hospitals, schools, Magdalen-asylums, orphanages, convalescent homes, trade-schools and sewing-schools, all the various efforts to enhance the ability for self-support among the female sex, and many other philanthropic agencies.

That within the Church of England, with all the appreciation given to its Catholic character, the spirit of the Reformation has more and more triumphed, is proved, among other things, by the pan-Anglican councils, held since 1867, with their anti-papal decrees.   It was by the suggestion of Dr. Pusey that the pan-Anglican conferences took their stand, not upon the first four general councils, but upon the first six, and by that act included in their doctrinal basis the condemnation of an heretical pope by an ecumenical council.   To German Protestants a good deal will still appear strange in these formularies.   But German Church history knows of similar attempts at union upon the basis of the undivided Church of the first six centuries.   The disputes oc-

casioned by the Syncretism of Calixtus, early in the
seventeenth century, drove many converts into the
Church of Rome; but Syncretism became in the end
the forerunner of Pietism and of the general reinvigor-
ation of Reformation ideas. Such appears to be to-day
the prospect in the Church of England.

CHAPTER XVIII

THE NEW PAPAL HIERARCHY IN ENGLAND AND THE FRUITS OF THE PAPAL SYSTEM IN IRELAND

WE have already mentioned the "restoration of the Episcopal hierarchy" as coincident with the climax of English conversions; this was the requital on the part of the pope for Catholic emancipation. The consideration of this subject was interrupted in order to trace the Anglo-Catholic movement through its various stages to the final outcome. By so doing we have now been placed in a position to follow the interferences of the Vatican in the affairs of England, not as an isolated phenomenon, but in connection with what went before and with what came after.

Our survey of the progress of papalism couples the history of Ireland with that of England. For we must keep in view the long series of Irish conspiracies, charitably ignored by the Papacy, in order to comprehend the reactionary step which England took when she sent Errington on a mission to Rome (1880). From the establishment of the papal hierarchy by Pius IX. to the secret mission of Errington to Leo XIII. the papal policy runs a straight course.

It was in the middle of October, 1850, when England was surprised by the announcement that the pope in secret consistory had ordered the "restoration" of the "Catholic" hierarchy in England, had nominated the apostolic vicar Wiseman as archbishop of Westminster, and had divided all England into twelve bishoprics under him. By this " restoration " the Church of England, as by law established, was simply treated as non-existent and given to understand that she, no more than any other schismatic church, could claim any rights over against the authority of the Propaganda.

In view of the care with which the Anglo-Catholic Church had always guarded the apostolical succession of her bishops, there was in this action a much larger degree of assumption than if such pretensions had been made towards bishopless Protestants. The title " archbishop of Westminster " was particularly outrageous, because by it the royal court and the Parliament were submitted to the jurisdiction of the Roman prelate, who at the same time received the title of cardinal.

The consequences of this proceeding were just what had been counted upon in Rome: intense momentary excitement without any real fruits. Every fibre of the national feeling vibrated with excitement. It seemed almost as if all the gains that the papal Church had hitherto made had become jeopardised.

Everywhere there were meetings, loyal addresses were adopted, and impetuous demands made for interference by the government. All non-Tractarian pulpits thundered against the Roman antichrist and the false prophets in their own Church. These sermons were loudly re-echoed by the press. It was a harmless but significant act of vengeance, that on the commemoration day of the gunpowder plot Guy Fawkes processions on a magnificent scale and attended by a general concourse of people paraded the capital. At the conclusion of the celebration the pope, Wiseman, and Pusey were burned in effigy.

Even the ministry was drawn into the popular movement. By a curious coincidence Lord John Russell, the

principal author of Catholic emancipation, stood at its
head. The action of the pope was a bitter requital for
the trustfulness of those English statesmen who had
omitted to take the necessary precautionary measures
against papal aggression when emancipation was carried
through in obedience to the just demands which the
spirit of the times made. They had meekly accepted
the policy of the Curia with regard to Ireland. And
after the Curia had been suffered to set up in Ireland,
against the bishops of the state Church, its opposition
bishops with the same titles, a like measure could not be
prevented in England. What did it avail that the prime
minister wrote a letter to the bishop of Durham (November 4, 1850), in which he spoke with indignation of
papal pretensions and promised decided counter-meas-
ures ? The bishops of the state Church might unanimously re-echo his sentiments, — that did not put their
rivals out of the way. What real advantage was gained
by the ecclesiastical titles bill, which was introduced by
the ministry in February, 1851, and accepted by Parliament ? It forbade the Roman bishops the public use of
their titles, assumed from the cities of England, and it
prohibited the wearing in public of their costumes by
clergy and monks. But even this prohibition remained
a dead letter. And what finally came of the state over-
sight of the monasteries which was now made law ? It
remained disregarded, like the numerous older laws that
have never been repealed, which have as much validity as
ever, but " exist only not to be applied." Too frequently has, since then, this pernicious form of speech
been used in Parliament, when motions have been made
for the enforcement of the prohibition of the Jesuits and
for the investigation of abuses in the monasteries. These
motions have always been rejected with derision.

While thus legal measures proved as fruitless as the
popular excitement that preceded them, the papal cohort

was all the more energetic in carrying out the programme which had long been secretly prepared.   The policy of the Curia officially permits dissimulation *temporis ratione habita*, until the favourable moment has arrived for the practical enforcement of theoretical claims.   So long as the " anti-papal aggression " lasted, the act by which the rights of the English bishops had been usurped was defended as a self-understood consequence of freedom of worship.   But this tone was afterwards changed, and the address to the English people, which Wiseman issued at the time, is to-day as antiquated as the declaration of the Irish bishops in 1826 to the effect that the Church of Rome does not teach the infallibility of the pope. Indeed, they understood admirably at the time how to represent themselves as the lamb whose water the wolf had muddied.   Even the most zealous of the converts, such as Spencer, Northcote, and Lady Fullerton, in their popular writings, assumed the air of innocent lambs.

Wiseman's successor, immediately after his nomination, spoke in a very different tone.   We have already noticed his prognostication of the future of the state (page 295).   The assurances which it was customary to give before the Vatican Council are to-day no longer considered necessary.   The Roman Church in England now counts its resources with pride.   The strata of the populace which she controls are as good as hermetically sealed from the rest of the population.   They have their own historians: Cobbett, Lingard, MacCarthy; their own novels, their own collections of poems and poets, their own newspapers and periodicals, their own tract-societies. A number of orders of monks and nuns have spread themselves over all parts of the country.   The educational institutions of St. Edmond and St. Cuthbert have been founded upon the model of those of St. Omer and Douai in France.   The privileges of a university have been extended to Stonyhurst.   Since 1874 there has been

established a special " free " university in Kensington.
The number of Roman Catholic pupils was calculated
some years ago to be 140,000, distributed among 1400
private schools, which are under strict confessional management. The teachers are trained in their own seminaries. Every year new minsters and cathedrals are built.
In the one year 1878 there were erected in the single
diocese of Liverpool nine magnificent churches; nine
more were in the process of construction. The Jesuits,
driven out of Germany, had the choice of a number of
asylums and endowments, which were simultaneously
offered them. Of the other orders also, which left Germany on account of the *Kulturkampf*, Great Britain
received a fair share.

The complete change of conditions, however, since the
" restoration of the Catholic episcopate " in England
was nowhere more strikingly shown than by what happened when Leo XIII.— in his first consistory, March,
1878 — applied the same measure to Scotland. It was
accepted quite as a matter of course; it received hardly
any attention. The Scotch Act of Union of 1707 had
expressly provided for the unconditional perpetual exclusion of every kind of Roman Catholic hierarchy from
Scotland. Now the peace-pope set up with one stroke
two archbishoprics and three bishoprics. And the *fait
accompli* was calmly accepted. The Propaganda had
been so successful among this most Calvinistic of all
people that the German historian Alzog could boastfully
say: " Open conferences were held in the Scotch cities,
and the misrepresentations of the Protestant ministers
had only the effect of making non-Catholics desirous of
learning the principles of the reviled faith." Scotland
has its papal periodicals and newspapers of all kinds as
well as its higher and lower schools.

The history of the English Parliament in our own time
brings before our eyes the increasing influence of the

Ultramontane party upon the parliamentary proceedings. The British party of the Centre, like the German, has understood admirably how to maintain the balance of power and to make Whigs and Tories outdo each other in the price paid for their votes. Even the social movement is taken advantage of, as is the case in Germany. The writings of Lord Montague rival those of Bishop Ketteler of Mayence in all the arts of the social demagogue. MacCarthy's *History of England* makes very clear the kind of future " loyal Catholic subjects " have planned for the British empire, and it was hardly necessary to emphasise the teaching by the dynamite propaganda of O'Donovan Rossa.

These last names have carried us over from England to the smaller neighbouring island. We shall now have to examine more closely into the consequences of Catholic emancipation as it affected Ireland. The result of the Irish insurrections of the last years of the eighteenth century was to intensify the opposition between the two hostile races as well as the bitter feeling against the English Church on the part of the Roman clergy, who were especially involved in the insurrections. This state of things in Ireland co-operated to bring about Catholic emancipation. It was seen to be a social necessity. And the further history of Ireland is in fact nothing but a series of efforts to heal abuses transmitted from former generations.

It is, however, a characteristic of Irish history, and one which has to be realised in order to understand the course of affairs, that every concession has been answered by a new rebellion. And there has been no rebellion where the Church did not have her hand in the game. The Irish clergy is more uneducated than in other countries ruled by the Vatican, but for that very reason is closely bound up with the people. A detailed description recently given of land and people (by E. Goegg)

characterises the Irishman as " strictly orthodox," and
adds: " Everywhere one meets at the crossroads wooden
and stone crucifixes, and even in the poorest parts are
many and imposing churches.   Priests there are in superabundance.   Every Catholic Irishman humbly uncovers
his head to every priest.   The women salute by kneeling."

The effect of the Emancipation Act (1829) was only to
increase the excitement in Ireland.   It seemed as if the
Irish clergy were bent upon justifying the dark forebodings of the opponents of the bill: a measure which justice
demanded, but which overthrew the legal basis of the
state as it had hitherto existed.   Very soon after, in
1831, a large number of agrarian murders were committed.   The new demand, which these murders were
intended to emphasise, and which was raised especially
by the Roman priests, was the abolition of tithes paid to
the Church of England.   The Russell ministry at once
obediently made the motion in Parliament to remit the
tithes to leaseholders and to substitute for them an
annual ground-rent to be paid by the owners.   This
motion passed the House of Commons, but was repeatedly rejected by the Upper House.   The parliamentary conflict lasted from 1833 to 1838, until at last
the Upper House yielded, as it had done in the question
of emancipation.   Even that part of the tithes which
was to remain was allotted to a fund for popular education among Catholics.

At the same time the government applied itself seriously
to remedy the bad condition of the public health.   Father
Mathew's famous temperance movement, which began
in 1840, received extensive aid from England.   But
hardly had it begun when O'Connell's Repeal agitation,
the demand for complete separation of Ireland from
England, diverted popular attention from the temperance movement.   His treasonable agitation (represented
by the papal press of all countries as a battle for the

faith) remained long unpunished. At last he was condemned by a Dublin jury in 1844. But the influence
he exerted from prison was all the greater. And his
death in 1847 gave to the Irish people another national
saint.

The agitation begun by O'Connell was carried on without intermission through the next ten or twenty years.
And, all through it, sectarian fanaticism made itself
prominent. The cynical brutality which marked the
proceedings even of the highest prelates appears in other
countries almost incredible. When on the 5th of November, 1855, the Redemptorists made a bonfire of Bibles,
the archbishop primate praised the deed as a laudable
imitation of the occurrence at Ephesus (Acts xix., 19).

The extensive emigration of the Irish to America,
which, it was thought, might have proved a remedy for
the overpopulation of the island and the evils consequent
upon it, only made the condition of affairs worse. From
his new home across the sea, where the Irish voters,
under the discipline of the clergy, have exerted an immense influence, where the government of the state of
New York has come entirely under the control of the
Jesuits, young Erin has not only sought in every way to
disturb the friendly relations between the Union and the
British empire, but has taken an active part in every
insurrection in the old country.

After an endless series of murders and street-fights (as,
e. g., in 1865, in Belfast), the conspiracy of the Fenians
began in 1866 to spread nearly over the whole island.
The higher clergy now changed their attitude and placed
themselves officially on the side of the state. What the
lower clergy did in the confessional is beyond the knowledge of the historian. As a reward for the loyalty of the
prelates the general oath of allegiance was modified, and
by this modification all restrictions upon the mental reservation characteristic of the papal system were removed

(1866). In the following year, in a Catholic convention at Aix-la-Chapelle, '' the present aspect of the movement towards Catholicism in the English high Church " was represented as more hopeful than ever.

We find in the seventies, even more than during the preceding years, the same alternation of assassinations and concessions. The Clerkenwell explosion [1] and the disestablishment of the Irish Church (January 1, 1871), the establishment of the Land-League (1879) and the reduction, by law, of rents, the so-called Kilmainham treaty with Parnell and the atrocious murder of the viceroy Cavendish and secretary Burke (1882)—these stand in the closest mutual relations the one to the other. The detailed account of the renewed agitations and assassinations which followed upon each new concession is a part of political history. It is, however, a matter of interest to the ecclesiastical historian that the offer of £20,000 as a reward for the discovery of the murderer of the viceroy proved futile, but that the crown-witness Carey was immediately found after the higher clergy had intimated that it was permissible to '' open the mouth " of those murderers who desired to add immunity from the state to the absolution of the Church.

That in the Irish revolutionary movement there exist rivalries among the various parties is beyond a doubt. But, precisely as in the case of Russian nihilism, the milder factions serve only to cover the backs of the '' men of action." The murder of the viceroy has since been outdone by the dynamite explosions in the London

---

[1] December, 1867. The explosion at the Clerkenwell House of Detention was intended to release the Fenians, Burke and Casey. '' Six persons were killed outright; six more died from its effects, according to the coroner's inquests; five, in addition, owed their deaths indirectly to this means; one young woman is in a mad-house; forty mothers were prematurely confined, and twenty of the babes died from the effects of the explosion on the women; others of the children are dwarfed and unhealthy," etc.—*The Times*, April 29, 1868.

ministry and in the office of *The Times*. These deeds were vociferously applauded by the Irish in America through their spokesmen, and greater acts of heroism were promised; while at the same time Egan, the treasurer of the Land-League, found it prudent to withdraw to America. It shows how close was the connection between Ireland and America, in that both the Land-League and the "Invincibles," who butchered the unarmed viceroy, found their model in the Irish-American secret society of the Molly Maguires, whose statutes were not long after this revealed by detective MacParlan, who had become a member of the society.

The public programme of the Molly Maguires was "Christian Charity and Philanthropy." The conditions of admission were Irish descent and the Catholic religion. The supreme control of this association, whose proper field of activity was America, was in the hands of the *Board of Erin* in Ireland. This board gave the watchwords, the grips, and the toasts. The secret language of the society, taken mostly from commercial life, is remarkably similar to that of the Frisian Jesuits, as it was made known in the year 1616 through the confiscated papers of Father Warighem, and published in the official pamphlet (now rare), *Der Jezuyten Negotiatie ofte Koophandel*. Most of the members of the Molly Maguires are not informed of the plans of their superiors, as is the case with the lower degrees in the Jesuit order. But while they suppose themselves to belong to a philanthropic association, a secret lodge is in the background.

Like the "German Catholic associations," they endeavoured to influence public elections and to bring both political positions of honour and civil administrative offices into the hands of "believers." That in so doing they did not stop short of violence, murder, and arson is proved by the reign of terror which for a number of years existed under the secret rule of this association in several

21

states of the Union. In the judicial investigation which was brought about through the devotion of MacParlan, there were revealed not only the watchwords, which were mostly of a political or sectarian character, but also the methods by which the murderers and incendiaries had hitherto escaped the arm of the law. This was done by choosing, for the execution of the crimes, men who were unknown in the respective neighbourhoods. Other conspirators then swore to an alibi. The ample means of the secret association permitted the engagement of the best legal talent in behalf of the accused. And absolution for sins committed was assured where the "Catholic religion" was a condition of admission to the society.

These methods passed from the Molly Maguires in America to the "Invincibles" in England. The English prime minister was called upon to face the situation brought about by the activity of the latter. And, just as fear of the nihilists brought about the "peace" between Russia and Leo XIII., so Gladstone now found that the Curia alone was able to discipline its faithful sheep. This is the background of the much-talked-of Errington mission, with which the English ministry, in the spring of 1883, played such a mysterious game.

The member of Parliament for Longford, "a Catholic faithful to his convictions," was not officially accredited to the pope, either by the queen or by the ministry. The official disclaimers are right in denying this. But this did not prevent Errington from serving as "love-messenger" between the ministry and the Curia as early as the winter of 1880 to 1881. The result of this mission was a papal brief to the twenty-six Irish bishops, forbidding their participation in agitations which, according to all appearances, led to murder and arson and other inhuman atrocities. The bishops remonstrated, and there followed another brief, in which the prohibition of participation in the secret meetings of the Land-Leaguers was rescinded. Thereupon Errington again went to Rome ; and Leo XIII. wrote another letter to the bishops, in which he sought to unite the two factions among the latter (the one led by Archbishop MacCabe of Dublin, the other by Archbishop Croke of Cashel). At about this time the notorious Carey became crown witness and began his revelations of the secrets of the gangs of assassins. Carey (as was officially stated at the trial) had belonged to a " Catholic society " whose members took communion once a month.

Errington brought back to England, in November, 1882, an autograph letter to the queen, in which the pope expressed his gratitude for the interest manifested by their sovereign in the Catholics of the British empire. The Vatican press at the same time expressed the hope that, after Germany had set the example and Russia had followed, England herself would soon send an official representative to the Vatican. This, however, excited the violent opposition of the English press, which recalled the papal encyclical of December 28, 1878, against the Reformation. Errington meanwhile remained the semi-official representative of the ministry and secret delegate of the state. A Catholic scholar describes the cause of his mission as follows: " Since infallibility in moral affairs (to which surely belong murder and arson) and the unconditional supremacy of the pope in all dioceses is an article of faith for all Roman Catholics, Gladstone wants to draw some profit from it."

Since then the Irish " martyrs " have been placed in a corner by the Curia, just as was once done with the Polish. When Archbishop Croke made a contribution to the Parnell fund, Cardinal Simeoni issued a letter (May 11, 1883), which forbade the agitation for this fund on the part of the clergy. Rome considered itself the more called upon to take this step that Parnell had exchanged courtesies with the infidel French radicals. Croke himself was called to Rome, as was said, *ad audiendum verbum papæ*. But, according to his own statement, he did not by any means fare ill in Rome, and the agitation in behalf of the Parnell fund only increased after the Simeoni letter. In the beginning of July, 1883, the Irish bishops went so far as to issue a joint address to the British government, in which they prescribed further agrarian measures.

How close was the connection between the " shepherds of souls " and the " martyrs " has been more and more strikingly shown by every new trial. Carey was member both of a religious and a revolutionary association. Mullagh's diary began by stating that he received the communion on the first of January, 1882, and immediately afterwards was admitted into the league of conspirators. Whitehead, the manufacturer of dynamite in Birmingham, stood in close relations with several priests. When treasurer Egan fled to escape arrest, he had just before been visited by a priest, in whose clothes he escaped. The mystical Number One (Tynan) proved to be a pupil of a religious order.

In all this there was nothing new: the Ravaillacs and Balthasar Gerards have at all times had numerous predecessors and successors, and Syllabus and Vatican Council have publicly re-inaugurated the Hildebrandian policy. Only one thing was new; and that was, that after all such experiences proud Albion should fly to the pope as the protector against revolution.

The history of the country has sufficiently proved that renewed concessions to the Curia do not further the welfare of the Irish people any more than they do that of any other country. We notice, however, since the beginning of the dynamite era, a gradual revulsion of public opinion in regard to Irish matters. Until that time, the

Irish, like the Poles, were the favourites of that sentimental liberalism which judges after the outward appearance. At present we find that not only have men in
England and Scotland come to the conclusion that affairs
cannot go on in the way they have been going, but in
America also the customary coquetting with the Irish
element has received a serious set-back.

It is even more significant as a sign of the times, that
those organs of the German press which had been used
to look upon Poles and Irishmen as their ideals begin to
subject the Irish conception of liberty and its results to a
searching criticism. This was first done in connection
with Bradlaugh's refusal of the parliamentary oath. The
government, to put a stop to endless troubles, brought
in a bill providing for a liberal parliamentary oath, where-
upon the home-ruler M'Callan made an opposition motion. This called forth from a liberal authority the
following judgment upon the Irish idea of liberty : " The
League, the Fenians, all the numerous open and secret
associations of discontented Irishmen call for freedom.
But the freethinker is to be denied the right in place of
the oath to make a simple affirmation."

This contradiction of principles, as the same author
proceeds to say, is not without reason. For, not only
have the liberty-loving Irish in large numbers borne arms
against the liberty of Italy and Germany ; the spirit of
religious persecution has always dictated their sympathies
and antipathies. " Nationality, self-government, liberty
—all these lofty words form with leaguers, home-rulers,
Fenians, and Invincibles only a covering for dark intrigues, just as was the case with the Swiss Sonderbund."
Hence, in MacCarthy's *History of Our Own Times*, the
malicious attacks upon Garibaldi. Hence the charge
which O'Shea, the negotiator of the Kilmainham treaty,
makes against minister Forster as the friend of Mazzini.
Hence, in the *Freeman's Journal*, the characterisation of

the Italian liberators as a band of intriguers and hirelings, of Victor Emanuel as a puppet of the revolution, and Cavour's and Ricasoli's deaths ascribed to the interposition of God.

It is in view of such facts as these that the question has been asked " whether England has not a mission of civilisation to perform towards Ireland." The success of this mission, we may say, depends in the last instance, upon how far Vaticanism is able to extend its sway over the life of the people in England. It has already reached alarming proportions. For under the regimen of the converts, all the modern Jesuit cults, the fraternities of the scapulary and the rosary, devotions of the Sacred Heart, and Madonna visions have been greatly extended; and the belief in evil spirits is brought forward with an unreservedness which may be fitly characterised as the most significant sign of the times.

CHAPTER XIX

AMERICAN CATHOLICISM AND THE ROMAN CHURCH IN THE NORTH AMERICAN UNION

OUR attention has already been called, in the general survey of ecclesiastical conditions at the time of the Restoration, to the remarkable difference between the state of affairs in Europe and in America. In Europe we find reaction following upon the heels of the Revolution; when we pass over to America we enter the modern world of ideas, the new world which dates from the English double reformation. Upon the virgin soil of the American free states it was possible for modern Protestantism, in the turbulent years of the Revolution, freely to develop the various individualities of its ecclesiastical systems. But here, too—and likewise immediately after the successful issue of the struggle for liberty—the ideal of Catholicism in its anti-papal form, supplementing Protestant individualism, struck its roots deep into the soil. From small beginnings the American Episcopal Church, which was the first to restore this idea to its rights in the Protestant world, has raised itself to a position of moral power, which has enabled it to oppose a true Catholicity to the false Catholicity of the Papacy, and to be the means of a higher unity to the diverging Protestant bodies.

Every ecclesiastical gift and prerogative has its own advantage, but has also its own peculiar danger, and the

Episcopal Church of Great Britain was no exception to
the rule. The high value which this Church laid upon the
apostolical succession (through Rome) of its episcopate
was the most important factor in the recent numerous
secessions to Rome. It called forth sharp criticism even
from so warm an admirer of the Anglican ecclesiastical
system as Bunsen, to whom it represented a distortion of
the true ideal. But of much greater moment is the opposition which it excites among German Protestants
whenever the idea of restoring the episcopal system is renewed. Bunsen himself was made to feel this opposition
in all its force at the institution of the English-Prussian
bishopric of Jerusalem (1841).

The most illustrious representatives of German Protestantism have been and are the most decided opponents of
the episcopal system. And after the moral suicide of the
papal bishops at the Vatican Council only one thing more
was needed to check any desire for the restoration of the
episcopate among German Protestants, and that was the
fact that those nominal Protestants, who were responsible
for the serious defeat of the state in its conflict with the
Roman Curia, should show their liking for an episcopal
hierarchy. But however strongly the peculiar line of development that German Protestantism has taken for
more than three hundred years may emphasise the duty
of preserving historical continuity and of avoiding the
imitation of any foreign fashion, this condition of affairs
need not oblige us to form an unfavourable judgment
upon the episcopal system as such.

No one who has studied the sources of ancient Church
history needs to be told that there could be hardly any
greater contrast than that between what the old-Catholic
conception of the Church as it was held by Ignatius,
Irenæus, and Cyprian, involved touching the equality of
bishops chosen by the congregations, and the universal
episcopate of the pseudo-Isidorean papal system. We

may also assume that all who are familiar with the history of the Reformation agree upon no other point with the same unanimity as upon this, that Luther's break with the episcopate, which Melanchthon had sought by every means to prevent, was the one fatality which befell the young German churches and the principal cause of the ignominious Byzantinism to which they too soon fell a prey.

The latest researches concerning the elector palatine, Frederick the Wise, have pointed out again how great a calamity for the German people, passing through the most violent convulsions of its history, was the premature death of this high-minded prince (1525). As long as his guiding hand restrained the impetuosity of Luther, the break with the elements which were friendly to reform in the German episcopate was avoided. Left to himself and even treated by the princes as a superior authority, Luther's volcanic nature lost the power of self-control and of moderation. From this time on we trace the dependence of princes and statesmen upon the political counsels of the theologians, with their increasingly dangerous direct and indirect consequences, until finally there came the equally ominous recoil to the opposite extreme: disgust among the leading classes with all theology. From this time, on the other hand, began the suppression of episcopal privileges, which till then had theoretically at least been conserved, and at the same time the inauguration of a cæsaro-papism among the petty princes, who indemnified themselves for the loss of political influence by making the Church into a department of police.

A clearer appreciation, therefore, of the injury inflicted upon the German Church by the loss of the episcopate makes us understand much more fully why not only the English, but also the Danish and the Swedish Reformed Churches recognised the preservation of the episcopal

system as the necessary guarantee of the independence
of the Church, and why even the United Brethren and
Methodism returned to it.   But beyond all others it was,
in Europe, the national Church of England whose particular *charisma* seemed to be the union of the ideal-
Catholic and the Protestant principles.   The most striking
proof, however, of what Episcopalianism is capable of
accomplishing is presented, not by monarchical Europe,
but by republican America.

American Episcopalianism is indeed nothing less than
a mere copy of the English type.   It is a significant fact
that before the American revolution the English Episcopal Church in the colonies had no bishops.   It was a
peculiarity, fatal for England herself, of her colonial
policy, that it maintained the ecclesiastical dependence
of Episcopalians, in order thereby to strengthen the
political dependence of the colonies.   The heel of Achilles of Anglicanism, the fact that the Church could be
turned only too easily into a tool of the crown or of a
parliamentary majority, was more painfully felt in the
fresher and freer atmosphere of New England than in
the mother-country.   Nevertheless, after the conclusion
of peace the adherents of the Episcopal Church remained
true to the Church's ideal.   But when they demanded an
independent American bishop, the English bishops refused to consecrate one.   To such an extent had the
Anglicanism of the time lost its consciousness of the
great heritage of the English Reformation in the combination of its Protestant and its Catholic character.
    It is the merit of the little Episcopal Church of Scot-
land to have divested the ideal-Catholic heritage of the
English national Church of its particularistic one-sidedness
and to have made it once more a power for good to the
whole Christian world.   The Scotch Church itself had
only come into existence in the year 1661, under the

influence of the reaction against the division into sects which was prevalent in the Republican era, through the consecration of Scotch bishops by the English; and this Church had, as a true child of the Restoration, long preserved its sympathies for the Stuarts against the Hanoverian dynasty. This very fact, however, effected a greater independence on the part of the Scottish Church than had ever been enjoyed up to that time by the Church of England. And it was a manifestation of this independence when, after American Episcopalians in the year 1784 had elected Samuel Seabury bishop, upon the refusal of the English bishops under the influence of George III., the Scotch Church conferred upon him their consecration.

Thus by its origin the Episcopal Church of America, in equal measure Catholic and Protestant, was led to emphasise the truly universal, all-comprehensive character of Christianity. At the same time the political constitution of the American states has given to the religious interests of the country a much larger degree of independence and freedom, and this has been greatly to the advantage of the Episcopal Church. This made it possible to create a Church constitution which has united the aristocratic form of the bishopric with the democratic congregational principle. The highest legislative authority of the American Episcopal Church (which for its constitution Bunsen chose as the type of his " Church of the future ") consists in the General Convention, which meets every third year. This body, like the English ecclesiastical Parliament, is divided into a House of Bishops and a House of Deputies of the dioceses; but it is not, as were the Anglican convocations for so long a period, a mere empty form; on the contrary, it is full of fresh, energetic life. The American Church has applied its fundamental principles in the manner of choosing bishops, which in this Church cannot take place by the authority of the

crown or of its ministers.   The organised dioceses themselves, in their annual diocesan synods, choose their
bishops; while the General Convention acts for the newly
projected dioceses.   As soon as the latter (the so-called
missionary jurisdictions) are able to support themselves,
they receive the same rights as the older dioceses.

As men who know how to use their liberty, the official
representatives of the Church have themselves restricted
their sphere of liberty, so that in their ecclesiastical
capacity they do not intrude in the agitations of political
parties.   All political parties are represented in the
Church, but the latter serves no party.   So too, the
high, the low, and the broad Church have equal rights
in theology.   But everywhere the same prayer-book is
used.   A liturgy " understanded of the people " has
taken the place of dogmatic formularies.   The old ecclesiastical confessions have retained their canonical and
theoretical validity, but their injurious effect upon the
Church's life has passed away, and there is a happy absence of trials for heresy such as have disgraced the
Church in Germany in our own time.

Even those who are familiar with the very large interests of American Church life in comparison with the
insignificance of the corresponding activity in Germany
will be filled with astonishment by a mere review of the
special literature which this Church has brought forth.
A comparison of the minutes of the triennial conventions
is of great interest.   The first *Journal of a Convention*
covers only a few small sheets.   This was the convention
that sat from September 27 to October 7, 1785 (the
year of Seabury's consecration), in Philadelphia, and
was made up of deputies from New York, New Jersey,
Pennsylvania, Delaware, Maryland, Virginia, and South
Carolina.   Two conventions met in the following year, the
one following close upon the other: in Philadelphia, June
20th to 26th, and in Wilmington, Delaware, October

10th and 11th. From the first of these conventions we have the opening address of the Rev. William White (shortly after chosen bishop), whose strong faith and hope of the future show a remarkable parallel to the character of the national Congress during Washington's presidency.

The men who in a free state founded a really free Church, in contrast to the slavery of the Papacy, had an instinctive presentiment of the interest with which later generations would follow the beginnings of this work, and a series of important acts as well as the signatures under the documents were in these first years preserved in autograph. In the year 1789 there were again two conventions held, both in Philadelphia, the first July 28th to August 8th, the second September 29th to October 16th. The ecclesiastical organisation had now so far progressed that future conventions met in regular order once in three years, and that ever after the convention of 1789 the members were no longer spoken of as the deputies from the several states, and there was no more a *Journal of a Convention*, but that now the " Protestant Episcopal Church in the United States of America " appears with its *Journal of the Proceedings of the Bishops and of the Clerical and Lay Deputies*. At the convention held in Trenton in 1801, Bishop White consecrated his newly elected colleague, Bishop Moore; at the same time the *Articles of Religion* were adopted and published.

Few historical documents are so impressive to the historian as the minutes of these conventions with their constant increase in bulk and contents. Up to the year 1856 their size was still so limited that several years' issues could be bound up together. In the last ten years (to 1889) the Journals, with all possible brevity, present a wealth of material which in Germany is not even approximately equalled by any similar ecclesiastical publication.

Whoever finds the study of the convention journals too

tedious will find in *Perry's Manual*, published in 1877, of
the conventions held up to that time, an admirable guide.
Another historical source is the biographies of the bishops,
published by Butterton in 1878. To the first of these,
Samuel Seabury, a special memorial is devoted (1873),
and his son's lectures, published by his grandson, on *The
Nature and Work of the Holy Spirit*, prove that his ability
has been transmitted in his own family. The active
historical interest which animates the leaders is proved
by the organisation of an Historical Association of the
American Church. One of its most valuable publications
consists in a large volume of facsimiles of ecclesiastical
documents.

The German members of the Church have been provided with prayer- and hymn-book in their own language.
A special " Church German Society " is devoted to the
religious needs of the German congregations. There
exist large numbers of other societies. To the Anglo-
Continental Society, which has extended the warmest
sympathy to the old-Catholic movement in Germany and
Switzerland from its first beginning, corresponds the
Anglo-American Society. We say nothing of the numerous year-books, almanacs, catechisms, and tracts of
all kinds, in which the American " Church " vies with
Methodists, Baptists, and Lutherans.

In order, however, fully to understand the importance
of the Episcopal Church for the entire development of
the American commonwealth, the historian must have
recourse to statistics. For here it is not a question of
meaningless numbers, as in the advertisements in the
papal organs of the 200,000,000 who are supposed to believe in papal infallibility. In the case of American
Catholicism we have to do, if anywhere, with numbers
that are full of significance, which represent the power of
an idea. Out of the one diocese in 1784 there have grown
48 independent dioceses (1889). The total number of

bishops, including those of the missionary jurisdictions, is 65. The 592 clergy of the year 1832 had become 1052 in 1841, 1558 in 1850, 2286 in 1862, 3082 in 1877, and in 1889 their number is above 3400.

Equally significant is the increase of baptisms, marriages, and funerals, the only facts upon which can be based a true calculation of the membership in the various religious denominations in America. In the year 1832, when these statistics were first recorded in the journal of the convention, the number of baptisms of the three preceding years was 23,127. In the three years before 1841 the number was 34,465, in the same space of time before 1850 there were 42,925, before 1862 71,533, and before 1877 129,757. Only the Lutheran Church in America shows a similarly rapid increase.

The well-known advertisements of the papal press are fully justified in this one point, that the papal Church of to-day has been able to amass the largest ecclesiastical property. But the statistics of the year 1880 count altogether only 6,143,322 Roman Catholics. If only the descendants of the Roman immigrants had remained true to the faith, the total number would have been about 15,000,000. One of the organs of the German papal press has confessed that " the total result is not by any means so brilliant as the common reports of the American Church have led us to expect," and makes an effort to investigate the " cause of this immense defection from the Church." No stronger proof could be given that Roman Catholic immigrants, who feel the influence of American Church life, in time turn to a Church which is in sympathy with the national life.

The Episcopal Church in America shows quite the opposite tendency. Born Anglicans make up only the smallest part of its membership; for Anglican Englishmen form a much smaller contingent of the total immigration than, *e. g.*, the Irish, because the former in contrast

to the latter represent the stable and well-to-do element
of the population of the mother-country.   By far the
largest increase therefore comes from former adherents of
other churches.   Seven German clergymen belong to the
Episcopal Church in New York; they have all come from
other denominations, most of them from the Church of
Rome.   And, although it is a well-known fact that many
European immigrants consider it a part of true liberty
to have nothing to do with any church, and although
America has developed a proselytising atheism with a
regardless frankness such as Europe has rarely known,
nevertheless the second or certainly the third generation
is usually carried away by the power of religious impulse
in the land of liberty.   As representing the most strongly
organised Church in America, the Episcopal Church
draws from all this the greatest advantage.   As early as
in Cooper's time this Church began to grow with striking
rapidity; to-day it must appear to most European
Churches as a worthy model.

The special danger growing out of the present situation
is that the American Episcopal Church should become
in a certain sense the Church of the aristocracy; and yet
the institutions founded for the general good of the public have a tendency to counteract this danger.   The social
benevolence of the members of this Church is, measured
even by an American standard, extraordinary.   Its hospitals, asylums, and schools are among the best endowed
and among the best arranged.   The Episcopal Church
has taken up missions among the Indians as its special
province.   But its activity extends in other directions.
In the island of Haiti there has been organised an Episcopal national Church; in Liberia the first steps have
been taken with the same object in view; and in Mexico
there are now three bishops active, who are in communion
with the North American Episcopal Church.   From here
their path would seem to lead them almost directly to

the South American states, where the lamentable condition of the Roman Church has long cried out for a remedy, which the one-sidedness of purely Protestant forms of worship is not able to supply.

Most significant of all the hopes for the future which the American Episcopal Church has brought forth appears to be the " intercommunion " of Catholicism and Protestantism, which has for the first time been realised by her action. It is indeed a wonderful cycle of events which has led up to this crisis, and one in which the most diverse nations have each rendered its own service to the cause of the kingdom of God, just as happened in the struggles of the sixteenth and seventeenth centuries against the counter-Reformation. Transferred from England to America by way of Scotland, it has been given to the youngest of the episcopal churches to be the first to offer a friendly hand to the inner-Catholic movement for reform, whose seeds the Netherlands preserved through a century and a half, in order to hand it down first to the German old-Catholics and through them to their Swiss brethren in the faith. Through the consecration given by the ancient Church of the Netherlands, the German Bishop Reinkens was enabled, in behalf of Germany, to enter once more into the heritage of the ancient Church-ideals, which in no part of Catholicism had wholly died out. He in his turn transmitted the consecration to his Swiss colleague, Herzog. The latter, at the General Convention in the year 1880, solemnly ratified the " communion with the Anglo-American Church," which is valid as well for Switzerland as for America, and which may form the point of departure for similar unions in a wider sphere in the future.

This latter consideration applies especially to Italy. The hindrances which here oppose themselves to Protestant missionary enterprises do not exist for evangelical

22

Catholicism.   It was therefore a true instinct which led
the American Episcopal Church to understand that to
her was given that particular *charisma* which would enable her in the home of the Papacy to set the gospel,
which the latter had placed under a bushel, once more
upon its candlestick.   The successes which have rewarded
the work of the rector of the Church of St. Paul in Rome
(Dr. Nevin) are not to be judged in the light of a sectarian
proselytism.   In this young Catholic Church of Italy
Canon Campello, with his many like-minded followers, has
found a firm support; and Bishop Herzog, acting under
the authority of his American colleagues, has performed
the rite of confirmation upon a number of young Christians (Easter, 1883).   The foundation of a Catholic
bishopric in opposition to the pseudo-Petrine and pseudo-
Isidorean Papacy may not be ventured by any of the
European state Churches, but American Christianity is
not prevented by diplomatic considerations from supply-
ing this most urgent need of the Church in Italy.   Italy
offers a large harvest for the evangelical Catholicism
which she represents.[1]

Bishop Herzog, in his *Pastoral Letter upon Ecclesiastical Communion with the Anglo-American Church*, sets
forth the significance of this fact in a manner most convincing and impressive, such as characterises only those
ideas which are weighted with a future significance.
This letter was followed by an address, in which he

[1] The author elsewhere speaks as follows of the Church in Italy:
" Europe has quietly allowed the pope to start his opposition hierarchies in
England and Holland and has permitted the bishops under him to claim
jurisdiction over the Protestants in their dioceses.   No state, no Church in
Europe has requited the papal arrogance with the foundation of a Christian
bishopric in Rome.   But the confirmation of Catholic children in Rome by
the Swiss bishop, Herzog, has brought to the light of day the steps that
have been quietly taken by the Americans.   The election and consecration
of a Christian-Catholic bishop of Rome is probably only a question of
time."

treated of the history of the American Episcopal Church. We extract from this historical survey the comparison between the Episcopal and the papal Church in America:

The American Episcopal Church is apostolic in her constitution, she has made no change in the apostolic episcopate and in the equality of the apostles which St. Paul so strongly emphasises; the Roman Church is no longer apostolic, but papal; she has nullified the word of the Saviour: "Call no man your father upon the earth: for one is your Father, which is in heaven. Neither be ye called masters: for one is your Master, even Christ," and has made one man "holy father" and the infallible teacher of all men, and in open defiance of God's word has given to this one man all power over all churches and all believers in all matters of faith, of morals, of discipline, and of Church government.

The former is primitive in her doctrine; she acknowledges the creeds of the ancient undivided Church and the principle that only that is to be received as binding in the faith which has been believed from the beginning, everywhere and by all in the Church. The latter receives the insipid phantasies of mediæval monks and the cunning inventions of the Jesuits, which have been made dogma under Pius IX.

The former is primitive in her liturgy; especially does she celebrate the Holy Communion in a manner most dignified and elevating, and with prayers in which no one will miss anything essential. The latter, with her dead language and her many and serious abuses, has driven the faithful more and more from the sanctuary.

The former is humane; she opens her benevolent institutions to all, even Jews and heathen, who apply to her for help. The latter brings sacrifices only where she can further her hierarchical and political ends.

The Episcopal Church of America is national and is anxiously careful to avoid forcing her forms and peculiarities upon others; on the contrary, she delights in seeing independent national churches arise upon other continents, to which she can offer her hand. The Roman Church is only Roman and

everywhere anti-national ; she endeavours to force everything
into her own forms and formulas, and does not rest until she
has obliterated the national character of the Church and stifled
all national life in the Church.   She has strangled the Gallican
Church, she has subjected the theological universities of Germany to Jesuitism, she has wiped out the various national lit-
urgies, and down to our own day she has either broken or
anathematised every character of any independence.

Our sister Church is tolerant ; she tolerates within her own
bosom various tendencies and various forms, and looks upon
herself, not as *the Church*, but as a branch of the Catholic
Church.   The Roman Church, on the other hand, is the only
saving Church, and whosoever does not hold to her loses
eternal salvation ; for, says Boniface VIII., it is necessary, for
the salvation of every human creature, to be subject to the
pope.

Our sister Church is patriotic ; she does not mix herself in
affairs which do not concern her, but is satisfied to be the
heart and conscience of the people, and to stimulate the heart
and the conscience of all her members ; and by so doing she
seeks to accomplish in behalf of the welfare of the people
something which no school and no police can do.   She has no
conflicts with the civil authorities of the country, but meets
with ready recognition from all who have the public welfare
at heart, in her activity for the education of the young, for the
spiritual and moral elevation of the people, in her struggle
against the many social evils and needs.   In spite, therefore,
of the separation of Church and State there is, so far as I
know, no country in which the most eminent organs of the
press take such favourable and willing notice of Church events
as in the United States.   The Roman Church, on the other
hand, is everywhere a foreigner, even in Italy ; for she everywhere pursues tendencies which are opposed to the tendencies
of the country—in Italy, in France, in Belgium—wherever the
nation has become of age and has attained to a certain liberty
and independence.

Our sister Church stands in no conflict with the civilisation
and the progress of our time ; her members are among the

best educated and the most prosperous inhabitants of the new world. The pope, on the other hand, has solemnly declared that he cannot reconcile himself with modern civilisation,[1] and the Roman Church in time crushes the strength of a people ; it is her fault that such earthly paradises as Spain have gradually become desolate and have lost their dominating influence in the world ; and it is her shame that Catholic nations, if they would regain their ancient importance and rouse themselves once more to active spiritual, physical, and national work, inevitably come into conflict with the Roman hierarchy.

We find ourselves in entire accord with the Catholic bishop, and see in the ideal Catholicism of the American Episcopal Church the exact reverse of the papal universal monarchy. The papal press, on the other hand, dwells with particular predilection upon the Church's conquests in America. Alongside of the English secessions, it is especially the extension of the papal power in the free states of the new world which it paints in the most glowing colours. And as with each new English convert the amount of his income is generally the first thing which they publish, the same is done in America with the value of newly acquired ecclesiastical capital, which, according to papal canon law, belongs no longer to the parishes but to the Roman bishop.

Whoever has not been sufficiently taught by European events to appreciate the true nature of the " ideal " of world-renunciation which prevails in the papal Church, will find it worth his while to study American conditions such as they actually are. He will learn to know the whole Roman Church as a solidly compact political power, which at present draws its advantage by forming alliances with one and the other of the old parties, but for the future has far more ambitious schemes in view.

[1] See the last article of the Syllabus (Introduction).

The statistics of the increase of the Roman communion in America may be very much exaggerated; nevertheless, the dangers which the papal system has introduced, which threaten the peace among the various religious societies and thereby endanger the firmest pillar of the constitution, are—so we are forced to judge—considerably greater than in the European states. Some time ago a distinguished authority called attention to the plans of the Vatican in the new world, which had hardly been noticed in America itself:

The Americans are like the French : whatever lies outside of America is totally unknown to them. Of the organisation, the unity, the power, and the influence of the Vatican, by far the largest majority has not even the most shadowy conception, for the reason that their history shows no record of struggles with Rome like those of the old world. But the danger here is even greater than on the other side, because here republican liberty is used for dark purposes and misused for the strangling of liberty. Soon we shall have in America more monasteries, congregations, and associations than are in France and Italy together, and the untaxable property of the Vatican grows in mighty proportions ; and money is power. If you were to look through Sadlice's *Catholic Directory* (New York, 1875), you would be astonished at the power which Rome now possesses here, and the book of the Redemptorist father, Michael Müller, *Public School Education* (New York, 1875), would give you an idea of the boldness with which they operate.

The author of this quotation is Frederick Hecker, the revolutionary hero of 1848, who took refuge in republican America, and who expressed this judgment in one of his last letters. He can certainly not be said to lack either the knowledge adequate to the criticism which he makes upon the American conception of liberty or a familiarity with Roman Catholicism, which he brought with him from his South German home. There prevails in young America very generally the same infatuation concerning the power of the Vatican as did in Germany before the days of the *Kulturkampf*. Men do not reflect upon how many new strongholds the Papacy has added to its old centres in the states of Florida and Louisiana, originally colonised by Spaniards and Frenchmen, and the Jacobite colony of Lord Baltimore in Maryland. Canada, in spite of the British dominion, is one of the most important arsenals of the Church of Rome. More than half of the inhabitants are of French or Irish origin; in the southern part of Quebec the Roman priest exercises a sway as unrestricted as in Ireland. In the Union itself Irish voters have acquired more and more influence over political parties, and thereby have made themselves strongly felt in politics.

At the time of the Rebellion, the action of President Jefferson Davis may have been considered a sort of curiosity, when he invoked the arbitration of the pope, and received from Antonelli a very adroit answer, calculated to suit every possible issue of the crisis. But how often since that time have not the Presidents of the Union been obliged to submit, whenever Irish revolutionary committees made their demands! The mission of Archbishop Bedini under Pius IX. has been followed by that of Cardinal Howard under Leo XIII., who transacted the papal business without the title of nuncio, but also without hindrance by any kind of state control.

Nor are there wanting zealous converts, theological as well as non-theological. A number of German and English divines in America have taken refuge with the rock of St. Peter, and children of mixed marriages are trained to be the tools of the Propaganda. A son of the celebrated General Sherman has been educated by his zealous Roman Catholic mother as a Jesuit. This is the same who, as teacher at the Jesuit college at Woodstock, sprang into fame by his defence of the humane institution of the Inquisition.

The papal Church in America, besides its efforts to influence politics, directs its attention particularly to the schools. At a convention held in Frankfurt in 1882, Father Müller, referred to above as the author of the book *Public School Education*, spoke of the immense conquests in the sphere of education made during the past ten years. The Jesuits, he said, driven out of Europe, were free to travel over the whole Union. Very many educational institutions, and especially the higher schools, were in the hands of Jesuits, and half of the pupils were not of Catholic parentage. The Catholics themselves no longer sent their children to the godless public schools, but to their own parochial schools. And these were almost exclusively under the direction of men in religious orders whom the *Kulturkampf* had driven to America.

To these communications from Father Müller we may add that since then a " free " university [1] with a rich endowment has been started by the Jesuits. All these educational institutions of various kinds stand under the same direction and play into each other's hands. It can hardly be long before the same consequences will show themselves, only very much intensified, as in the schools of Belgium and Holland.

The political and pedagogical activity of the Church militant is supported by a skilfully organised press, which likewise owes its great influence to a unified direction, while the unhealthy condition of American party life is the cause of innumerable petty divisions and rivalries. Over against the dreadful corruption in the civil service, the venal ring administration in the cities, and the fierce competition among the railroad kings, the work in behalf of the papal universal monarchy appears like the pursuit of a noble ideal. As in Germany, so there are in America a number of high-minded characters who have been so charmed by the magician of Rome that they have given

[1] See page 246, note.

all their powers to his service. At the Vatican Council the most learned of the North American bishops were among the most energetic representatives of the opposition: Quirinus (Döllinger) has given a series of interesting communications concerning the hopes and the fears which they then cherished. We speak of the " latent powers " of genuine religion, which the Papacy has bound: the figure is nowhere more applicable than in the new world.

Under the feverish effort for extension of its sphere of power, the moral task of the Church suffers more even than in Europe. In order to win rich and illustrious members, or at least not to lose their contributions, much is overlooked. The defects which to-day attach themselves to the Church life of America in all denominations are to a large extent due to the worldly political features of the Roman Church, whose lead in this respect is followed by the other communions. But in a rivalry of this nature no other Church can hold its own against the Church of Rome. In a masterly way she understands how to use her compact organisation so as to profit by the divisions among the Protestant sects. And this will not be changed until the unadulterated Catholic ideal, which in the Episcopal Church alone has been combined with the Protestant ideal in a higher unity, takes deep root in the whole great body of American Protestantism. A noteworthy movement in this direction has been made by the convention of the Evangelical Alliance in New York. The dogmatic character of its statutes has perhaps made co-operation impossible for all but a fraction of those who are in sympathy with the ideals of the first founders. But that which has proved unattainable by European state-ecclesiasticism has been clearly recognised in the birth-land of the free Church as the task of the future: the conquest of papalism by evangelical Catholicism.

CHAPTER XX

THE LATIN STATES OF AMERICA IN THEIR RELATIONS TO THE ROMAN CURIA AND IN THEIR ECCLESIASTICAL DEVELOPMENT

THE development of civilisation among European states has been largely determined by the religion which they professed. And in America the contrasts between Germanic and Latin states, even more marked than in Europe, are traced to the differences of religion among the first colonisers. English Protestant antecedents furnish the key to the history of the North American Union, and similarly we shall understand the condition of affairs in the Spanish and Portuguese colonies only by taking into account the nationality and the religion of the conquestadors. From the very beginning, the Roman clergy in Central and South America ruled with a power almost more unrestricted than in Spain or Portugal. Nowhere had religion become so completely externalised as here; nowhere did it exhaust itself so entirely in the veneration paid to the clergy, the diligent hearing of mass, and the strict observance of the many feast-days, while the excessive worship of saints impressed even European Catholics as a kind of new idolatry. To this day there prevails in the remoter regions the grossest superstition, which is used to great advantage by the priests for their trade in indulgences and amulets. With the increasing impoverishment, neglect, and ethical degradation of the people has gone hand in hand the increase of wealth among the clergy.

Into this paradise of the clergy, which had attained its climax in the Jesuit state of Paraguay, the war of independence against Spain entered as a disturbing element. When Joseph Bonaparte, upon his accession to the throne of Spain in 1808, demanded the subjection of the Spanish colonies, the latter, instead of obeying, followed the example of the Spaniards themselves, and established provisional juntas in the name of Ferdinand VII. At the same time they demanded of the Spanish Cortes in Cadiz to be placed on the same level with the mother-country. When this was denied, there followed, in the majority of the colonies, the declaration of independence. After the Peninsular war and the expulsion of the French, King Ferdinand [1] might by timely and just reforms have won back the colonies for Spain. But in the spirit of the unimproved absolutism which he restored in Spain, he demanded the unconditional subjection of the colonies. The consequence was that one colony after another separated itself definitely from Spain. Buenos Ayres was the first, in 1816; Chili followed in 1817; Colombia, Venezuela, and New Granada, in 1819; Peru in 1821. The same happened in those parts of Central and North America which by their origin belonged, not to the Germanic-Protestant, but to the Latin-Catholic category: in Guatemala (1820), Domingo (1821), Mexico (1822 and 1823). And even Brazil followed the general example, and separated itself in the year 1822 from Portugal and proclaimed an independent empire.

Since then all these new states have been subjected to numerous internal revolutions, and in the midst of all the confusions, internal and external, these countries, formerly so isolated, have been more and more affected by modern ideas. But revolution has broken only the

---

[1] Restored to the throne of Spain in 1814.

political, not the ecclesiastical, absolutism. For the clergy, consisting mostly of natives and hating the Spanish bishops, made common cause with the people, and in return the constitutions of the young republics confirmed the monopoly of the Roman Church. The Mexican constitution of 1824 expressly declared in its third article: " The religion of the Mexican nation is and ever remains the Apostolic-Roman-Catholic; the nation will protect this religion by wise and just laws and forbids the exercise of every other worship." So with the constitutions of the Central and South American states.

Although, therefore, Pope Pius VII., in 1824, advised maintaining the connection with Spain, Leo XII., in 1827, not only recognised the governments *de facto*, but filled the vacant bishoprics and sent his legates. In this manner the clergy retained the sympathy of the people and their power. Only gradually, beginning in the coast towns, in which commerce and industry had established themselves and where Protestant churches were soon organised, a change began to take place, which, however, is not everywhere equally noticeable. For still there exists in many places a most chaotic condition of affairs and the various parties are engaged in bitter conflicts. It is no mere chance that both Garibaldi and Pius IX. had been active in the South American republics. The conflict of principles which in Italy is associated with their names has been carried over to those remote countries.

The country which has passed through most revolutions is Mexico, and in almost all of these revolutions the attitude towards the clergy has been the party shibboleth. For at the time of the declaration of independence, not only was there the inordinately large number of 3200 clergymen, 146 monasteries, and 39 nunneries, together with 11 bishops and 1 archbishop; but the clergy possessed about half of all the real estate. And yet, the taxes in behalf of the Church had been immensely increased, and were collected with the aid of imprisonment and the whipping-post. A number of pretenders and regents, such as Santa Anna and Miramon, found their support among the clergy; while the liberal governments sought to deprive the clergy of their influence. The liberal party, finally victorious, secularised the real estate of the Church, provided for the gradual dissolution of the monasteries, took away the jurisdiction of the clergy in civil and criminal cases, introduced civil marriage and civil register, and in the end even proclaimed liberty of conscience. The clerical party, bankrupt in the country itself, called in foreign help.

Pecuniary difficulties, which were added to the confusion, finally brought about the Spanish-English-French expedition, from which, after the withdrawal of the first two powers, there was developed the French occupation and the empire of the Hapsburg Maximilian I. Although called in by the clerical party, yet the Emperor Maximilian could maintain his position and could successfully meet the pressing difficulties of the situation—the Roman Curia refusing to grant any, even the most essential, reforms—only by instituting of his own motion such measures as were absolutely necessary. And so it was that the prince who had made a special pilgrimage to Rome and had been dismissed with the particular blessing of the pope, came himself into decided conflict with the Vatican. At the same time, after the victory of the Union over the rebellious slave states, his throne, which had been founded upon the expectation of an opposite issue of the struggle, became very insecure.

In the year 1867 the tragedy of poor Maximilian came to an end at Queretaro, where he was shot. Before his own death he had received the news that the Empress Charlotte had become hopelessly insane in the ante-room of Pius IX., after the audience in which the pope had rudely reproached her when she came to implore his help. Since then she remains under the care of her relatives in the castle of Tervueren in her Belgian home. The terrible fate of the princely couple, who were animated by the highest motives, has since been cleared up by a series of authentic publications from original documents found after the fall of the empire in the imperial archives. These documents have proved that the cause of all the difficulties with which the emperor had to contend were the pretensions of the Vatican, which were as insatiable as they were irreconcilable with the claims of the modern state.

Before their departure for Mexico the imperial couple had made a pilgrimage to Rome in order to receive the blessing of the holy father. Besides this blessing and the promise of the papal influence upon the Mexican clergy in favour of the new monarchy, Pius IX. also promised to send a legate with sufficient authority for composing all difficulties. But after the emperor had arrived in Mexico in May, 1864, he had to wait for the promised nuncio until the end of December. In the meantime the commandant of the French troops of occupation, Marshal Bazaine, in a report, dated November 3, 1864, on the condition of affairs in the several districts, had pictured the debased state of the clergy as a principal cause of the wretched condition of the country.

When finally the nuncio arrived in the person of Monsignore Meglia, he brought a letter from the pope (dated October 18, 1864) to the emperor, in which a detailed plan for the reorganisation of ecclesiastical affairs, which the latter had demanded, was laid down. But what a reorganisation! "Above all is it necessary that the Catholic Church continue, to the exclusion of every other form of worship, to be the glory and the support of the Mexican nation." Then follow other conditions:

that the bishops should be entirely free in the exercise of their pastoral office, that the religious orders be restored and reorganised according to the instructions of the pope, that Church property and all rights appertaining to it be defended and protected, especially that no one be permitted to spread false and subversive doctrines, that all instruction, public as well as private, be conducted and watched over by the ecclesiastical authority, and that finally all the fetters be broken by which until now the Church has been held in dependence upon the caprice of the civil government.

These were only preliminary demands, " in order to restore happiness to the Church "; they were also the first conditions for the consolidation of the empire and the restoration of social order.

The unhappy monarch was now placed before the alternative, of either satisfying the pope and the Church by renouncing the most essential rights of government and thereby depriving the state of the most important and the most indispensable sources of income, or of adding the opposition of the nuncio to the antagonism of his political enemies.

He attempted a middle course and put together in nine points all that he could concede and what he could not concede; these points, however, included concessions to the Papacy which it was impossible to fulfil. He declared himself ready to restore the Roman-Apostolic-Catholic worship as the " state religion "; but other forms of worship would have to be " tolerated." The other demands also of the Vatican were as far as possible sanctioned and only the most indispensable conditions attached to them. The state treasury was to provide for all the expenses of the Catholic worship, the Church receiving the same privileges as were accorded to the civil list of the state; in return the clergy were not to oppress the people with parochial taxes, tithes, etc. (as had been done in most cruel manner before the reform laws). The holy father was to be authorised, with the consent of the emperor, to determine what suppressed orders and religious organisations were to be restored and in what form.   In all places where the conditions made it possible, the Catholic clergy were to be intrusted with the care of the registers of births, marriages, and deaths.   The privileges of the clergy, especially the right of jurisdiction and the care of cemeteries, were allowed, but were to be defined in future negotiations.   The direction and superintendence of all instruction by the clergy was sanctioned without any question and was not even touched upon in the nine points.

All this was not enough for the Curia.   The nuncio immediately declared: he had no authority to negotiate, but simply to demand the repeal of the " reform laws " and, in general, of all laws which were contrary to the sacred rights of the Church.   The nine points contained reservations which were inimical to the doctrine as well as the discipline and the sacred canons of the Church. Above all, objection was made to the first point, concerning the toleration of other forms of worship, which violated the doctrine of the Church and injured the feelings of a Catholic people.   But he had also received instructions to insist upon the unconditioned restoration of the religious orders and the restitution of the churches and monasteries as well as upon the recognition of all former rights of the clergy in regard to the acquisition, possession, and the administration of property, real and personal.   With regard to the proposed payment of salaries to bishops and clergy, they would prefer to live upon the charity of the faithful; the renunciation of their plundered property by the Church was entirely out of the question.   And in general Meglia explained his mission by declaring that he had only been sent to demand the repeal of the laws inimical to the Church, compensation for all injury done to the Church, and complete independence and liberty for the Church in the future.

One must know the details of these transactions as they are given in the account entitled *The Relations of the Holy See to Mexico before and during the Episode of the Emperor*, which is based upon official documents, to get an idea of how far the poor emperor and his wife went and what pains he took to explain the actual condition of affairs, in order to make Monsignore Meglia understand the utter impossibility of his demands. The same answer was always given: *Non possumus*. In the meantime the president, Juarez, made daily increasing progress, and in the parts which came into his possession the clergy were energetically restrained within their limits. In order to overcome so dangerous an opponent, the emperor would have had to rival him in measures for the welfare of the people. Instead of this, he was placed in the dilemma, either to yield to the exorbitant demands of the pope or to make an enemy of the very party that had called him into the country.

On Christmas day, 1864, Monsignore Meglia replied to the concessions which the emperor had offered by asserting that the latter only intended to complete the work begun by Juarez. Thereupon the emperor, on the 27th of December, commissioned the minister of justice, Escuderò, to make the necessary proposals with a view to taking the control of ecclesiastical affairs into his own hands. On December 29th the nuncio protested against this proceeding. The emperor reminded him, on the 7th of January, 1865, of the law promulgated at the time of the declaration of independence, according to which all papal pronouncements intended for the country required the sanction of the state authorities. Meglia protested again on the 19th of January, and two days later diplomatic intercourse with him was broken off.

This ended Meglia's work. But still the emperor hoped to be able to appeal from the ill-advised to the better-advised pope. He now sent an embassy to Rome.

23

When this proved futile, he separated himself from his faithful wife, in order to let her appeal to the heart of the pope. Pius IX. declared that " he was surprised that a person of her age and her sex dared to present such a matter." The effect upon the empress of the pope's language has already been told: she became insane.

The *Old-Catholic Messenger* closes the discussion of the newly published documents with this question: " Can we suppose that the bloody sandhill of Queretaro and the insane woman of Tervueren never rose up to disturb the last dreams of the aged Pius ?" We reply to this question with a negative, simply because Pius at no time loved any other person than his own dear self.

When the princely couple, in response to the urgent appeal of the clericals, had taken upon itself the heavy weight of such a throne, the pope had declared that " with the establishment of the new empire he looked for the dawning of peaceful and happy days." He had expressed his particular pleasure " that there had been called to this crown a prince of a Catholic family which had given so many brilliant proofs of religious devotion," and who personally " would show himself worthy of the blessing of Jesus Christ, of the prince of the Church, and of her bishops." But when the emperor had begun his task, impossible demands were made upon him, and when he demonstrated their impossibility, the promised support was withdrawn at a time when the partial fulfilment of the papal wishes had vastly increased the number and the bitterness of his enemies.

With all this, the transactions in Mexico brought no advantages to the Curia, any more than to the Empress Eugenie and her husband, whom his pious wife influenced in favour of the " Catholic work " in America. The weakening of the French military power is traced to the Mexican adventure. And it was a fatal coincidence that the news of the execution of Maximilian arrived in Paris during the days of the Austrian emperor's visit, when the alliance against Germany was to be effected. This made an end of the alliance and thereby nullified the preliminary conditions, which were essential to guarantee to France the victory in the war against Germany so long planned by Eugenie's father confessors.

The republican constitution of Mexico was restored after the short episode of the empire, and with it the ecclesiastical reform legislation. This was subsequently carried still further, to the complete emancipation of the state from the Church. The Mexican government no longer recognises a papal authority, with which it is obliged to negotiate as sovereign with sovereign: it ignores the pope entirely. The consequences threatened by the pope have not been realised. Appointments of clergy have to be sanctioned by the government, monasteries and ecclesiastical possessions have remained secularised, the schools have been freed from the supervision and the control of the clergy. Toleration of other forms of worship has from time to time called forth crusades on the part of the priests against heretics in the remoter regions, but is making steady progress from year to year. The social position of the Roman Catholic clergy itself has been raised by the exclusion of unworthy priests. Even the revolutionary pronunciamentos, formerly so numerous, have become rarer in the course of the past years.

If the condition of affairs in Mexico is becoming gradually more worthy of a modern state, the best part of this result has been effected by the increasing influence of the neighbouring Union. So much the more glaring, however, is the contrast with the Central and South American republics, which are for ever distracted by revolutions, where hitherto it has been impossible to bring about settled conditions. Here, too, the fundamental cause of the political confusion lies in the ecclesiastical situation.

While North America, by the confluence of all those who were persecuted for their religion, became the arena of the most perfect religious liberty, the Spanish conquestadors brought the Inquisition.   The supremacy, externally, of the Church was more firmly established than that of the state.   But the same reaction into complete infidelity which Latin Catholicism experienced in Europe in the eighteenth century has in the nineteenth century assumed far greater dimensions in Latin America.   Hence the never-ceasing conflicts of both extremes, which renders a peaceful development impossible.

In the year 1867 we find a double war going on: Brazil in union with Uruguay and the Argentine Republic against Paraguay, where the dictator Lopez had revived the old Jesuit traditions; and the war of Chili, Peru, and Bolivia against the mother-country of Spain.   The consequence of the first war was the complete conquest and devastation of Paraguay.   The second brought, after peace had been made with Spain, new quarrels, which have finally ended in the conquest of Peru and Bolivia by the aspiring state of Chili.   At the same time the Central American republics have waged repeated wars with each other, and the Argentine Republic has been thrown from one revolution into another.   Even in imperial Brazil the conditions have not been much more steady.

Ecclesiastical conditions are no less changeable.   To-day a government devoted to the pope is at the helm and sanctions pretensions which elsewhere would appear absolutely incredible.   To-morrow ecclesiastical property is confiscated, monks and nuns are released from their vows and Church holidays abolished.   The day after to-morrow there are already signs of the first preparation for a clerical revolution.   Externally the daily life of the people is interwoven with ecclesiastical usages.   At every step one meets a *Botica Jesus y Maria* or a *Cervizeria Jesus Nazareno*.   The favourite female baptismal names are *Immaculata Concepcion* and *Maria de los Dolores*. At the same time the newspapers are full of complaints about the immorality of the ill-educated and illpaid clergy, and (to cite one instance) in Lima the number of illegitimate births has long ago exceeded that of the legitimate. People of education identify religion and the hierarchy to such an extent, that whoever speaks a word in favour of the former is usually put down as an Ultramontane.

The same papal Curia which in Europe chooses to appeal to liberty shows by the concordat concluded with Ecuador in 1862 to what lengths of arrogant demands it dares to go and what it is able to effect in Latin America. All that was demanded of Maximilian in Mexico has here been sanctioned by law. Only the Catholic form of worship was allowed by the concordat with Ecuador; every other form prohibited. The government pledged itself to the suppression of all erroneous doctrines. The entire school system was placed under the control of the clergy. Every book prohibited by a bishop was to be confiscated. The government, however, went far beyond the concordat. Under the influence of the Jesuits, who in this loyal republic found one of their most important arsenals, the dictator Garcia Moreno devoted the whole country to the Sacred Heart and allotted a large part of the yearly income to the poor prisoner in the Vatican. When the system of terror which he founded had come to its customary termination by his assassination, the papal organs of all countries printed eulogies of this greatest statesman of the nineteenth century. To what an incredible degree this delusion rose can be seen in the Dutch clerical press of the time. The actual consequence of the Jesuit episode for Ecuador was that this republic was entirely eclipsed by other states such as Costa Rica and Guatemala.

Peru, like Ecuador, rejoiced in a dictator after the

pope's own heart — Pierola. This is the Pierola under whom Peru suffered her crushing defeats by Chili.

Chili, on the other hand, which before had stood very much in the background, won by this war a position of power in South America which has been compared with the rise of Piedmont and of Prussia. For a long time the same countenance was given to the rudest superstition here as in the neighbouring states. It was in Santiago in Chili that in the year 1866, at the feast of the Immaculate Conception, eighteen hundred women met their death in a burning church, and where the priest Ugarte, who shortly before had instituted a mail service to the Virgin Mary, declared that the Virgin had taken her devoted children to herself, because Chili had needed a large number of saints and martyrs. Not long after, however, in spite of the opposition of the clergy, freedom of worship was proclaimed as the law of the state. The Vatican revenged itself in the customary manner, by preventing the filling of the episcopal sees, and thereby making the satisfaction of the religious needs of the people impossible.

When the archiepiscopal see of Santiago became vacant and the government proposed a candidate in every way fitted for the position (Dr. Taforo), his confirmation was refused under frivolous pretexts. The efforts of the Chilian ambassador in Rome against a procedure which imperilled the authority of the government led only to a painful procrastination. Appearances seem to indicate that the enemies of Chili endeavoured to revenge themselves for their defeat in the field by winning the Curia to their side and thereby producing internal confusion in Chili. Aside from this, however, it was but natural that the increasing strength of the Chilian state should reanimate the old principles of papal reactionism, which recognised its worst enemy in every powerful state organism. But since its triumph in the war, which exceeded every expectation, the young and strong state has assumed an energetic attitude against papal assumptions. The conflict between both culminated in the expulsion of the nuncio (January, 1883), and the proposal of a law for the separation of State and Church.

A similar development has taken place in the United States of Colombia, where also a liberal government has restrained the Church within its own proper limits and has raised the school system to a standard which, for South American conditions, is astonishingly high. Especially worthy of notice is the young university of Bogota, which has become the centre of a progressive system of education.

In the Argentine Republic likewise, as often as there is a pause in the customary civil wars, the school question occupies the chief place in the popular interest, and the two parties, clerical and liberal, have been violently opposed to each other upon the decisive question of religious instruction in the public schools.

In spite, however, of liberal aspirations there could be no greater error than to measure the religious conditions, even in states like Chili and Colombia, by a European standard. No educated German Catholic would recognise his religion in the fetichism such as is practised by the clergy. Nor has Protestantism exerted any influence upon the people of the country. Protestant diminution of the personnel attached to the heavenly court, which eliminates the most interesting figures, impresses the people as tiresome. The prevailing religious conceptions represent the climax of materialism, which would justify some of our historians in placing these countries at the top in the scale of advanced nations, in contrast to a country so behind the age as the North American Union.

Parallel with the development of the Spanish colonial states has been that of Brazil, both during its union with Portugal and after its separation. The clergy of Brazil

have never been so extraordinarily rich as the clergy of
Spanish America; and yet their power has been sufficiently great and their intolerance correspondingly intense.   The refusal to recognise Protestant marriages has
always been, and is now, a serious factor affecting internal
politics.   Nevertheless there is observable even in Brazil
a gradual and yet distinct diminution in the power of the
clergy.   After the Vatican Council, Brazil even had its
Kulturkampf, which the Berlin press in the days of the
German *Kulturkampf* often held up as a worthy example.
In this struggle with the government the policy of Leo
XIII. has been able to counteract the mistakes of his
predecessor and to cripple the state.

But the German Protestant immigration, which as-
sumes annually greater dimensions, may be expected in
time considerably to modify the condition, not only of
the coast lands, but also of the interior provinces.   And
besides this, the old-Catholic movement, which in Mexico
has already made itself noticeably felt, will meet with no
barrier in the Isthmus of Panama, especially now that
the projected canal prevents for all future time a seclusion
from the rest of the world such as the Jesuits for a while
effected in Ecuador.

Even in the negro republic of Domingo-Hayti, in spite
of the caricature of all forms of culture prevalent there,
the modern principles of religious liberty have been incorporated in the constitution.   And Cuba also, along
with the most hideous outbreaks of an incorrigible
fanaticism, nevertheless has profited by the progress made
by Spain in the republican episode.

CHAPTER XXI

CATHOLIC AND PAPAL

THE pope claims to be the " head of the Catholic Church." Few stop to reflect upon the arrogance and presumption of that claim, and in the tacit sanction almost universally given to the papal pretensions we find the most potent cause of that increasing power of the Papacy which characterises the history of the nineteenth century.

And be it remembered that the representatives of the state and of the Protestant Churches have, more than all others, fairly pressed upon the Papacy this its best weapon against those within its own fold who have fought the battle for a true Catholicism and who have been the most determined opponents of papal autocracy. Even in the official documents of secular governments it is customary to designate the pope as the " head of the Catholic Church." In the eyes of the great multitude " papal " or " Jesuit " and " Catholic " are synonymous, and Protestant authors have adopted a style of language by which those who in theory are the bitterest enemies of the curialistic system really do their best to smooth its path.

The intolerable pretensions of the Papacy are therefore largely the result of Protestant ignorance. Not until Protestants shall learn that the idea of Catholicism has its roots just as much in the soil of the gospel and is just

361

as important for the future as Protestantism, that Catholicism and Protestantism mutually condition each other, will there be recognised the opposition between Papalism and Catholicism, an opposition which has never wholly disappeared in the Catholic Church. But so long as the customary confusion of speech is maintained and men will persist in using language in a manner which is as false as it is contradictory of all history, the power of papalism will continue to increase.

By what right does the pope claim to be the " head of the Catholic Church " ? When have the oldest Christian Churches relinquished the name of Catholic Churches and accepted the overlordship of the pope ? Where have the English and the American Episcopal Churches in any of their official documents omitted to emphasise their Catholic character ? Do not even the original literary monuments of the Lutheran and of the Reformed Church, Zwingli's theses as well as Luther's writings, always speak of their adherents as members of the Catholic Church ? Have not the later symbols made a particular point of retaining this honourable designation ?

We trace to the terminology of the Peace of Augsburg [1] and of the Peace of Westphalia, [2] the fateful use of language which permitted the pope to proclaim himself the " head of the Catholic Church," to whom all baptised persons are subject. But another factor has recently contributed even more to this confusion of ideas and of language: the would-be wise diplomacy of the nineteenth century, which, following the example set by Niebuhr, [3] spoke the language of the Curia, quite as a matter of

[1] 1555. The Peace of Augsburg established the principle that the religion of the people should be that of the prince, either Lutheran or Reformed or Roman.

[2] Which ended the Thirty Years' War in 1648.

[3] See page 62, note.

course and in perfect innocence. Ancient and mediæval Church history abundantly teaches the distinction which the primitive undivided Church as well as the divided Churches of the middle ages made between Roman and Catholic, between whatever proceeded from one single city and what concerned the whole Christian Church. It is high time that this ideal of Catholicism be reinstated in its rights, in opposition to the assumption of its Roman caricature.

It was an historical necessity that the Protestant ideal, representing the principle of Christian individualism, should in the sixteenth century have been obliged to fight for its existence against the Catholic ideal, the principle of universalism. But upon the period of opposition there followed a period of adjustment: we find in the eighteenth century a mitigation of sectarian differences, and in the beginning of this century the more advanced on both sides, Catholics and Protestants, came together in a closer intercourse, which answered to the deeper feelings of all truly Christian minds. Roman Catholics began to appreciate the claims of Protestant principles, and in conventions of Protestant Churches attempts were repeatedly made to bring the idea of Catholicism again into prominence.

But soon after the opening of this century a great change took place. In 1814 the pope was restored to his capital, and with that restoration began a process of papal aggression which culminated in the dogma of infallibility. The principles which have governed the Papacy since 1814 have been directly antagonistic to the tendencies of a genuine Catholicism. The Catholicism for which the Papacy in this century has stood is a caricature, the distorted Catholicism of a pure autocracy, hitherto unknown in the Church; and the restoration of the Papacy marks the beginning of the modern contest between a genuine

Catholicism and its papal corruption. This contest is the most important factor in the ecclesiastical history of the century, and in its light alone can we understand modern national development in the various countries.

The preceding pages have endeavoured to draw the lines of that struggle: we have traced the continued aggressions of the Papacy and we have seen the resistance of those who could not forget the purer and the older principles of a time when the Church knew no such insolent tyranny. The crises which this contest has called forth and the character of this struggle in the various countries, in Europe, in the East, and in America, vary according to the conditions of each and the antecedents and character of the people; but everywhere there are the same essential antagonisms. In all nationalities we meet the influence of the spirit which again rules in the Vatican. The connection with Rome is drawn closer than ever; and Jesuitism, dominating Rome, intrudes everywhere. With the claims of the hierarchy grow the number of its allies; while at the same time we observe, among Roman Catholic populations, an increasing hatred of clericalism and a growing opposition to the ecclesiastical regime, running through all degrees, from ridicule and defiance to positive efforts for reform.

The struggles between the papal and national-Catholic parties reached their climax in the Romance or Catholic countries, but in Germanic nationalities also we find the same opposition between papalism and Catholicism as the historically dominating principle. And wherever, within the Church, papalism has suppressed the opposing tendencies, there the conflict becomes one between the Church and the State, and turns upon the emancipation of the state, of the family, and the school from the control of the hierarchy. We find therefore in Europe an increasing desire for the separation of Church and State, and we meet with repeated attempts to make religion independent of the Church and to realise a morality without religion, or at least without sectarianism.

Nothing in the sphere of ecclesiastical history is more astonishing than the triumphs of papalism in our century, but those who believe in Catholicism as an important factor in the progress of Christian civilisation will have confidence in the ultimate victory of truth; and the history of the latest times shows a few phenomena, such as the inauguration of the Christian-Catholic Church in Switzerland, the martyrdom of old-Catholicism in Germany, Döllinger's union-conferences, and the opposition to papalism in England and America, which hold out the promise of a better future—a future in which Protestantism shall have learned more fully to appreciate the ideal of Catholicism, and in which the Church of Rome shall have awakened to a renewed appreciation of her ancient heritage of liberty.

INDEX

The Story of the Nations.

MESSRS. G. P. PUTNAM'S SONS take pleasure in announcing that they have in course of publication, in co-operation with Mr. T. Fisher Unwin, of London, a series of historical studies, intended to present in a graphic manner the stories of the different nations that have attained prominence in history.

In the story form the current of each national life is distinctly indicated, and its picturesque and noteworthy periods and episodes are presented for the reader in their philosophical relation to each other as well as to universal history.

It is the plan of the writers of the different volumes to enter into the real life of the peoples, and to bring them before the reader as they actually lived, labored, and struggled—as they studied and wrote, and as they amused themselves. In carrying out this plan, the myths, with which the history of all lands begins, will not be overlooked, though these will be carefully distinguished from the actual history, so far as the labors of the accepted historical authorities have resulted in definite conclusions.

The subjects of the different volumes have been planned to cover connecting and, as far as possible, consecutive epochs or periods, so that the set when completed will present in a comprehensive narrative the chief events in the great STORY OF THE NATIONS; but it is, of course, not always practicable to issue the several volumes in their chronological order.

THE STORY OF THE NATIONS.

The "Stories" are printed in good readable type, and in handsome 12mo form. They are adequately illustrated and furnished with maps and indexes. Price per vol., cloth, $1.50 ; half morocco, gilt top, $1.75.

The following are now ready :

GREECE. Prof. Jas. A. Harrison.
ROME. Arthur Gilman.
THE JEWS. Prof. James K. Hosmer.
CHALDEA. Z. A. Ragozin.
GERMANY. S. Baring-Gould.
NORWAY. Hjalmar H. Boyesen.
SPAIN. Rev. E. E. and Susan Hale.
HUNGARY. Prof. A. Vámbéry.
CARTHAGE. Prof. Alfred J. Church.
THE SARACENS. Arthur Gilman.
THE MOORS IN SPAIN. Stanley Lane-Poole.
THE NORMANS. Sarah Orne Jewett.
PERSIA. S. G. W. Benjamin.
ANCIENT EGYPT. Prof. Geo. Rawlinson.
ALEXANDER'S EMPIRE. Prof. J. P. Mahaffy.
ASSYRIA. Z. A. Ragozin.
THE GOTHS. Henry Bradley.
IRELAND. Hon. Emily Lawless.
TURKEY. Stanley Lane-Poole.
MEDIA, BABYLON, AND PERSIA. Z. A. Ragozin.
MEDIÆVAL FRANCE. Prof. Gustave Masson.
HOLLAND. Prof. J. Thorold Rogers.
MEXICO. Susan Hale.
PHŒNICIA. Geo. Rawlinson.
THE HANSA TOWNS. Helen Zimmern.
EARLY BRITAIN. Prof. Alfred J. Church.
THE BARBARY CORSAIRS. Stanley Lane-Pool.
RUSSIA. W. R. Morfill.
THE JEWS UNDER ROME. W. D. Morrison.
SCOTLAND. John Mackintosh.
SWITZERLAND. R. Stead and Mrs. A. Hug.
PORTUGAL. H. Morse-Stephens.
THE BYZANTINE EMPIRE. C. W. C. Oman.
SICILY. E. A. Freeman.
THE TUSCAN REPUBLICS. Bella Duffy.
POLAND. W. R. Morfill.
PARTHIA. Geo. Rawlinson.

JAPAN. David Murray.
THE CHRISTIAN RECOVERY OF SPAIN. H. E. Watts.
AUSTRALASIA. Greville Tregarthen.
SOUTHERN AFRICA. Geo. M. Theal.
VENICE. Alethea Wiel.
THE CRUSADES. T. S. Archer and C. L. Kingsford.
VEDIC INDIA. Z. A. Ragozin.
BOHEMIA. C. E. Maurice.
CANADA. J. G. Bourinot.
THE BALKAN STATES. William Miller.
BRITISH RULE IN INDIA. R. W. Frazer.
MODERN FRANCE. André Le Bon.
THE BUILDING OF THE BRITISH EMPIRE. Alfred T. Story. Two vols.
THE FRANKS. Lewis Sergeant.
THE WEST INDIES. Amos K. Fiske.
THE PEOPLE OF ENGLAND IN THE 19TH CENTURY. Justin McCarthy, M.P. Two vols.
AUSTRIA, THE HOME OF THE HAPSBURG DYNASTY, FROM 1282 TO THE PRESENT DAY. Sidney Whitman.
CHINA. Robt. K. Douglass.
MODERN SPAIN. Major Martin A. S. Hume.
MODERN ITALY. Pietro Orsi.

Other volumes in preparation are :

THE UNITED STATES, 1775-1897. Prof. A. C. McLaughlin. Two vols.
BUDDHIST INDIA. Prof. T. W. Rhys-Davids.
MOHAMMEDAN INDIA. Stanley Lane-Poole.
THE THIRTEEN COLONIES. Helen A. Smith.
WALES AND CORNWALL. Owen M. Edwards.

HEROES OF THE NATIONS.

A series of biographical studies of the lives and work of certain representative historical characters, about whom have gathered the great traditions of the Nations to which they belonged, and who have been accepted, in many instances, as types of the several National ideals.

The volumes will be sold separately as follows : cloth extra, $1.50 ; half leather, uncut edges, gilt top, $1.75.

The following are now ready :

NELSON. By W. Clark Russell.

GUSTAVUS ADOLPHUS. By C. R. L. Fletcher.

PERICLES. By Evelyn Abbott.

THEODORIC THE GOTH. By Thomas Hodgkin.

SIR PHILIP SIDNEY. By. H. R. Fox-Bourne.

JULIUS CÆSAR. By W. Warde Fowler.

WYCLIF. By Lewis Sergeant.

NAPOLEON. By W. O'Connor Morris.

HENRY OF NAVARRE. By P. F. Willert.

CICERO. By J. L. Strachan-Davidson.

ABRAHAM LINCOLN. By Noah Brooks.

PRINCE HENRY (OF PORTUGAL) THE NAVIGATOR. By C. R. Beazley.

JULIAN THE PHILOSOPHER. By Alice Gardner.

LOUIS XIV. By Arthur Hassall.

CHARLES XII. By R. Nisbet Bain.

LORENZO DE' MEDICI. By Edward Armstrong.

JEANNE D'ARC. By Mrs. Oliphant.

CHRISTOPHER COLUMBUS. By Washington Irving.

ROBERT THE BRUCE. By Sir Herbert Maxwell.

HANNIBAL. By W. O'Connor Morris.

ULYSSES S. GRANT. By William Conant Church.

ROBERT E. LEE. By Henry Alexander White.

THE CID CAMPEADOR. By H. Butler Clarke.

SALADIN. By Stanley Lane-Poole.

BISMARCK. By J. W. Headlam.

ALEXANDER THE GREAT. By Benjamin I. Wheeler.

CHARLEMAGNE. By H. W. C. Davis.

OLIVER CROMWELL. By Charles Firth.

RICHELIEU. By James B. Perkins.

DANIEL O'CONNELL. By Robert Dunlop.

SAINT LOUIS (Louis IX., of France). By Frederick Perry.

LORD CHATHAM. By Walford Davis Green.

Other volumes in preparation are :

MOLTKE. By Spencer Wilkinson.

JUDAS MACCABÆUS. By Israel Abrahams.

HENRY V. By Charles L. Kingsford.

SOBIESKI. By F. A. Pollard.

ALFRED THE TRUTHTELLER. By Frederick Perry.

FREDERICK II. By A. L. Smith.

MARLBOROUGH. By C. W. C. Oman.

RICHARD THE LION-HEARTED. By T. A. Archer.

WILLIAM THE SILENT. By Ruth Putnam.

JUSTINIAN. By Edward Jenks.

G. P. PUTNAM'S SONS, PUBLISHERS, NEW YORK AND LONDON.

HISTORY AND BIOGRAPHY.

THE STORY OF THE CIVIL WAR.

A Concise Account of the War in the United States of America between 1861 and 1865. By JOHN CODMAN ROPES, author of "The Army Under Pope," "The First Napoleon," etc. To be completed in four parts, printed in four octavo volumes. Each part will be complete in itself and will be sold separately. Part I. Narrative of Events to the Opening of the Campaign of 1862. With 5 maps, 8vo, $1.50. Part II. The Campaign of 1862. With 13 maps. $2.50.

"His (Mr. Rope's) name bespeaks for him instant attention on any subject on which he may write. He is putting the student of American history under immeasurable obligations by laying this philosophical, two-sided, and expert disquisition on our civil war before him. A just narrator and critic."—*Detroit Free Press.*

FRANCE UNDER MAZARIN.

With a Sketch of the Administration of Richelieu. By JAMES BRECK PERKINS. With photogravure portraits of Mazarin, Richelieu, Louis XIII., Anne of Austria, and Condé. Two volumes, 8vo, $4.00.

"Our pleasure in reading it has been so great that we fear only that we shall use language that seems too laudatory. . . . 'France under Richelieu and Mazarine will introduce its author into the ranks of the first living historians of our land. He is never dry, he never lags, he is never prolix ; but from the first to the last, his narrative is recorded *currente calamo*, as of a man who has a firm grasp upon his materials."—*N. Y. Christian Union.*

OLIVER CROMWELL: A HISTORY.

Comprising a Narrative of his Life, with Extracts from his Letters and Speeches, and an Account of the Political, Religious, and Military Affairs of England during his Time. By SAMUEL HARDEN CHURCH. With portrait and plans of Marston Moor and Naseby. 8vo, $2.50.

THE WINNING OF THE WEST

And Southwest, from the Alleghanies to the Mississippi, 1769-1807. By THEODORE ROOSEVELT. With maps. 4 vols., 8vo, each, $2.50.

A HISTORY OF THE THIRTY YEARS' WAR.

By ANTON GRINDELY, Professor of German History in the University of Prague, Translated by ANDREW TEN BROOK, recently Professor of Mental Philosophy in the University of Michigan. With twenty-eight illustrations and two maps. With an introductory and a concluding chapter by the Translator. 2 vols., 8vo, $3.50.

THE WRITINGS OF THOMAS PAINE.

Political, Sociological, Religious, and Literary. Edited by MONCURE DANIEL CONWAY, with introduction and notes. Complete in four volumes, uniform with Mr. Conway's "Life of Paine." Price per volume, cloth, $2.50.

GUSTAVUS ADOLPHUS,

And the Struggle of Protestantism for Existence. By C. R. L. FLETCHER, M.A., Fellow of All Souls College, Oxford. 8vo, fully illustrated. $1.50

"We know of no book that so clearly and satisfactorily covers this confused but deeply significant period of European history, and we know of no more consistent and intelligent account of one of its master spirits."—*Christian Union.*

G. P. PUTNAM'S SONS   -   -   PUBLISHERS